Ande Manners'
POOR COUSINS...

"THIS IS A REMARKABLE STORY OF ALMOST EPIC PROPORTIONS, REMARKABLY WELL TOLD. . . . A SCHOLARLY BOOK OF HISTORY MADE MORE DELECTABLE BY FAST-PACED WRITING AND ROLLICKING HUMOR."
—*Nashville Tennessean*

"The most fascinating of many popular works published in recent years on Jewish communal history."
—*Kansas City Times*

"AN ENGROSSING CHRONICLE. . . . ANDE MANNERS HAS SOME FUNNY TALES TO SPIN AND SOME FASCINATING FACTS TO BARE IN THIS OFTEN HILARIOUS HISTORY OF THE 'OTHER JEWS.' "
—*Newsweek*

"As the son of two of the poorest of the Poor Cousins, I am grateful to see the moving story so well told. It is a fine addition to the literature of freedom."
—*Sam Levenson*

"MRS. MANNERS HAS CAUGHT THE COMPLETE SPIRIT OF THE LOWER EAST SIDE JEWS, THE POVERTY AND THE STRUGGLE TO BECOME AMERICANS, AND BEST OF ALL, THE TREMENDOUS INTELLECTUAL DRIVE THAT WAS EVERYWHERE ON THE EAST SIDE."
—*Harry Golden*

POOR COUSINS

Ande Manners

A FAWCETT CREST BOOK

Fawcett Publications, Inc., Greenwich, Conn.

To Bill

and to Julie
and to Jane
and to Tracy

Contents

Acknowledgments

Obviously, I required the assistance of many people in the researching and preparation of this book, and I wish to thank them all. Since such written amenities have a formidable, studied aspect, I ask that the warmth and informality of a personal expression of gratitude be read between the lines.

I'm obliged to the staffs of the Ferguson Library in Stamford, Connecticut; the Bridgeport, Connecticut, Library; and the Jewish Division of the New York Public Library; they were immensely helpful. My special thanks to Ruth Adams of the Westport, Connecticut, Library, for her diligence in tracking down hard-to-find material, and to Stanley Crane of the Pequot Library in Southport, Connecticut, for his exuberant resourcefulness in uncovering sources I might otherwise have missed. Dr. Jacob R. Marcus of the American Jewish Archives in Cincinnati, Ohio, kindly provided needed material. Dr. Gladys Rosen and Dr. Lloyd Gartner of the American Jewish History Center of the Jewish Theological Seminary and Zosa Szajakowski of the YIVO Institute of Jewish Research offered valued suggestions. I am particularly grateful to Ezekiel Lifschutz, archivist of the YIVO Institute, for his unfailing courtesy and extensive knowledge; to Dr. Theodore Norman of the Jewish Agricultural Society, who kindly made available to me records and reports of his organization; and to Judge and Mrs. I. Harry Levin of Vineland, New Jersey, for their hospitality, and for

7

Judge Levin's generous permission to examine his collection of materials dealing with the Alliance colony and the papers of his grandfather, Moses Bayuk.

The wonderful facilities, remarkable holdings, lovely situation and cooperative staff of the American Jewish Historical Society at Waltham, Massachusetts, made my visits a great pleasure. I would especially like to express my appreciation to the society's librarian, Dr. Nathan Kaganoff, and to Kitty Bernack, Ellen Friedman, and Everett Fox.

Rabbi Samuel Silver of Temple Sinai, Stamford, Connecticut —with characteristic ebullience and good humor—took time from his always busy schedule to meet with me. In addition to conjuring up anecdotes from his inexhaustible supply, he also directed my thinking along fruitful lines. My visits with the late Bernard G. Richards and the late Gilbert Seldes clarified whole areas that they knew at first hand. I benefited greatly from Ida Libert Uchill's wide-ranging knowledge of Colorado Jewish history and her generosity in answering my queries. I also wish to thank Charles Gorham of Westport, Connecticut, for leading me to fascinating pathway of research, and William Miller of Roselle, New Jersey, and Averil Toker of Elizabeth, New Jersey, for apt anecdotes.

My affection and appreciation go to Roberta Pryor of International Famous Agency for her customary fortitude, persistence, and bonhomie. At Coward, McCann & Geoghegan, I am greatly indebted to Ellis Amburn, for his encouragement and discerning criticism, as well as for his extraordinary patience during the writing of this book. And my warm thanks to Linda Grey, for her keen editorial eye and enthusiastic interest.

I must also express obligation to my daughters, Julie, Jane, and Tracy—or run the risk of having them point it out to me— for valiant periods of cooperation. As for my husband, he has my deep gratitude for the special insights he possesses as a Midwestern Orthodox Rabbi's son (who delivered round patrician matzos to the *Yahudim* on the hill and ate square plebeian matzos at home), as a former farm school student, a former rabbinical student, and a former professional boxer (who wanted me to include Benny Leonard and Sid Terris and all the other fighters who wore a Mogen David on their trunks)—and also for his acute editorial counsel and perceptive *nudzhing*.

8

PART I

"FROM THIS LAND OF PAIN"

When an American Jew returned from a visit to Russia in 1960, his father, who had emigrated from Russia to the United States more than a half century earlier, had this exchange with him in Yiddish: *"Vas hert sich in der alter heim?" "Ich hob zeh in drerd." "Es hot sich gornisht geenderet in die letzte fufzig yahr."* ("How are things in the old home?" asked the father. "For my part they can go to hell," the son replied. His father nodded understandingly. "Ah, nothing has changed in the last fifty years.")

A Simple Formula

Just as every Frenchman is a lover, every Irishman a lepre-
chaun, every Mormon a saint, so every Jew in czarist Russia
was a philosopher. His philosophy did not have the transcen-
dental majesty of Plato's Ideas, the scope of Bergson's *élan
vital;* rather it was comprised of the homey, practical insights
indigenous to adversity. After generations of incessant religious harassment and persecution, "it was hard," they said,
"to be a Jew." And while life in Russia was a trial, "to a worm
in horseradish, the horseradish is sweet." And when conditions in that sweet land offered the alternatives of starvation,
death, conversion, or emigration, their probing approach to
life presented limitless options: They could either leave or not
leave. If they left, they could go either to Palestine or to the
United States. If they went to the United States, they could either become farmers or stay in New York City. If they stayed
in New York City, they could either work in a sweatship or
get a pushcart and peddle. If they peddled. . . .

And when they swarmed off the boat and were herded
wide-eyed into Castle Garden, the huge, round-domed immigrant depot—and, after 1892, onto the institutional bastion of
Ellis Island—and were asked: "Who are you? Where are you
from? Where are you going?" and their eyes were scrutinized
for trachoma, the scourge of East European Jews, and when

they peered outside to Battery Park and saw awaiting them a covey of agents from immigrant boardinghouses, cabbies willing to take them anywhere by circuitous route, cousins from their mother's side, and an assortment of potential employers, some eagerly offering suspiciously high wages to young girls, and others mentioning low wages, but a wholesome life to shoemakers willing to go to Nashville, Tennessee, and work in a shoe factory, and still others—sweatshop operators from New York—negating low wages with the opportunity of working with *landsleit*—people from one's own *shtetl*—a blacksmith from Minsk gubernia declared philosophically, "So, it's not *Eretz Israel*, but it's not Russia either."

By 1881, when Jews determined that they must leave Russia, they had been seeking *Eretz Israel*—a homeland—for 1,811 years. Their departure for the United States— 2,798,046 from 1881 until the passage of the American Immigration Act in 1924—evolved from a century-old dramatic relationship with the Romanovs and, even before that, from their having lived for hundreds of years in what became modern Russian territory.

Indeed, according to legend, Russia at one point could have become a Jewish country rather than a Christian one. The legend maintained that in 986, in the days of Russian paganism, the Grand Duke Vladimir, seventh ruler of Russia, decided to abandon paganism. Consequently, he summoned the proponents of Judaism and Christianity so each might try to convince him of the supremacy of his faith. When Vladimir was just at the point of accepting Judaism, he posed an awkward question for the Jewish representative. "Where," he asked, "is your country and your great temple?" Upon hearing the lame account of Roman pillage of country and temple, Vladimir declared flatly, "Your God could not think much of you or He would have taken better care of your country." Thereupon, he accepted Christianity.

Five centuries after this momentous decision there began expulsions of Jews, which continued for the next 200 years, and Russia allowed no Jews within its boundaries. However, after the Crusades, an orgy of religious persecution in Germany drove German Jews eastward; by the fifteenth century they had settled in Poland. Then, as a result of the various partitions of Poland, Russia acquired 5,000,000 Ashkenazic (Hebrew for German) Jews who were confronted by Catherine the Great—a synthetic Russian, a Romanov only by marriage, and an autocrat by conviction. The ideal conditions for exacting complete obeisance to imperial will (as Torquemada had assured Ferdinand and Isabella) are those in which the subjects conform to one culture, one set of customs, and one religion. The nineteenth century, therefore, saw the Herculean efforts of reigning Romanovs and their governments to force not only Jews, but all the millions of other Russians into one obedient, Russian Orthodox mold.

The Russian imperial government was not a monolith surmounted grandly by the autocratic czar. Rather, two establishments supported him: a monstrous professional bureaucratic hierarchy and the Russian Orthodox Church. At one time the bureaucracy was composed primarily of the nobility, but by the late nineteenth century there had developed a large civil service class whose progress up the twelve ranks of officeholding was facilitated by strict maintenance of the status quo. As for the Russian Orthodox Church, its spirituality was alloyed by the materialistic dross of political nationalism, and it served as the greatest cementing power of the empire. All those who failed to follow the faith, therefore, weakened its cohesive hold.

The Romanovs could have pointed with pride and accuracy to their family's achievement in assuming the Russian coloration—though they didn't—because, for all their Slavic posturing, the Romanovs, from Catherine to the end of the line in 1918, were predominantly German. Their only blood link with Russia was Catherine's son, Paul I. His father was either Catherine's German husband (but a grandson of Peter the Great) or a Russian friend of hers.

Indeed, Catherine herself exemplified complete Russification. And if she, a German princess, could change her name from Sophia Augusta Frederica to Catherine, her religion from Protestant to Russian Orthodox, and her personal habits from the stolid dull vices acceptable in a small German court to the more individual depravities for which the court of the Romanovs had a partiality, why then couldn't Orthodox Jews become Christians of the Russian Orthodox denomination?

The six czars who followed Catherine—Paul I, Alexander I, Nicholas I, Alexander II, Alexander III, and Nicholas II—possessed minds that ran on substandard gauge tracks. Although some accounts of Paul I—sporadically insane and in his sane moments not a very pleasant chap—credit him with more perception than was possessed by his sons, grandson, great-grandson, and great-great-grandson, his five-year reign ended when several of his palace officers, intent on persuading him to abdicate, inadvertently strangled him. As for the other czars, they had only one basic objective: to cling to their autocratic power. Their sensibilities having been bruised by the harsh implications of the French Revolution and the Napoleonic Wars (Paul I was so hypersensitive he prohibited members of the Academy of Science from using the word "revolution" in reference to the course of the earth around the sun), they endeavored by deifying a Slavic Russia, and themselves, to resist the decadent democratic ideals of the West.

In 1791, Catherine established the Pale of Settlement for the confinement of her Jewish subjects acquired by the partitions of Poland. Comprised of fifteen state governments—gubernias—the Pale extended from the shores of the Baltic Sea south to the Black Sea: Vilna, Grodno, Kovno, Minsk, Vitebsk, Mogilev, Volhynia, Podolia, Kiev, Chernigov, Poltava, Bessarabia, Kherson, Ekaterinoslav, Taurida, plus the ten provinces of Poland.

The efforts of Catherine's descendants to transform those Jews into Christians ranged from Alexander I's offer of bribes for conversion to Alexander III's reliance on wet and dry—hot and cold—pogroms. But it was in the reign of Nicholas I, grandson of Catherine and grandfather of Alexander III, that Russian Jews were subjected to the greatest variety of czarist malevolence, to the most persistently cruel attempts to destroy Judaism and Jewish life, for Nicholas aimed "to diminish the number of Jews in the empire" by means of forced conversions. In 1854, the year before his death, a record 4,439 Jews converted, and this figure substantially exceeded the previous high in 1848, of 2,446.

"Perhaps all the things he says are not very intelligent," Baron Christian Friedrich von Stockmar said charitably, when the twenty-year-old Grand Duke Nicholas visited London in 1816, "but at least they are very pleasant." To this pleasantness there was the additional attraction of Nicholas' superlative good looks—six feet three, "slender as a young pine-tree," his regular features set off by a fine open brow, a perfect line of nose, clear complexion, well-cut chin. If in later years, his hairline receded, and he resorted to a toupee, if his eyes grew chilly, the lines of his mouth severe, even cruel, "the harshest man I ever met," he was, undeniably, a spectacularly fine-looking despot.

Nicholas' bloody accession to the throne in December, 1825,

succeeded despite an uprising of young idealistic aristocrats demanding a constitution, inspired in part by the American Revolution and, naturally, in part by Nicholas. His subsequent implacability, hanging five of the Decembrists and exiling a hundred of them to Siberia, created an unbroken line of revolutionaries that reached to 1917 and the extinction of his great-grandson, the second Nicholas. In the delicate phraseology of Andrew White, then a young attaché at the American ministry in St. Petersburg, Nicholas had reason for becoming so stern a reactionary: Two czars, his father and grandfather, "had both been murdered in obedience to family necessities."

So splendid an image of an emperor did Nicholas project, so impressive was his gift for authority, that he could make pronouncements in somewhat exotic spheres without seeming to have overstepped the bounds of his power. When as head of the Russian Orthodox Church, he was presented with a long memorandum from the Holy Synod asking for a declaration on "whether or not the existence of purgatory was an Orthodox doctrine," he simply scribbled unequivocally in the margin, "No purgatory." And, again, upon signing a marriage annulment, he pronounced categorically in the margin: "This young person will be considered a virgin."

But in spite of his obligation to oversee the spiritual and temporal condition of his empire, "the principal occupation of the Emperor is always the army and this absorbs three-quarters of his day." From the time he received his first uniform at the age of three and the rank of general several years later, he directed all his hopes, dreams, and almost all his attention to military affairs. When he was czar, practically all his ministers at one time were generals, and even in music, he "preferred the drum to the piano." "I hope," his mother wrote to him, "military service will not make you adopt a brutal, harsh and imperious manner." But, alas, devoted as Nicholas was to the army and his officers in the guards, the guardsmen detested him precisely for his "brutal, harsh and imperious manner." With no regard for the pride of his officers, he snapped out coarse insulting reprimands on the parade ground and inflicted pitiless punishment on the men themselves. For a soldier to be dragged through a double line of men armed with sticks, which would literally skin him alive, struck Nicholas as sound practice for a disciplined force. "He is quick, severe, nothing moves him," Princess de Lieven wrote admiringly of Nicholas to her lover, Metternich. "His heart is of stone." But the princess, wife of the Russian ambassador to England, sat in London, where perhaps a stony-hearted czar conveyed more of a Gothic appeal than he did in the guard barracks, on the parade ground, or in the Pale.

Yet all that rigid discipline and incredible brutality were not directed at a goal of military superiority, for according to Prince Kropotkin, camp life, battle strategy were "of quite secondary importance. . . . The true military man of those times," wrote Kropotkin, "was the officer who was enamored of the military uniform, and utterly despised all other sorts of attire; . . . and who could show on parade a row of soldiers as perfectly aligned and as motionless as a row of toy-soldiers. 'Very good,' the Grand-Duke Michael [a young replica of his brother Nicholas] said once of a regiment after having kept it for one hour presenting arms—'only *they breathe!*' " Thus instead of receiving combat training, Russian soldiers were trained to groom and curry their horses to a magnificent sleekness and to practice elegant parade ground maneuvers. Advance sharpshooters received orders to keep neat alignments, rather than run for cover.

So obsessive was Nicholas on the matter of uniforms—he himself hadn't been in civilian dress since his adolescence—that he uniformed everyone: students, professors, engineers, civil servants. To him the sight of a man in a frock coat held sinister overtones of civil insurrection, "the ever recurring specter of the French Revolution." Consequently, to a czar so dedicated to a myopic insistence on conformity that he commanded his officers to wear sweeping black mustaches like his own, dyed if necessary, that each of his guard units had to be made up of men according to size, facial type and hair color,* to such a man, the appearance of his Jewish subjects—*payess* (earlocks), long scraggly beards, black caftan reaching to the heels, and broad flat-brimmed hat—was a personal affront. "The Czar's voice," his doctor wrote, "without being especially strong or even harmonious, seemed to vibrate through the air and increase in volume, penetrating in a marvelous way to the ear of the most distant soldier." It also penetrated to the Pale, for in 1827, barely two years after his ac-

---

* The Preobrazhensky Guards had all to be tall; the Semenovsky all handsome; the Ismailovsky all dark-haired; and the Pavlovsky all snub-nosed in memory of his father, snub-nosed Paul I.

cession, Nicholas devised a horrendous plan for converting Russian Jews, and it was, not too surprisingly, through military means.

On August 26, 1827, Nicholas handed down a ukase that specified special military conscription laws for Jews. At every conscription, Jewish communities had to furnish ten recruits for every thousand of the population, but non-Jews had to furnish only seven per thousand and at intermittent conscriptions. Moreover, at the age of twelve, Jewish boys were to be taken from their families and sent to military posts in the eastern provinces of Russia and Siberia for six years, far from any Jewish influence. Then at eighteen, they were subject to the regular twenty-five-year military service to which non-Jews were also liable. An additional diabolical stipulation of the cantonist system made it a duty of the kahals—the Jewish self-governing body in the *shtetlach*—to hunt down the young cantonists for the czar's army. Thus, Nicholas' plan set Jews against one another, for the kahal appointed recruiting agents —the *khappers*—who terrorized the Pale for almost three decades, sometimes snatching children as young as six or eight from their parents if there weren't enough twelve-year-olds. Parents resorted to nearly any means to keep their sons from the dreaded fate—hiding them in the woods, marrying them off at even a younger age than usual, because a rumor asserted that the czar wouldn't take "married children," even maiming them. Once the *khappers* had carried off a son to the army, kaddish—the mourner's prayer—was recited, for few such young men were ever seen again by their families.

Since the purpose of the system was conversion, it was necessary to make the cantonists agree to baptism. And to make them agree, they were flogged; made to go days without sleep or food; fed salted fish and then refused water. No torture could be too brutal if it achieved the victim's purification from sin by the sacred immersion of the baptismal service. Nicholas' great personal interest in the matter resulted in a high rate of conversion. In 1845, for example, in the battalion of Saratov, the 130 cantonists submitted to baptism two weeks after their arrival. "Faithful to the principles inherited from my brother [Alexander I]," Nicholas wrote the Pope, "I have reverently garnered from his legacy the sentiment of religious tolerance."

Yet despite this seeming success in converting children, adult Russian Jews continued their stubborn adherence to the religion of their fathers. So Nicholas struck at them as part of his general campaign of literary censorship—*Uncle Tom's Cabin* and *The Scarlet Letter* were banned as harmful to Russian morals—and he had Hebrew and Yiddish books confiscated and burned. One Hebrew book, *Rambam*, was reported to the czar as particularly pernicious; his informant claimed it commanded Jews to capture and murder Christian children and drink their blood. In reality, Rambam was the acronym for Moses ben Maimonides, the preeminent philosopher and physician of the Middle Ages, whose exposition of the Jewish faith, *A Guide of the Perplexed*, delved into the nature of God.

Although Nicholas never felt inadequate to any task, it was clear that despite his rewards for conversion—he offered to exempt baptized Jews from paying taxes for three years, to pardon Jewish criminals, and to permit the formation of Jewish farm colonies in Siberia (then issued a ukase limiting their residential rights there)—millions of Jews remained Jews and did not become Russian Orthodox. So Nicholas turned to a more subtle means of conversion. His minister of education, Count Sergei Uvarov, who had crystallized the ideology of Nicholas' reign—autocracy, orthodoxy, and Russian nationalism—studied the situation and concluded: "The Russian Jews are different from other Jews; they are orthodox and believe in the Talmud." In his travels, Uvarov had seen modern Jews of Western Europe who had had a secular education, had abandoned the Talmud, and had assimilated with alacrity. Consequently, he reasoned, the influence of the Talmud had to be removed from Russian Jews, too. To this end, a commission was appointed: "Commission for Finding Ways and Means for the Radical Transformation of the Jews in Russia." The "Ways and Means" Count Uvarov favored was a system of crown elementary and secondary schools for Jewish children at which secular subjects would be taught and the Jewish religion "according," he explained to the czar, "to Holy Writ." In order to overcome the deep suspicion of Jews in the Pale that this was a scheme to convert their children, Uvarov finally persuaded a respected young German rabbi, Dr. Max Lilienthal, to head the schools and travel throughout the Pale to convince Jews, as he had been convinced, of Uvarov's high-minded motivations.

"Doctor," a Jewish leader in Vilna said to Lilienthal, "are you fully acquainted with the leading principles of our Government? . . . The Government intends but to have one Church in the whole Empire. . . ." For good reason, the religious leaders of Vilna believed that "education without emancipation leads to conversion." Lilienthal assured the Vilna rabbis that if he found this to be the case, he would immediately disassociate himself from the project.

A year later, after one of Uvarov's officials suggested to Lilienthal that he should consider becoming Russian Orthodox, Lilienthal awoke to the fact that he had been duped. He left hurriedly for the United States; there he wrote: "The horrible hatred against the Jew in Russia is nothing more to me than a crazy remembrance." At his death, in 1882, many of those Russian Jews he tried to help injudiciously had just begun a belated escape similar to his own.

By 1850 Nicholas had abandoned the crown schools despite their lucrative source of income—textbooks brought in one kopeck and a half tax per page, and pages were always set in large type with wide margins—and his campaign to make docile Russian Orthodox subjects out of Russian Jews had floundered—in the vernacular, *farblonjet*. In that year he therefore issued a ukase banning the Jewish form of dress and ritual adornment. To enforce it, the imperial government encouraged the most bizarre kind of harassment. Police lurked at street corners, ready to spring out at any Jew wearing the customary long black caftan and earlocks, *payess*—worn in strict observance of the command in Leviticus 19:27: "Ye shall not round the corners of your heads, neither shalt thou mar the corners of thy beard." Armed with shears, they would cut the skirt of the caftan, trim away the *payess*.

Soon after these skirmishes with the Jews, the disaster of the Crimean War dispelled the great myth of Nicholas' military genius. While he, with his insistence on parade ground maneuvers and properly buttoned-up uniforms, may have been esthetically invincible, he managed to lose the war to the British despite a seemingly insurmountable obstacle—the monumental incompetence of the British General Staff. Shortly before the war ended, Nicholas died of influenza and, it was maintained by a few fanciful courtiers, of a broken heart.

His son and successor, Alexander II, disliked Jews, and any suggestion of extending them full civil rights appalled him. But there was a spirit of liberalism abroad among the Russian people, or perhaps Nicholas' policy of repression had grown too fatiguing. Consequently, the accession of Alexander II resulted in one profound improvement in Jewish life. The czar abolished juvenile conscription; the "soldier" children were free. "Get up, children!!" cried a voice outside a barracks where twelve-year-old conscripts lay sleeping. "A deliverance! You are free! An *ukaz* from the czar to release you!"

Alexander also abolished serfdom and thus became entrenched in history as the "Czar Liberator" (a type of czar not easily confused with the others). It was a golden age, Jews told one another. Perhaps, at last, the answer to the "Jewish Question" would be emancipation.

A long series of other reforms of Jewish policy took place within the first decade of Alexander's reign. Areas formerly closed to Jews were opened. Jewish university graduates were permitted to enter government service; merchants and artisans and their families might leave the Pale, live anywhere in Russia. Those who had no legal right to leave the Pale also left, because the congestion and restrictions of the Pale had grown worse while the punishment for illegal presence in interior Russia had eased. And since government-sponsored efforts to convert Jews through schools and colleges had halted, Jews flocked to them "like starving persons suddenly treated to a delicious meal."

Haskalah—the movement to spread Western culture among Jews, begun a hundred years earlier in Germany by Moses Mendelssohn, Felix Mendelssohn's Jewish grandfather—had already taken root in the Pale, particularly in Lithuania, a hotbed of intellectualism. And notwithstanding the extreme disapproval of Orthodox leaders, young men and women developed an appetite for secular knowledge. When the son of the great scholar Rabbi Israel Salanter went off to Berlin to study medicine, his father sat *shivah*—the seven-day mourning period. Many a yeshiva *bochur* bent over the Pentateuch which held an opened clandestine math or geography book or a Victor Hugo novel. One of Chaim Weizmann's teachers affected by the Haskalah went so far as to have his students read aloud from a book on natural science and chemistry, and so that passersby wouldn't suspect, they chanted these secular words with a singsong rhythm and traditional swaying of the body, as though they were reading from the Talmud. No longer did affluent Jews yearn for a Talmudic scholar for a son-in-law; now they wanted their daughters to marry university graduates.

Convinced that a benign era had arrived in Russia, Jewish intellectuals jubilantly urged their co-religionists to embrace the Russian language, Russian life, and the Russian fatherland. They greeted every sign of civility on the part of non-Jews with a lyrical awe appropriate for the parting of the Red Sea.

"What happened! What miracles!" exclaimed a Jew who had been admitted to a gentile club. "They elected me not in spite of my being a Jew, but because of it, so that I might serve as an instrument for the expression of their highest ideal." Their gratitude, a Jewish historian observed sourly, "bordered on flunkeyism."

However, in addition to lifting many Jewish restrictions, Alexander II did three things—although one wasn't voluntary —that initiated the pogroms and started the flood of Jewish immigration toward Castle Garden. He made a disastrous choice of tutor for his heir; he set aside his wife and took a mistress; and he was assassinated.

Infected, perhaps, with the concept of liberation—if serfs were freed, why not czars?—Alexander II cast an admiring eye on Princess Catherine Dolgoruky, twenty years his junior, fell wildly in love, and despite a pang or so of guilt ("Don't speak to me of the Empress," he would say occasionally to one of his ministers; "it makes me suffer too much"), he established her as his mistress. The czarina did the conventional, sportsmanlike thing by turning her attention to piety and by dying in 1880. However, her eldest son, the Grand Duke Alexander, reacted to his father's infidelity with open resentment, nor did he try to hide his animosity for Princess Catherine and the three children she bore the czar. Six weeks after the czarina died, Alexander II married Princess Catherine and legitimatized their children. As a consequence, the bitterness of the Grand Duke increased; it was further intensified by the presence of his father's new wife at the dinner table, sitting above the grand duke and his wife.

Even before the marriage, two rival camps existed in the palace: A liberal—at least by Russian standards—set of advisers, headed by Count Mikhail Loris-Melikov, rallied around Princess Catherine, and a reactionary one around the grand duke. Among the latter, Konstantin Petrovich Pobyedonostzev proved himself the grand duke's unfailing source of comfort and advice. Formerly a professor of civil law at Moscow University and the grand duke's tutor, Pobyedonostzev was now procurator of the Holy Synod—lay leader of the Orthodox Church.

To say Pobyedonostzev was a reactionary was stark understatement. Emaciated, with a skin like parchment, possessing "pinched features cast in a Byzantine mould," cold sharp eyes framed by steel-rimmed glasses resting on his pointed nose, his appearance reflected his character. Sentiment, though not a frequent indulgence, may have moved him—a flower in bloom, a bird in flight, properly filed documents—but he more often gave the impression of being "a kind of wooden ruling machine in human shape to whom the living units of mankind are nothing, while the maintenance of bureaucratic order is everything." His smile, according to a nihilist hiding in London, was "ghastly." He worshiped autocracy and the Orthodox Church, and every year he retired to a monastery for a period of meditation and austere living. As for his political philosophy, "on those occasions," wrote an impressed colleague, "when in his excitement, he raised both arms and pictured the horrors awaiting the Empire if the measure he happened to be opposing would be adopted, he was something worth seeing." And the numerous measures Pobyedonostzev opposed were similar in nature. The nations of the West were "rotten"; constitutions were "a fundamental evil"; universal suffrage "a fatal error"; a free press "one of the falsest institutions of our time"; democracy was "The Great Falsehood of Our Time"; and public education should be extended only to the ruling class, for it made the lower classes dissatisfied. "Humanity," he believed, "is endowed with another very effective force: inertia. This force which the superficial thinkers of the new school confuse with ignorance and stupidity is absolutely essential to the prosperity of society." Indeed, the march of human progress made him extremely uneasy. "I wish," he once remarked wistfully, "people would stop inventing things."

To the Jewish people, whose long history had provided experiences with a Haman, a Torquemada, and a Nicholas I, Pobyedonostzev was no novelty. In much the same way that world wars have been distinguished by number, Nicholas I was branded the "second Haman," and Pobyedonostzev was classified as the "second Torquemada." Be that as it may, on Sunday evenings between nine and twelve o'clock, while in his beautiful library—surrounded by evidence of his love for art and literature and under the salutary influence of a glass of hot Russian tea—Pobyedonostzev appeared to American Ambassador Andrew White as "a scholarly kindly man" who "seemed to have no harsh feelings against Israelites as such." But out of the library and its benign glow, the procurator could be quite another man.

Though he claimed to keep a volume of Emerson's essays on his study table at all times, Emerson's influence obviously hadn't stayed his hand in his "war upon ideas and crusade of ignorance." But the American Revolution and the establishment of the United States *had* served as an ideal to Pobyedonostzev's bitter enemies, Russian liberal intellectuals, from the Decembrists on.

Following the reforms of the early days of Alexander II, it became clear that the imperial commitment to reform was not wholehearted and that the idea of a constitutional monarchy horrified a liberal Romanov quite as thoroughly as it had reactionary Romanovs. According to Prince Kropotkin, Alexander II wasn't "what one could describe as a truly reliable man either in his policy or in personal sympathies. . . ." Faced with this situation, the liberal and radical movements in Russia, in their desperation, fragmented still further into a kind of utopian socialism and into nihilism. Jews, having suffered most from autocracy, were to be found in all these groups—and had been especially attracted to the less violent idealism of socialism.

In the eradication of existing social and economic institutions—in order to make a pristine, viable beginning—nihilists encouraged individual initiative in bomb throwing and assassination. Such irrevocable incidents were occurring with alarming frequency. One afternoon while Alexander rode along the Catherine Canal, a group of nihilists who had been living in the home of a Jewish woman, Hesia Helfman, hurled a nitroglycerin bomb directly at him and blew him to pieces.

As he passed the bier of his assassinated father, Alexander III, a huge, simpleminded man, not given to acute thought or fanciful expression, remarked with sincerity of feeling, "I should not like my son to ascend the throne under such circumstances as the present." If the new czar had any aptitude at all—and from the start of their relationship, his tutor, Pobyedonostzev, had feared he hadn't—it was for absorbing the intricacies of repression. His remarkably large head, more immense even than his father's, led the New York *Times* to speculate that "this form of head may have been produced according to Darwinian theory, by several generations of autocratic power."

Shortly after Alexander II's death, Alexander III conferred secretly with the proponents of two distinct ideologies in one of the 900 rooms of the imperial palace at Gatchina. ("The palace was surrounded by moats and protected by a watch tower," with "trap doors in the study for suddenly throwing an enemy on the sharp rocks in the water underneath" and with a "secret staircase leading to underground prisons and to an underground passage which opens on a lake.") Present were his imperial majesty's minister of the interior, Count Mikhail Tarielovich Loris-Melikov, and Konstantin Pobyedonostzev. Loris-Melikov wished to combat revolutionary activity with a series of moderate reforms; he therefore urged Alexander III to carry out his plan of a modified form of representative government, outlined in a document which the late czar had signed several hours before his murder. But moderate reform was no less evil to Pobyedonostzev than revolutionary activity. And Pobyedonostzev's position now was secure; his former pupil was czar. Moreover, a government dominated by the procurator's fanatically nationalistic policy of Russia for the Russians, doomed the position of Loris-Melikov, an Armenian. In addition to having an alien heritage, Loris-Melikov had been the adviser of the new czar's despised stepmother. Consequently, soon after the conference at Gatchina, it was reported that "the Princess Dolgoruky, the morganatic wife of the late Czar, has left St. Petersburg and will not return." And Count Loris-Melikov handed in his resignation, retiring to the more salubrious climate of Nice, France.

Within two weeks of Loris-Melikov's departure, an imperial manifesto that bore the unambiguous stamp of Pobyedonostzev, who had drafted it, declared: "The voice of God hath commanded us to take up vigorously the reins of government, inspiring us with the belief in the strength and truth of autocratic power, which we are called upon to establish and safeguard."

However Olympian the sentiment, however divine its origin, one technique of safeguarding the "strength and truth of autocratic power" rested on a staple always popular in imperial circles and one which Pobyedonostzev readily utilized—anti-Semitism. Jews were incapable of assimilation—*i.e.*, conversion—as all the futile efforts of the Romanovs up to this time made evident; therefore, it was necessary to pursue "a repressive policy toward them. . . ." That a Jewish woman had harbored the czar's assassins served the procurator's purposes admirably.

One of Pobyedonostzev's weapons was a secret society, the Sacred League, which he organized to protect the life of Alexander III. The league consisted of about 300 army officers who received triple salaries as an inducement to join and whose duties included the covert surveillance of all classes of society. It was "said to be much superior to that of the ordinary secret police." The excessive zeal of these *agents provocateurs* at times appeared sheer *opéra bouffe*. ("Two officers without knowing that they both belonged to the league would entice each other into a disloyal conversation, during a railway journey, and then proceed to arrest each other, only to discover at the last moment that their pains had been labor lost.") The league also organized pogroms and sent emissaries to cities in the Pale to prepare police for inaction in the event of riots against Jews and to dispatch "the bare-foot brigade" (tramps) to arouse hostility to Jews among the peasants in the Pale.

Because of their "temperance and industry," Pobyedonostzev maintained, Jews endangered Russia's very existence. Still, their real threat lay not in these two virtues, menacing as they may have appeared to the procurator, but in their failure to bow before his three gods; a trinity of autocracy, orthodoxy, and nationalism. In any event, the Jews had to be eradicated, and Pobyedonostzev had a formula for their destruction, a simple one, but aptly a trinity in form and certain—he thought—to be effective: "force one third to emigrate, another third to embrace Christianity and the remainder to die of starvation."

Although the Romanovs—particularly from Nicholas I on—had not been as methodical as to formularize their objectives, the elements of Pobyedonostzev's plan had dwelled in their hearts. They also held failure in common and for the same reason: They did not understand their adversary, the singular complexity that made the Russian Jew invincible from that kind of attack.

2

"Scattered Islands in a Gentile Ocean"

The Russian code of laws classified the aliens inhabiting the Russian empire as: (1) the Siberian aliens; (2) the Samoyeds of the government of Archangel; (3) the nomadic aliens of the government of Stravropol; (4) the Kalmyks leading a nomadic life in the governments of Astrakhan and Stavropol; (5) the Kirgiz of the Inner Ord; (6) the aliens of the territories of Akmolinsk, Semipalatinsk, Semiryechensk, Ural, and Turga; (7) the alien population of the Transcaspian Territory; and (8) the Jews. Of these eight groups, the Jews proved the most stubborn, vexing, puzzling, and contrary, for though they appeared vulnerable—pallid, scrawny scholars, shabby artisans, isolated in a curious world of piety, righteousness, and love of God—the might of the Russian imperial government could not, paradoxically, penetrate the armor of their identity.

Five million of them—half the world's Jewish population—had been forced by imperial decree to live in the Pale, which was, except for the Crimea, a 313,000-square-mile monotonously flat, sand-arid prison. This 300-mile-wide plain—about the size of Texas, stretching along Russia's western border, sustaining scrub pine and producing harvests that to American observers "scarcely appeared worth cultivating"—also served as a buffer zone, a barricade against invaders from the West. In attempting to traverse it, Napoleon had lost 400,000 men, thus proving that no army could subsist on land virtually as barren and unproductive as a firebreak. In the southern part of the Pale—the more fertile part, in the gubernia of Ekaterinoslav—the soil was black, but droughts destroyed crops so frequently that only one year out of five yielded any crop at all. Sometimes water had to be carried from as far as five miles. But it was here, in the 808 *shtetlach* —townlets, "scattered islands in a gentile ocean"—that Russian Jews found not only the strength and fortitude to endure, but a spiritual reserve that made them flourish. It was during this period, wrote Abraham Heschal, that the Jews "attained the highest degree of inwardness . . . the golden period in Jewish history, in the history of the Jewish soul."

Most American Jews of East European descent can recall their parents' or grandparents' stories of *shtetl* life. Sometimes as these memories were evoked, former residents of different *shtetlach* insisted no other place anywhere in the world could be so dirty, so exposed to jeopardy, and so unbelievably poverty-stricken as theirs. ("Zosleh was so poor that there was no glass for the windows." "So who had windows?" "Who said windows? A board fell out, so there was a hole, a window." "Boards? *You* had boards? The Graf Pototski* had boards, not us.") All agreed the vast forest surrounding the *shtetl* held constant dangers—wolves, bears, and Russian or Polish peasants—as ferocious, when inflamed by vodka, as the beasts. And in the *shtetl* itself the local police officials preyed on them. Yet in these reminiscences could be heard a lingering strain of longing, of nostalgic affection for old Motel, Neustadt, or Kimanye.

What made *shtetl* life so memorable, such a unifying force —and consequently, a substantial irritant in the workings of the Romanov autocracy? It could hardly have been the *shtetl*'s physical attributes, thatched old wooden one-story hovels, leaning precariously on makeshift foundations, clustered together on streets of viscous black mud (the unforgettable

* The Graf Pototski may have originally referred to an eighteenth-century Polish count—Valintin Potocki—who was supposed to have converted to Judaism and was burned at the stake in Vilna. But whoever he really was, Graf Pototski became the generic name among *shtetl* Jews for rich, imperious, and often cruel Polish and Russian noblemen, such as Prince Czartoryski, who hunted Jews in Podolia "because there was so little game left in the neighborhood." "Look," a mother would say to a child waxing arrogant in the kitchen, "look, a regular Graf Pototski!"

shtetl blotte) or, in dry weather, of choking dust that transformed the atmosphere into a yellow haze. The water supply consisted of a barrel of water in the kitchen, frequently the only room. There was no sewage system, and the smells of the dishwater thrown into the streets revealed, sensitive *shtetl* dwellers noted, "what day of the week it is."

Shtetl life centered on the marketplace, often too grand a name for a mere collection of pitifully shabby stalls frequently run by women whose husbands spent their time in the study of the Talmud. Of the entire *shtetl* population—of which, generally, at least two-thirds was Jewish—only 5 percent lived in any degree of comfort. The rest adjusted to abject poverty and engaged in such occupations as shoemaking, tailoring, carpentry, lime burning, and blacksmithing.

While these occupations had the substantial sound of subsistence, in reality they provided only a hand-to-mouth existence. A *shtetl* shoemaker, for example, could cover peasants' homemade moccasins with leather, make boots by stitching leggings onto shoes, repair soles and heels; but in summer the peasants went barefoot. The work of a *shtetl* tailor might not be as seasonal, but it offered a meager income. He could charge only 20 kopecks—ten cents—for making a shirt. Blacksmithing, an almost exclusively Jewish occupation in Lithuania, was slightly more rewarding in that the smith received vegetables and grain in addition to a small amount of money. Apart from making and repairing tools, shoeing horses, and fashioning iron runners for sleds and spokes for wheels, Izek the smith, Schloma the smith, and Velvil the smith also turned out cooking utensils. (Their work lives on through the ubiquitous heavy black iron skillet, displayed in ancestral splendor from condominiums in Miami Beach to contemporary aeries with a view of the Pacific and Catalina). Yet they, too, like all *shtetl* artisans, could not make a sufficient income from one trade. "The best cobbler of all the tailors," *shtetl* wits would say, "is Yankel the baker." They were rich in irony, but little else. "I am a little cobbler/Living day in and day out/Jolly, merry and fine," they sang, concluding, "I am a cobbler, but I go barefoot." And in the Yiddish folk song, the little tinsmith, too, lived day in and day out, "jolly, merry and fine/I sit and hammer on other people's roofs/But by me in the house it leaks."

There were also those without a regular trade at all. They —the *luftmenshn*— lived on air. To ask a *luftmensh* how he made a living might elicit this reply: "I'm a little bit a *shammes* [sexton], a little bit a matchmaker, before the holidays I sell palm branches for Sukkos, in the season I help out the tailor, and besides, I have a brother in the United States who sends me every month a little something."

Attached diagonally to the doorpost of every house, a mezuzah, a small metal receptacle containing a piece of parchment on which monotheism is proclaimed, served as a reminder to Jews of the heavenly source of all their material wealth. In the *shtetl*, understandably, the mezuzah became an object to ward off evil spirits, which, of course, included the czars.

Though small and primitive, the *shtetl* was a highly organized entity, with its own culture, language, governing body, and social system. Essentially theocratic, all but the smallest *shtetlach* supported their own shul, rabbi, cemetery, *khevreh kedisha* (burial society), *chedar* (school), *mikveh* (ritual bath), *shochet* (ritual slaughterer), and a dozen or more charities that assisted orphans, dowerless brides, students, and destitute strangers. Those who could afford it were also called upon to contribute a ruble or two to some family for Passover, for that holiday required not only interruption in work, but special food, dishes, pots, and pans. "In fact," reported a 1907 American Bureau of Labor study of the economic condition of the Jews in Russia, "the Jewish family that lives from hand to mouth finds itself facing the approaching Passover absolutely unable to meet it according to the commands of the Hebraic law, and consequently in danger of committing a serious sin." One-fifth of the Jews in Russia needed some assistance at Passover, though sometimes a family received as little as 75 kopecks—39 cents.

In addition to such community obligations, there were special taxes imposed on the Jews by the imperial government. Not only were they confined to the Pale, but the government also attacked them through the externals of their religious life: the candle tax on Sabbath lights, and the box tax, divided into two classifications—general and subsidiary. The general tax was levied on every ritually slaughtered animal or bird and on every pound of kosher meat. The subsidiary tax applied to the rents of houses or shops, business profits, inheritances, and clothing specially worn by Jews. To wear a *yarmulke* (skullcap), for instance, one had to pay a tax of five silver rubles a year.

The constant expense of buying immunity from police harassment added still more to their burden. "Each restrictive measure passed against the Jews is a living source of bribes for the Russian policemen." And in the Russian code of laws there were 650 such measures directed specifically toward Jews. (Though a non-Jewish peasant suffered intense poverty too, "police favor was retailed at a lower price to him than to the Jew.")

Despite destitution and the punitive regulations inflicted by the imperial government, the *shtetl* prevailed, unified by its spiritual life; by a constant dream of a homeland, Palestine; and by what had shielded Jews since the Exodus—their Covenant with God. For His part, God promised to protect and guide the Jewish people, though the capriciousness He had shown in carrying out this promise often caused *shtetl* Jews to reproach Him, for their relationship with God was an informal one derived from long acquaintanceship. (As a child, Abraham Cahan, editor of the *Jewish Daily Forward,* visualized Him as another boy, sitting high in the clouds and wearing a *yarmulke.*) For their part, Jews accepted God—one God—and promised obedience to His Law as given to Moses at Sinai, for the children of Israel. It had been an onerous undertaking, for the demands of this Covenant, as set down in the Torah, involved 613 commandments. Among all the injunctions, those dealing with education received the greatest emphasis. That the Jewish religion made learning an integral part of its theology accounted in large measure for the Russian Jews' ability to survive in spite of the Romanovs. Learning linked inextricably with the inner life provided strength and dignity and a superiority to ephemeral, demeaning externals. The most desirable marital catch was therefore not the richest, the handsomest, or the hardest worker, but the scholar of repute. And the highest honor—*koved*—a family could achieve was to produce a man of erudition. In East Europe, this tradition of learning focused for centuries on religious subjects, but when the hundreds of thousands of *shtetl* dwellers settled in the United States, they applied themselves to secular subjects. (After all, even William Rosenthal, founder of the Maidenform Brassiere Company, received a Talmudic education in Rakov, Russia.) And they produced—out of all proportion to the size of the immigration—an incalculable number of intellectuals—and even pseudointellectuals.

It naturally followed that the rabbi should be the man of the highest status in his *shtetl* and that ritual regulate every aspect of *shtetl* life, from the morning prayer—Shaharith—recited upon awakening, through the late-afternoon prayer—Minhah—to the evening prayer—Maariv. In between, the devout recited a hundred blessings: a separate benediction for each item of food or drink in a meal, for the first time in a season that a particular food was eaten, for fragrant odors, upon washing one's hands, on the occurrence of natural phenomena—from earthquakes to rainbows. . . .

Though these benedictions—by the weight of their number and repetition—may at times have deteriorated to mere reflex, their beautiful intent shone through: The individual should be ever aware of the Divine, the omnipresence of God.

Equally thorough was the Talmud's argumentative commentary on the Torah. These interpretations were subjected to the most minute scrutiny by scholars, whose pilpulistic legerdemain led them to debate shades of meaning imperceptible to others. Consequently, each rabbinical scholar had his own fervid following, supporters who displayed all the intense devotion that someday many of their more secular American descendants would give to the Brooklyn Dodgers.

At an early age every boy was sent to *chedar*—Hebrew school—usually one dismal room in which the teacher and his family also lived. And the ferocity of *shtetl* Hebrew teachers was legendary. Rabbi Joel Margaretten, whose son emigrated to the United States and became a founding partner of Horowitz Brothers & Margareten, Matzo Bakers, recalled that in his youth there was one *chedar* teacher who had three kinds of straps: "One for meat, one for milk and a third for vegetable days. The child would be asked 'what did you eat today, meat or milk?' The strap would be suited to the diet."

"Everything comes second to learning," a Vilna rabbi told his son. "It is more important than prayers, more important than anything else."

But, of course, this rabbi was a Litvak—a Lithuanian Jew.

In the southwestern Pale, the Polish provinces, particularly in Galicia, the Hassidim were zealous followers of a gentle children's teacher and lime digger, Isaac ben Eliezer, known as the *Baal Shem Tov* and affectionately by an acronym, Besht. He had rebelled against the cold intellectuality, the everlasting probing and verbal hairsplitting of Lithuanian Talmudic scholars. The Hassidim emphasized the Jewish heart rather than the Jewish head. God, they believed, was more impressed with excessive zeal than with incessant learning. To bury oneself in books in the name of piety—as the Litvaks did—actually affronted God, for He wanted men to enjoy His sensual gifts—food, drink, love. So the Hassidim laughed, danced, sang, worshiped through joy. (Eventually, there was a reaction among Hassidim against anti-intellectuality, and they, too, began turning out eminent scholars.)

From this mind versus emotion conflict, the great Litvak-Galitzianer feud developed in the close-knit Pale and, paradoxically, in the process of dividing the Pale, gave it a unifying controversy. Litvaks scorned Galitzianers as common, uneducated dolts—*prosteh*—and Galitzianers derided Litvaks for their cold pedantry. In the United States, as generation succeeded generation and the basis for the antipathy was forgotten, the feud mellowed to more or less good-natured Litvak-Galitzianer jokes.

But even when the animosity raged, neither Litvak nor Galitzianer would say that the other did not possess *Yiddishkayt*. In contemporary idiom, *Yiddishkayt* might be defined—though inadequately—as Jewish "soul." Yet it was the Jewish heart—the *Yiddish hertz*—that figured more intrinsically. To have *rachmones*—compassion—was vital to *Yiddishkayt,* which evolved in the *shtetl,* as a blend of religious, ethical, and cultural values. *Yiddishkayt* blessed one with an ineffable way of viewing life, its divine mysteries, as well as its superficialities—and you either had it or you didn't. In the United States the close ties of religion and nostalgia enhanced the essentials of *Yiddishkayt*. And it was there that East European Jews would regard themselves as the upholders of *Yiddishkayt*. They were the "Jewish Jews" as opposed to their American co-religionists of German descent who were—what were they?—*gornisht*, nothing.

Indeed, *Yiddishkayt*, in diluted form, would be one of the few elements of *shtetl* life to survive in the United States. As one generation after another became more secular, and piety became shul attendance solely on Rosh Hashonah and Yom Kippur, and Talmudic scholarship was displaced by the mastery of Bar Mitzvah speeches, only a tenuous *Yiddishkayt* lingered, a mere link with the past. But the culture developed by Russian Jews had served as a citadel of civilization in the midst of an oppressive society and a spiritual refuge, steadfast in spite of all the attempts of the imperial government to subvert it.

3

Baron de Gunzburg,
Baron de Hirsch, et al.

In 1911, an American Immigration Commission report on the reasons for the enormous immigration concluded, as government reports have always done, with the obvious: "that the Jews are emigrating, not because it is impossible for them to find sufficient earnings in Russia, but because the Government deprives them of the most elemental conditions of life and property. . . . Let but the pogroms cease and the emigration of the Jews will immediately and considerably diminish. . . ."

"Pogrom" is a Russian word whose literal meaning is devastation and destruction. Before 1881 there had been three other pogroms in the nineteenth century, two of them in Odessa, considered the most cosmopolitan city in Russia. But in 1881 the imperial government, driven by its pathological (but not, by any means, paranoid) fear of revolution, used pogroms as a strategic *divertissement* and also as a weapon in their continuing war on all dissenting minorities.

To the illiterate muzhik, sunk in squalid poverty, frightened by the revolutionary movement, galled incessantly by his condition, how simple, how efficacious, how like a trusted old ally for the agents of the imperial government to say the *Zhyds*— "Yids," the Russian pejorative for Jews—had caused it all.

Thus, to "beat the *Zhyds*" was to do one's duty to God and country, a gratifying sensation.

In the quarter century from 1881 to 1906 there were three periods of pogroms: 1881–1882; 1891–1892; 1903–1906. The pogroms of the first two periods had a desultory amateurish quality: a few hundred feather beds slashed; houses and shops looted; several dozen people killed; here and there, a few skull fractures, broken limbs, and women and girls raped. But from October 17, 1905, to the end of 1906, 661 towns and cities were devastated, 38,000 families or 162,000 individuals affected; 985 people were killed; 1,492 badly wounded; 387 women became widows; 177 children were completely orphaned; 1,474 lost one parent.

From its vantage point on Park Row in New York, the *Times,* with an air of romantic adventure, described the ringleaders of the pogroms as "strangers from the North"; more specifically, they were a road company of tough, mean tramps, recruited from the slum warrens of the cities. These men turned up at railroad stations in any city destined for a pogrom, sowed rumors of Christian sacrilege committed by Jews, read articles aloud from anti-Semitic papers, and declared that everyone could oblige the czar—the Little Father —by "beating the *Zhyds*." Further prodding continued in taverns. Then, the fury, the savagery of drunken peasants, intoxicated not only with vodka, but with the heady brew of imperial sanction, spilled over into the streets, where they began assaulting passing Jews. Within a few days, 125 Jews suffering mutilations were carried into one hospital in Odessa. "Kishinev," wrote Simon Dubnow, the noted Jewish historian, in 1919, concerning the pogrom in 1903, "was the scene of bestialities such as find few parallels even in the history of the most barbarous age."*

To an accompaniment of whistling, jeering, and hooting, the mobs of vodka-exhilarated muzhiks would demolish Jewish homes and stores, "whole streets literally razed." Thousands of impoverished Jewish families lost whatever they possessed, were homeless and dependent on charity, although "authorities have forbidden the opening of subscriptions for their relief." The mobs threw themselves on synagogues, shredding Torah scrolls, the word of God laboriously penned by scribes on parchment, and trampling them in the dust; they

---

* Dubnow underrated civilization's capacity for barbarism. He was killed by the Nazis in 1943.

were comforted, no doubt, by the Special Restrictive Law Sections 219 to 233, Penal Code 1885, Number 170, which stated that such an offense was not sacrilege.

Even before the broken windows and unhinged doors of homes were thrown into the street, thick clouds of goose and duck feathers loosed from innumerable feather beds—*perinehs*, the dowries of Jewish brides—would swirl through the air and descend gracefully on the destruction below. These feather beds served a secondary but vital function: Occasionally apprehensive parents rolled up their pretty young daughters in them, to conceal the girls from predatory, lustful Cossacks. (As a child, Beverly Sills' mother was hidden during a pogrom in a pickle barrel.) Many years later, when an elderly woman from Bialystok viewed with awe the activities of her teen-age American grandchildren, she recalled that she had spent most of *her* adolescence rolled up in a feather quilt.

Police and army troops were among the detached observers of most pogroms. They stood silently by, regarding the violence and looting with what most generously might be called a bemused expression. In some cities, such as Kiev, the police waited until the mob had demolished one Jewish area and then escorted them to another; in still other cities after two days of violence and looting went by ("Two days shalt thou plunder and on the third shalt thou rest"), the police made a show of doing their duty: fired a few admonishing shots; arrested a few rioters, but more of their victims.

Before many pogroms had occurred, a fiery ideal gripped young Jews. Even many of those young revolutionaries whose attitude had been "We, as international socialists, may not feel any particular responsibility for one's brothers according to origin" reacted to the pogroms by identifying themselves with other Jews. Rallying around a Jewish nationalist movement, the students determined to organize and fight to defend themselves and their families from the mob, despite the imperial government's declaration that "self-defense societies should not be tolerated." At one synagogue in Odessa, a group of radical students appeared one evening to rouse the people to self-defense. Long alienated from the religious community, they "spoke to the people in Yiddish . . . quoting from Biblical and rabbinic literature [and] evoked a strong response. Many burst into tears at the sight of this rapprochement . . . children who have returned after many years in an alien world to their mother."

However, for the middle-aged, for family groups, for the

old, self-defense usually consisted of a few families agreeing to band together when a pogrom struck. Sometimes self-defense merely meant finding sanctuary in a cemetery or hiring rooms for one's family for a night in a brothel, the only place offering temporary shelter. Self-defense also took the curious form of fast days of mourning proclaimed from the great Lithuanian religious centers, Vilna and Kovno. So when St. Petersburg—pogrom headquarters—signaled a pogrom, Kovno—fast headquarters—struck back with a fast day.

"True," wrote Zionist leader Shmarya Levin, "the war was conducted with unequal weapons. But the Jews had one advantage: their ammunition was cheaper. . . ." His mother, he recalled, found the formally decreed fasts insufficient; so she proclaimed an extra fast or so a week of her own, which caused family arguments. "Elke," his father would implore, "is it your business to provide the entire world with piety?" "Let me fast, Samuel Chaim," his mother would answer, "let me get some sort of pleasure out of my life."

Since the specific goal of pogroms was to destroy Judaism, perhaps fasts, in their way, were a more irritating response in the government's eyes than violence. Another irritant stemmed from pogroms that went beyond the second day; the mob got out of hand, and non-Jewish property was destroyed, too. Thus, inevitably, rioters—driven by momentum into continuing their depredations despite police demands that they stop—were arrested. This, understandably, made them aggrieved. "They told us we had permission to beat the Jews," a peasant complained indignantly, "and now it appears it was all a lie."

Czar Alexander III was equally distressed. Upon reading a report of the Warsaw governor-general for 1882 which referred to the necessary inhibition of *pogromschiks* by the army, the czar noted glumly in the margin, "This is the sad thing in all these Jewish disorders."

Every fifth man in the Pale was a *luftmensh*—an individual without visible means of support—but there was only one Baron Horace de Gunzburg. To live in St. Petersburg or any city outside the Pale, a Jew had to be a merchant of the first guild, or an artisan practicing his trade, or a prostitute following hers. To live in Paris and commute to St. Petersburg for business and philanthropy, a Jew had to be the Baron de Gunzburg.

His father, Baron Yevzel de Gunzburg, a native of Vitebsk,

had left his *chedar* and yeshiva studies behind him for the more ephemeral satisfaction of acquiring great wealth, of having his family regarded as the "Rothschilds of Russia." During the early palmy years—the golden age—of Alexander II's reign, Gunzburg (the baronetcy and the accompanying aristocratic prefix "de," bestowed on the Gunzburgs by the Archduke of Hesse-Darmstadt and graciously acceded to by Alexander II, were not conferred until 1872) founded the first private banking house in Russia: Y. E. Gunzburg of St. Petersburg. When the Russian government could not raise the capital to build railroads, the Gunzburgs, with their ready access to West European banking houses, secured the capital to lay 14,000 miles of track. Having achieved a wary amity with the imperial government, Gunzburg at the same time attained the status of *shtadlan,* a wealthy, influential individual who represents and intercedes for his fellow Jews with the government. His major accomplishment had been in gaining those residential rights outside the Pale for merchants of the first guild and artisans. (The individual who won residential rights for Jewish prostitutes disappeared into history, anonymous and uncelebrated.)

The means Gunzburg used in having the residential restrictions raised were the tried-and-true methods of generations of *shtadlonim.* He petitioned the czar humbly and compliantly to lift the disabilities "from the best among us," so that "the whole Jewish people, seeing that these few favored ones are the object of the Government's righteousness and benevolence and models of what it desires the Jews to become would joyfully hasten to attain the goal marked out by the Government."

As the "golden age" of Alexander II began to tarnish and restrictions against Jews mounted, the Gunzburgs—Yevzel, until his death in 1878 in Paris, and Horace—worked tirelessly to ameliorate conditions. The imperious quality of Horace's erect, almost defiant bearing, the determined positioning of his domed, spade-bearded countenance were apt in a financier, but the sadness of his eyes, full-bagged and somber, bespoke a lineage of philanthropy and compassion. Undeniably, Baron de Gunzburg was swayed by the most acute compassion for his fellow Russian Jews, but he also displayed a remarkable innocence regarding the motivations of the imperial government. Distance, perhaps, enhanced the view from Paris; those in Kovno gubernia were onstage participants in the drama. And it may have been that Baron de Gunzburg

saw in the government's demands for Jews to assimilate a reflection of his own desire that Russian Jews abandon, not
their religion, but their separate Yiddish and Hebrew culture,
that they adopt Russian as their language. Yiddish, Baron de
Gunzburg believed, along with his fellow Jewish financiers in
the United States, "was no language at all, but a jargon."
Proof of its illegitimacy was "it has no grammar." And its
persistent use by Russian Jews was ruinous to any possible accommodation between Russians and Jews. Moreover, he had
every reason to believe it was possible to negotiate with the
imperial government. Had not he and his father successfully
dealt with it for years? One need only accommodate oneself
to their predilections. It was merely necessary to placate,
show suitable humility, present them with some advantage un-
available elsewhere, and make a large enough monetary sacrifice to their greed, and they were almost as amenable as one
could wish. To further the goal of Russification, the
Gunzburgs in 1863 had organized the Society for the Diffu-
sion of Culture among Jews in Russia. As one of the organization's founders explained:

> We constantly hear men in high positions, with whom we
> come in contact, complain about the separation and fanaticism
> of the Jews and about their aloofness from everything Russian,
> and we have received assurances on all hands that, with the re-
> moval of these peculiarities, the condition of our brethren in
> Russia will be improved and we shall all become full-fledged
> citizens of this country.

After the outbreak of the spring pogroms in 1881, Baron de
Gunzburg, accompanied by several other representatives of
Russian Jewry, drove out to Gatchina Palace for an audience
with Alexander III. Surely, it would be possible for the most
influential Jews in Russia—while declaring their "boundless
gratitude for the measures adopted to safeguard the Jewish
population at this sad moment"—to plead for a halt to the pogroms. And it *was* possible. De Gunzburg and his colleagues
weren't thrown into prison as some, more plebeian—Jewish
and non-Jewish—petitioners were. The czar with a degree of
civility told them, "State all this in a special memorandum,"
and refrained from repeating a comment he had privately
made: "In my heart, I am very happy when they beat the
Jews even though the practice cannot be permitted."

In September, 1881, when the National Line steamer *Egypt*

was on its way to New York carrying forty-eight Russian Jews among its steerage passengers, Baron de Gunzburg tried to deal rationally with the situation by conferring with a few of his affluent co-religionists in St. Petersburg about the problem of Jewish emigration. Before that meeting, the czar had appointed a man to succeed Loris-Melikov as minister of the interior, an office that embraced the Central Committee on Jewish Affairs. The new minister, Count Nikolai Pavlovich Ignatiev, had been recommended by Pobyedonostzev as a man of "healthy instincts and a Russian soul." Count Ignatiev was a fine-looking vigorous military figure, and elegant mustachios, reminiscent of Nicholas I's, embellished his commanding appearance. A member of the old nobility, he had earned great success in diplomatic posts, for his philosophy contained the proper elements of fanatical nationalism and anti-Semitism. He was also a pathological liar, with a celebrated reputation as the "Father of Lies" (among Turks as "Liar Pasha"), but the czar regarded this flaw as minor since he "lied only in little things." Thus when Baron de Gunzburg and his confreres consulted Ignatiev, the count blandly assured them of the "benevolent intentions of the Government."

Seven months later, a four-day conference—attended by twenty-five representatives from the Pale and fifteen prominent Jews of St. Petersburg, referred to by their lesser co-religionists with a tinge of sarcasm as "notables"—was called by Baron de Gunzburg with Ignatiev's permission. The purpose of this conference was to consider the question of emigration (though almost 10,000 Jews had already gone to the United States by the end of the previous year, and the end of 1882 would see three times that number disembark at American ports).

Many of the Pale delegates spoke out passionately for a Russian emigration organization. "Either we get civil rights or we emigrate," exclaimed Dr. Max Mandelstam of Kiev. "Our human dignity is being trampled upon, our wives and daughters are being dishonored, we are looted and pillaged; either we get decent human rights or else let us go wherever our eyes may lead us." Others, including Rabbi Isaac Elhanan Spector of Kovno, maintained that to turn to emigration as the solution would defeat all hope of emancipation. For their part, Baron de Gunzburg and the other notables were hesitant, apprehensive lest the desire to emigrate appear a criticism of Russia, and thus unpatriotic, even seditious. Yet not only had Ignatiev sent word to the conference that it should deliberate on ways of "thinning out the Jewish population in the Pale of Settlement, in view of the fact that the Jews will not be admitted into the interior governments of Russia," but the previous January he had plainly stated, "The Western frontier is open for the Jews." Nevertheless, by the end of the conference, the formation of a central emigration committee was rejected.

While the *shtadlonim* pondered mass emigration, Count Ignatiev had other plans afoot. His Central Committee drew up three special measures: No new Jewish settlers were permitted outside cities or townlets—*shtetlach*—of the Pale; Jews were forbidden to own or manage real estate or farms outside the cities of the Pale; Jews were not to transact business on Sunday or other Christian holidays. But before the count presented these measures for the czar's signature, he had his mother renew the twelve-year contracts with the Jewish managers of his estates in Kiev gubernia, and he intimated to Baron de Gunzburg that under proper terms he might change his mind.

"I have heard," he said to the baron, "that the Jews have collected a million rubles for me, and have deposited it in your bank."

"I know nothing about it," Baron de Gunzburg answered stolidly. "You have been misinformed."

So on May 3, 1882, the three measures were enacted as "Temporary Rules," though "temporary" was pure terminology, for they lasted thirty-five years, as long as the Romanovs themselves did.

The patent viciousness of the May Laws lay in their administration and elaboration, for as Chaim Weizmann wrote, they were "prolonged and broadened and extended until [they] came to cover every aspect of Jewish life; and as one read, year after year, the complicated ukases which poured from St. Petersburg, one obtained the impression that the whole cumbersome machinery of the vast Russian Empire was created for the sole purpose of inventing and amplifying rules and regulations for the hedging in of the existence of its Jewish subjects until it became something that was neither life nor death."

For a police state, the May Laws were consummate legislation—the perfect dry pogrom. The first of the May Laws forbade further Jewish residence in villages but failed to define a village. So cities like Palitski and Rechilovko could be arbitrarily declared villages, and a man who left Palitski for a few days to be married was expelled on his return because, he was told, he was a "new arrival." By classifying the suburbs of a large city like Vilna a village, any Jewish families who had settled there after May, 1882, could not remain. Even if a family moved from a house in which they had lived for many years to one across the road, they might be termed "new residents" and expelled. Often, *shtetlach*—shabby, muddy townlets—were transformed, as by a touch of a wand, into full-fledged villages. In 1893, 300 Jewish families of Jousovka, in the gubernia of Ekaterinoslav, were informed that their townlet was a village and they would have to leave. Someone, however, recalled that five years earlier when Alexander III and his family had miraculously escaped unhurt from a train wreck, the people of Jousovka had sent the czar a wire of congratulations, to which the czar had replied, "Thanks to the population of the *townlet* of Jousovka." So Jousovka Jews petitioned the czar. If he himself—his imperial majesty, autocrat of all autocrats—had said Jousovka was a townlet, wasn't Jousovka a townlet? Back from St. Petersburg came the answer. Jousovka was a townlet.

But such happy incidents were exceedingly rare. More often, in the late eighties and early nineties, thousands upon thousands of homeless Jewish families spilled out of authentic and pseudo villages into the few hundred teeming cities of the Pale. So congested had these cities become that three Jews were compelled to occupy the space used by one non-Jew. Entire families would rent a corner of a room.

As for those Jews who had special residential rights in cities outside the Pale, they, too, with the exception of Baron de Gunzburg and other influential St. Petersburg Jews, were no longer safe. Mass expulsions began from St. Petersburg, Moscow, Novgorod, Riga. The expulsion order from Moscow came on Passover and was carried out with merciless enthusiasm. Police and the citizenry hunted down artisans, merchants, and university graduates and their families—the reward for capturing one Jew was equal to that of capturing two non-Jewish looters. After a Jew's capture, he was arrested, placed in chains or handcuffs, and sent back to the teeming Pale like a criminal. There, in addition to the swarming population, new education restrictions contributed to the oppressive atmosphere. The number of Jewish students admitted to Gymnasiums—high schools—and universities would be determined by 10 percent of the Christian student body. And so "the classes in many classical and technical high schools remained half empty, for in the cities where the Jews constituted from 50 to 75 percent of the population, only 10 percent of the high school boys could be of the Jewish faith." To acquire a secondary education, then, a Jewish student, in effect, first had to recruit ten Christian students to make one opening for a Jew and then hope for admission. Indeed, a Jew in Russia found obtaining an education of any kind difficult. A young girl who wished to study shorthand in Moscow registered as a prostitute and received the yellow ticket, the only means of staying in the city legally. But when the police learned she was merely studying shorthand and not walking the streets, she was sent back to the Pale.

Though Baron de Gunzburg had made every attempt within his power to wrest some forbearance, some small mercy, all the much vaunted negotiative skills of the *shtadlonim* were in vain. The imperial government spoke with practiced glibness to the baron of commissions to study the "Jewish Question," while it tightened the noose around his fellow Russian Jews.

Baron de Gunzburg's was not the only failure. Baron Maurice de Hirsch, a German Jew, whose heavy long mustaches made him look more "like an Austrian cavalry officer than a financier," also possessed enormous wealth—inherited and accumulated. De Hirsch money stemmed from railroads and banking and was even more abundant than that of the Gunzburgs; with it, the baron tried desperately to rescue "his unhappy Russian co-religionists" from their government. In 1888 he informed the czar's ministers that with their permission, he would establish technical and agricultural schools for Jews with a donation of 50,000,000 francs. The government had no objection, if De Hirsch would give it, rather than the Jewish agencies, the money to dispense. Baron de Hirsch refused. Then one of his aides suggested that if he gave Pobyedonostzev 1,000,000 francs for Russian Orthodox parochial schools, the government might have a miraculous change of heart. So he gave Pobyedonostzev the 1,000,000 francs, which the minister pocketed. Baron de Hirsch again proposed his establishment of technical schools, and again the government turned down his proposal.

If an interview with De Hirsch, published in the New York *Times* at the beginning of 1889, was an accurate reflection of his views, then it was just as well his Russian co-religionists were not as yet *Times* readers. For in it, he, too, declared that the chief problem of Russian Jews was their isolation. "They do not even know the Russian language . . . speaking a sort of Hebrew of their own." (German Jews always found it heavy

weather trying to describe Yiddish.) "The salvation of the
Jews is in assimilation," he asserted, "let them be amalgamated by Christianity and merged into Christianity. Let the fusion be complete. Let Jews as a distinct sect disappear. This is
the tendency of the age. This will be the solution of the Jewish
Question and a blessing to civilization."

And in 1895 Baron de Hirsch revealed his unhappiness
with yet another Jewish characteristic in a discussion with
Theodor Herzl. The latter—just beginning his Zionist
campaign—tried to interest the baron in providing Jewish political leadership. He also suggested that Baron de Hirsch
sponsor a contest for Jews in the major anti-Semitic countries
for "deeds of great moral beauty, for courage, self sacrifice,
virtuous conduct, notable achievements in art and science . . .
in short for everything great." When Herzl assured him that
this would achieve "a general uplift among Jews," Baron de
Hirsch interrupted, crying out piteously: "No, no, no! I do
not want to raise the general level. All of our misfortunes
come from the fact that the Jews want to climb too high. We
have too much brains. My intention is to restrain the Jews
from pushing ahead. They shouldn't make such great progress. All of the hatred against us stems from this. . . ."

If, indeed, Baron de Hirsch did hold these opinions, he pru-
dently never expressed them to East European Jews. Nevertheless, as word of one after another of the unsuccessful negotiations trickled down to the Jews in the Pale, their faith in the
omnipotence of their *shtadlonim* wavered. They now began to
feel that they would have to be the masters of their own fate,
an attitude which they carried with them to the United States
and which would affect their lives there. (Hundreds of university students who had been certain that a rejection of Judaism
and belief in the nobility of the Russian peasant would swing
the pendulum toward a utopian society now lost their faith in
these verities. In fact, the pogroms and May Laws had
blacked out the effulgence of assimilation and enlightenment,
and many of these young men who had taken pride in their ir-
religion turned back to piety, at least symbolically, by order-
ing tefillin—phylacteries—posthaste from Vilna.)

Baron de Hirsch, disillusioned, too, though it took him several years longer to reach the decision that the future of Russian Jews in their own country was unmitigatingly bleak, organized the Jewish Colonization Association to establish "colonies in various parts of North and South America." In Sep-

tember, 1891, he addressed an open letter to "my co-religionists in Russia" urging them not to flee precipitously:

> You know that in the near future regular committees will be established in Russia, with the consent and under the supervision of the Russian Government. These committees will aim to organize emigration on a businesslike basis. All those wishing to emigrate must apply to their local committees, who alone will be authorized to give the necessary information. . . .
>
> Bear in mind that I can not do anything for you without the benevolent and generous assistance of the Imperial Russian Government. . . .

This cautious attitude—which epitomized the *shtadlonim* approach—those inexplicable references to "the benevolent and generous assistance of the Imperial Russian Government" galled Russian Jews. They wanted feeling—*rachmones*—not efficiency; they wanted their representatives—even at some risk to themselves—to stand up to the oppressors and speak the truth. (Was it not written there is "a time to keep silence, and a time to speak"?) As open-handed and philanthropic as they knew the Baron de Hirsch to be, his letter with its plea for circumspection didn't smack of a Yiddish heart.*

Nine years earlier a far more positive response had been made by a goy with a Jewish heart and with the fire lacking in the *shtadlonim*.

In the midst of a great meeting at New York's Chickering Hall, protesting Russia's treatment of her Jews, Judge Noah Davis—Republican justice of the New York Supreme Court —despite his austere appearance, had risen to the podium and proclaimed with *rachmones:* "Let them come! I would to Heaven it were in our power to take the whole three million Jews of Russia. The valley of the Mississippi alone could throw her strong arms around and draw them all to her opulent bosom, and bless them with homes of comfort, prosperity and happiness. . . ."

---

* What constitutes a *Yiddishe hertz,* of course, may vary. In 1860, for example, a French Rothschild—Salomon—visited America and met a number of Jewish Confederate leaders. "What is extraordinary," he wrote home, "is how all these men have a Jewish heart and show an interest in me because I represent the greatest Jewish house in the world."

4

"God, What Pandemonium!"

In Zitomir, Russian Christians "hesitated to order garments" from Jewish tailors, for fear the tailors might leave before they finished them. And in London, Paris, and New York, endless discussions took place on the subject of a refuge for Russian Jews. Spain, in a gesture of reconciliation for past offenses, had offered itself as a sanctuary; the 400 years since the onset of the Inquisition, however, hadn't dimmed enough memories. A group of Jewish students in Kharkov organized a Zionist group, Bilu, and aimed to emigrate immediately to Palestine. Am Olam, a larger student group, chose the United States in which to pioneer. Its goal was to establish agrarian communes, rejecting "unproductive callings" of traditional Jewish petty trades.

As for the rest of Russian Jewry, "America was in everybody's mouth":

> Business men talked of it over their accounts; the market women made up their quarrels that they might discuss it from stall to stall; people who had relatives in the famous land went around reading their letters for the enlightenment of less fortunate folk; the one letter-carrier informed the public how many letters arrived from America, and who were the recipients; children played at emigrating. . . .

Frequently, those letters contained a photograph in which the former *shtetl* dweller was not beardless but sported a flourishing mustache. He wore a short jacket, draped gold watch chain, stood erect with derby in hand. A *mensh!* "I have on the floor a velvet carpet," a letter might read, in Yiddish, "which is nicer than the tablecloth on your rich man's table."

Still, having a destination firmly in mind was not the answer to all difficulties. However glib Count Ignatiev had been in pointing out an open Western frontier to Jews, he was deceptive, as he so often was. One didn't just amble casually across the border. A passport, *pravozhitelstvo,* was necessary. This meant having five or six certificates, whose cost might be as much as 80 kopecks each (40 cents), a formidable sum for people who had barely enough to eat. Depending on one's locality, the acquisition of a passport might also require a visit to a city, entailing more expense, for "the sum necessary to move the police wheels, runs the cost up to twenty to twenty-five rubles." Since border guards would smuggle a person over the border for only a 5-ruble bribe, it was a simpler and less expensive, if slightly more dangerous, method than getting a passport. Some impulsive young men, subject to a call to the czar's army and thus unable to get a passport, dove in the Dniester River which at one point formed the border. They swam across, while holding aloft a drawstring bag, containing their tallis and tefillin—prayer shawl and phylacteries.

Whatever the method of getting over the border—by swimming; stealthy midnight scurries; striding past bribed guards; crossing legally or even, as in Sophie Tucker's case, being born en route—an exodus of Jews began, the largest since the one from Egypt. But unlike the Biblical Exodus, no Moses arose to lead these Jews. Instead, as befitted some nineteen centuries of progress, committees and an organization sprang into being. One of the most vocal of the former, the Committee for the Relief of the Russian Jews, was headed by Victor Hugo, who published his own personal protest: *Humanité, regard et vois!* However, the Alliance Israelite Universelle, an older organization based in Paris and intent on the defense of Jewish civil and religious rights, bore the greatest burden.

Led for twenty years by Adolphe Crémieux, an eminent French Jewish lawyer, the alliance and Sir Moses Montefiore of England had been Europe's most vigorous defenders of Jewish liberties. They had dealt with cases of forced baptism, blood libels, and the innumerable other oppressive facets of anti-Semitism. But Crémieux had died in 1880, the venerable Montefiore was ninety-seven years old, and now the alliance, controlled principally by French Jews and supported generously by Baron de Hirsch, was treading very delicately lest it impair French-Russian relations, on the threshold of a self-conscious contrived affability. All through late 1881 and the spring of 1882, when the May Laws restricted the lives of Russian Jews still further, the alliance sought some tactful way to help the victims without implying public criticism of their oppressor. Obviously, it wouldn't do to hold protest meetings, as had been done in London and New York. Instead, with genteel unobtrusiveness, the alliance collected money to care for the pogrom victims and held discussions on the feasibility of immigration to Africa, to South America, to the United States. But general reluctance to encourage emigration, particularly to their own countries, was shared by all European Jews; English and German Jews therefore provided aid in the form of food, clothing, *and* tickets to move on, generally to the United States. As late as 1890 Dr. H. M. Cohn of Berlin expressed the fears of German Jews that even "the existence of committees would excite the Russian Jews and increase emigration." But the trains carrying the emigrants to a German port stopped at Charlottenburg, a Berlin surburb, for six hours, permitting the emigrants to go into town and make personal pleas for aid. Their high visibility aroused public sympathy and Berlin newspapermen went out to Charlottenburg to see them. "Under the circumstances," Dr. Cohn admitted, "the Berlin Jewish committee could not remain idle. It arranged a meeting which elected the Central German committee for the relief of Russian Jews."

While the Central Committee of the alliance brooded over the feasibility of sending several "shipments," "consignments," of Russian Jews to the United States—the terminology invariably conjured up the need for longshoremen rather than immigration officials—the Board of Delegates of American Israelites dispatched telegrams expressing sympathy, but specifying that only young, strong, unmarried mechanics be sent. Innocent of all this, thousands of Russian Jewish families bundled up their meager possessions and fled to Brody, a Galician town on the border of Russia and Austria and under Austrian rule. Included in their baggage were any feather beds that had been left whole by the *pogromschiks;* for "feather beds are scarce in America," it was maintained. "In America, they sleep on hard mattresses even in winter."

In mid-August, 1881, the alliance arranged with a Belgian travel agent, Henri Strauss, to send 500 persons to the United States. As a matter of independent enterprise, Strauss had also distributed a Yiddish circular throughout the Pale, which declared, "cheaply calculated fares and all kinds of advantages guaranteed to all persons who will contact me." At the same time, subagents of the steamship lines, motivated by $1.50 commission per ticket sold, stumped the Pale and offered tickets at what they, too, claimed were bargain rates and also offered a great variety of misinformation on routes, baggage allowance, and what lay ahead for immigrants in the United States. Many of them circulated false rumors and forged letters which urged emigration to America and promised financial support by rich Jews to all those who did so. The letters were signed, ostensibly by Sir Moses Montefiore. All manner of frauds were perpetrated. It wasn't uncommon for an emigrant to purchase a ticket, believing it would carry him to America, only to find it would take him as far as an English port and that another payment was necessary to go on. The family of Samuel Chotzinoff, the pianist and music critic, waited expectantly on the dock for their cousin from Passaic to meet them, until they realized: "This is not America! We are in London." Since many had no money, they remained in England—the Chotzinoffs stayed for a year—which accounted for a further swelling of the huge Russian Jewish population in London's Whitechapel district.

In a period of four months, 24,000 Russian Jews steamed into Brody, a town whose normal population was 15,000. Frenetically, desperately, the alliance tried to cope with it all. "God!" wrote one of the emigrants. "What pandemonium!"

By the end of the year, well over 1,500 emigrants had been shipped to the United States—and more arrived daily. Officials sent some back to Russia; they quartered others in a factory in Brody and lodged still others in private homes. Three hundred were sheltered in a stable; many slept in the streets. In spite of the chaotic conditions, the relief at having got as far as Brody caused a certain fatalistic abandon among the immigrants. "One Friday morning," Abe Cahan recalled, "a young man I knew arrived from Russia alone, penniless and gloomy. The next night I found him dancing in one of the wedding parties. 'Whose wedding?' I asked. 'Mine!' he shouted. 'But,' I cried, 'you haven't a cent! You haven't even enough for a meal.' He laughed. 'True,' he said. 'But neither has she!' "

Out of this chaos, the alliance sought to achieve a semblance of order by issuing cards which would set off a predictable chain of events: The card would be exchanged for a ticket, which would then entitle an emigrant to be assigned to a train, which would carry him to a port, where he could board a ship to America. But first came the grim task of getting a card, and this created the disorder that the alliance had diligently worked to circumvent. Outside the factory, thousands of emigrants thronged, all frantically trying to get to one of the thirty windows of the building where an official "walks pompously from window to window and distributes cards at random." With a life-death ferocity, the emigrants twisted, pushed, fought, and clawed their way closer to the windows. One man even attempted to somersault his way over the heads of those in front of him, only to be mauled and shoved. Beaten, blood running from scratches and bites, faces dirty with blood and perspiration, they inched to the window with their last strength. Holding up a card in a clutched fist, one emigrant exclaimed, *"Gekrigen!"*—I got it!—and then dropped in a faint.

Anyone who had experienced the maelstrom of Brody would be more qualified than most to withstand the ten- to seventeen-day journey across the Atlantic in the steerage compartments of the great "greyhounds of the sea" of the Cunard, Inman, White Star, National, Hamburg-American, Red Star, and North German Lloyd lines. ("A boat!" Mordechai Edelstein exclaimed to his granddaughter, Gertrude Berg. "A boat. A captain! Only my enemies should go on such a boat.") Impelled by the pressures of the highly competitive steerage trade—profit was limited only by the number that would be packed in—the North German Lloyd Line issued a flyer warning emigrants "to keep away from English, Hollandish and other non-German steamship companies" and extolling their own steamers for "their seaworthiness, exemplary conduct of their experienced officers and effective crews, their celerity, combined with safety and good food for the steerage passenger. . . ."

In reality, steerage was steerage. On all the lines, "the persons carried are looked upon as so much freight with mere transportation as their only due," and the "disgusting and demoralizing conditions" varied little. (Though admittedly, it must have made a difference to anyone resting on the straw and seaweed-filled mattress and pillow issued each steerage passenger to know whether the steamship line on which he was traveling was one of the few on which the seaweed was changed each trip.)

Sleeping quarters consisted of "large compartments," accommodating either men, women, or families, and there were about 300 individuals in a compartment. Compartment floors were either wood or large sheets of iron, neither of which under the circumstances had overwhelming advantages, "for no sick cans are furnished, and not even large receptacles for waste. The vomitings of the seasick are often permitted to remain a long time before being removed. The floors, when iron, are continually damp, and when of wood they reek with foul odor because they are not washed." (But on the last day of the voyage they were washed, assiduously, in order to be ready for inspection at the port of entry.)

Above such uninviting floors—but not, surely, far enough above them—were berths in tiers of two. Each berth space of 6 feet 2 inches long by 2 feet 6 inches high—30 cubic feet—served as bed, towel and clothes rack, baggage space, and kitchen cabinet. The eating utensils, issued to each emigrant and stored in his berth, consisted of fork, large spoon, and a workman's tin lunch pail, the bottom of which was used for soup "and frequently as a wash basin," for which only cold salt water was available. A small tin dish that fitted into the top of the pail was used for meat and potatoes; a cylindrical projection on the lid served as a dish for vegetables or stewed fruits; a tin cup that fitted onto this projection was for drinks. Long before the voyage was ended, this untensil had rusted and was "not fit to eat from"—a suitable container for food that wasn't fit to eat.

After the turn of the century, most steamship lines established a separate galley for the preparation of kosher food, whose lack of quality was equal to that of the nonkosher. But until that time, Orthodox Jewish steerage passengers existed throughout the long voyage on soggy black bread and pickled herring. If one of the original purposes of the dietary laws was hygienic, then rarely had they served this purpose so admirably, for the food eaten or thrown over the side by the other passengers rated abysmally low. According to American law, an emigrant was entitled to one and a half navy rations per day: 1¼ pounds of salted or smoked meat; 3 ounces of dried or 6 ounces of canned fruit; 3 gills of dried beans; ¼ ounce of pepper; ½ ounce of dried mustard; 4 ounces of salt; ½ pound of macaroni. . . . Quality was not specified. Only the white bread, potatoes, and soup—and possibly the seasonings —were edible. Meats and fish, except for the pickled herring, could be relied on to be old, tough, and evil-smelling; "vegetables were often a queer unanalyzable mixture and therefore avoided"; and stewed fruit was the refuse that remained after the edible fruit was graded out. Hot water—"though not always boiling"—was poured over coffee grounds, sugar, and milk in a large galvanized tin can. "This was served as coffee."

After each meal, a steerage steward circulated among the diners, asking in sunny good humor, "Does the food taste good?" The replies he received in Italian, Hungarian, German, Rumanian, Polish, and Yiddish were uniformly surly and obscene.

And though noise—ear-shattering noise—surrounded the emigrants, each nationality tried to keep its spirits up. While children cried, exuberant Italians played accordions, Rumanians danced, Germans sang, Jews *davened* (prayed).

As each liner unloaded its unprepossessing, debilitated cargo of Russian Jews, frantic wires and letters from American organizations informed alliance headquarters in Paris: "Send no more emigrants. Committee must return incapables." "We as a Society and as American citizens," sternly wrote Augustus Levey of the Hebrew Emigrant Aid Society, "can not and will not be parties to the infliction upon our community of a class of emigrants, whose only destiny is the hospital, the infirmary, or perhaps the workhouse." Another HEAS official, on a note of hysteria, cabled: "Will not receive another refugee." And an outright threat came to New York from Milwaukee: "If you send many more Russians to Milwaukee, whether it be to this Society or 'to whom it may concern,' they will be shipped back to you without permitting them to leave the depot."

In 1891 a committee of American Jews (Jacob Schiff, Oscar Straus, and Jesse Seligman) appealed to President Benjamin Harrison to remonstrate with Russia for enacting special laws which "forced groups of its people to seek refuge in another country and that country our own." Harrison sent an immigration commission off to Russia to investigate. It was composed of Colonel John B. Weber, immigration commissioner of the new depot at Ellis Island, and Dr. Walter Kempster, a specialist in the pathology of insanity. Their report, a long, thorough account of the condition of Jews in Russia, urged the American government to protest Russian anti-Semitic policy, despite the American principle of nonintervention.

But while government reports were being written, and while officials exchanged letters, laid down stern stipulations, and formulated strict rules, down the gangplank came East European Jews at the rate of 1,000 a month, 2,000 a month, 5,000 a month. . . . They came, as though into welcoming arms, clutching their meager possessions—feather bed, an iron skillet, a worn velvet drawstring bag containing *tallis* and *tefillin,* and odds and ends of clothing carried in a worn wicker suitcase held together with rope, or merely wrapped in what they would later describe as a *shmatte*—a rag. *"Leben zol Columbus,"* they exclaimed. Long live Columbus!

To view the East European immigrants from a distance of almost a century, they might be a picture in the *National Geographic:* scrawny, pallid men with long scraggly beards and earlocks, dressed in frayed greenish-black caftans; women with sunken cheeks, scarves pulled tight over fierce black wigs; and children dressed as small adults, some appearing downright Oriental. They disembarked en masse, as anonymous as sparrows. They were statistics: 40,000 came in 1881–82; 62,619 in 1888; 136,742 in 1892; 106,236 in 1904; 153,748 in 1906. But they were individuals—appearance notwithstanding. They were greenhorns, too, and they knew it. They could, however, take solace in a shaky analogy: Just as in time a green apple becomes ripe, so eventually they would become Americans. They had refused to be Russians, because that meant giving up their religion, but here they would be Americans, because they could be Americans *and* Jews.

And so when a former yeshiva student came into a tenement to teach a child Hebrew and said to the child, "Open the *fenster,"* the child's mother objected. "Look at you," the mother said disparagingly, "an educated young man and you say '*fenster.*' You're in America now, say *vinda.*"

Because the immigrant in steerage had been transported in time, as well as spatially, from the seventeenth century to the late nineteenth century, he had an astounding amount to learn by way of adjustment. When one Jew saw another who was obviously green and just off the boat, standing on a street corner counting streetcars as they went by, he approached the greenhorn and asked in Yiddish what he was doing. The man explained that he had been told to take streetcar number 52. So far only fourteen streetcars had come and gone. So, God willing, he'd count until the fifty-second streetcar arrived.

PART II

THE TSITTERDIK *SYNDROME*

The mode of life of these people in Russia has stamped upon them the ineffaceable marks of permanent pauperism, only disgrace and a lowering of the opinion in which American Israelites are held . . . can result from the continued residence among us . . . of these wretches. . . .
   —AUGUSTUS A. LEVEY, Secretary, HEAS, 1882

It might be wise to send American-Jewish missionaries to Russia to civilize them rather than to give them the opportunity to Russianize us in the event of such colossal emigration.
   —*The Jewish Messenger,* New York City, 1882

The reputation that every Jew has is no higher than that of the lowest who professes his religion. We cannot therefore afford to permit this influx of poor deluded and oppressed Russians to become the standard upon which we shall be judged in the future.
   —*The American Israelite,* Cincinnati, Ohio, 1882

5

Matzos to Grover Cleveland

Two incontrovertible facts, early in the game, relate Jews with America: On August 2, 1492, 300,000 Spanish Jews who refused to convert to Christianity were expelled from their country. And the next morning Christopher Columbus sailed westward from Palos.

Four hundred years later Oscar Straus wrote to Dr. Moritz Keyserling, a Jewish historian, requesting that he begin a study of the role Jews may have played in the discovery of America. Mr. Straus' motivation wasn't historic curiosity. "You can well understand," he wrote Dr. Keyserling, "what an important result it would have if it were historically shown that our race had a direct part in the discovery of America, how this would be an answer for all time to come to any anti-Semitic tendencies in this country which doubtless will come to the surface sooner or later by reason of the large Russian immigration to our country. . . ." Sanguine Mr. Straus evidently believed that if, for example, it were known that Luis de Torres, Columbus' interpreter and the first European to set foot on the soil of the New World, was a marrano—a baptized Spanish or Portuguese Jew who practiced Judaism secretly—or if Dr. Keyserling could prove that Ferdinand and Isabella had financed Columbus' voyage with wealth confiscated from the expelled Spanish Jews, American anti-Semites would be placated and tolerate "the large Russian immigration to our country."*

Straus' anxiety (he also sent a case of matzos every year to Grover Cleveland) may have stemmed in small part from his childhood, for his family was the only Jewish one in Talbotton, Georgia. However, it also evoked a more common attitude among American Jews, a blend of defensiveness, apology, and anxiety—a condition expressed by the Yiddish word *tsitter,* whose very sound suggested trembling and uncertainty. To be *tsitterdik* was to be uneasy, wary, nervous. Among Russian *shtadlonim* like Baron de Gunzburg, it was an indigenous emotional state. In the case of American Jews, *tsitterdik* signified edginess about any Jew's behavior which might through glib generalization reflect badly on the position of all American Jews. Thus, when 2,000,000 indigent, unenlightened East European Jews, "badly dressed, unacquainted with any language save their own jargon," and warped by "outlandish medieval beliefs," began their entry into the United States, American Jews viewed them as a serious threat to their hardwon status, and *tsitterdik* manifestations appeared in one American Jewish community after another.

Such psychic turmoil was of recent vintage in America. No *tsitterdik* symptoms materialized among the first Jewish settlers in New York—the Sephardim, descendants of the victims of that fifteenth-century expulsion from Spain and, a few years later, from Portugal. They may have feared for their lives at one time or another, but never for their status. Peter Stuyvesant had been forced by the directors of the Dutch West Indian Company, among whose stockholders were several Jews, to allow twenty-three Jews who arrived aboard a French privateer from Brazil to live in New Netherland, "provided the poor among them shall not become a burden to the company and the community but be supported by their own nation." (One far-flung consequence of this promise was the development of federated fund raising.) Shortly after their arrival, the pioneers organized Shearith Israel, the oldest Jewish congregation in North America preceded in New York City only by the Dutch Reformed Church.

* An even more "direct part in the discovery of America" was suspected. But it wasn't until twenty years later that Straus found an article by a Spanish historian who set down nineteen specific reasons "for the conclusion that Columbus was a Spaniard and of Jewish ancestry."

For the next hundred years, sporadic immigration from Western Europe and a steady dribble from Russia and Poland increased the Jewish population. Nevertheless, all these Ashkenazic Jews—German and Russian—continued to be dominated by the Spanish-Portuguese Jews—the lordly Sephardim, whose attitudes were characterized by Spanish pride, not Jewish humility. Since Yiddish was as alien to the Sephardim as it was to non-Jews, and since regard for their own high status was as firmly fixed in their minds as it was in the British royal family, they literally and figuratively didn't know the meaning of *tsitterdik*. For more than a hundred years Ashkenazim had outnumbered Sephardim, but though the latter were in the minority, they saw to it that Sephardic ritual was followed in synagogue services. When a group of Ashkenazim asked that their ritual be used, they were haughtily refused. Nor did the Sephardim care to mingle socially or genetically with Ashkenazim (this total unapproachability relaxed somewhat when Ashkenazic millionaires began to surface). For the Sephardim harbored passionate feelings concerning the distinction between themselves and the German and Russian immigrants. In Jamaica, West Indies, where the Sephardim had lived for hundreds of years, a Sephardic lady confronted a young Ashkenazic rabbi, trying to preach unity. Pointing to her thin, blue-veined arisocratic wrist, she declared, "If I had a drop of Ashkenazic blood in my veins, I'd kill myself."

By combining a proud adherence to their faith, an ineluctable gift for achieving affluence and an impressively grand manner, the Sephardim were first among equals in the new democracy for which they had fought in the Revolutionary War. (Of course a few were loyal to King George III, and they packed up and went to England to live among the British upper class, where it was supposed they were happier with their own kind.) They were the elite, among the founders of such Establishment institutions as the New York Stock Exchange, Columbia University, New York University, the American Medical Association, and the Boston Athenaeum. (No less an institutional founder, but certainly less prestigious, Abram Mordecai founded the city of Montgomery and the first cotton-gin house in Alabama. A veteran of the Revolutionary War and an Indian trader, Old Mordecai lived fifty years with the Creek Indians and was firmly convinced American Indians were descendants of the Ten Lost Tribes of Israel. He never gave up hope that one day, someday, an Indian would step up to him and say something in Hebrew—possibly *shalom*. Described as "a darkeyed Jew of amorous disposition," Old Mordecai had his ear bitten off by an outraged Indian husband and lived to be almost a hundred.)

No pejorative adjective, such as "pushy," trailed in the wake of Sephardim, nor did they tremble before possible threats to their status. When the object of an offensive remark —"damned Israelite"—they might seek satisfaction, as Dr. Jacob Minis of Savannah did in 1832, by engaging in duels and killing their opponents. If a gentleman belonged to the Union, the Knickerbocker, the New York, and the Racquet clubs, the Sons of the American Revolution, and Seventh Regiment Veterans Association, he was above being *tsitterdik*.

By the mid-nineteenth century, when German Jews began to emigrate in large numbers, the Sephardim were personages of enormous prestige—not a peddler among them. A number of aristocratic, aloof merchants engaged in the then-patrician export-import trade or in the stock brokerage business. They also included erudite lawyers, but none had peddled stove polish like Meyer Guggenheim or lived in a room behind his store like Henry Lehman. In their own estimation, they were "the nearest approach to royalty in the United States" and, in the eyes of their East European brethren, the *shayna leit*, the beautiful people.

And as beautiful people will, they intermarried relentlessly, thus distilling the beauty of the *shayna leit* to an unadulterated essence of Seixas, Peixottos, Nathans, Franks, Florences, Cardozos, Lazaruses, and Hendrixes. Nowhere was the prevalence of such unions so evident as in the family descended from Seixas and Sarah Seixas Nathan (his first cousin) and revealed in name permutations: Hester Nathan Lazarus, Annie Florence Nathan, Rosalie Cardozo Florence, Rebecca Nathan Cardozo, Emily Hendrix Nathan, and, inevitably, Maud Nathan Nathan, whose first cousin and husband, Frederick Nathan, had ninety-eight other first cousins.

Eventually relationships grew complex and blood thin, and so some Sephardim married plebeian German Jews. Other Sephardic gentlemen wed non-Jews and began disappearing into the general population, while Sephardic ladies, unable to find a suitable match, remained unmarried. As a consequence, the Germans by virtue of their numbers became, after midcentury, the dominant nationality group in American Jewry.

Moreover, as the Sephardim faded away in assimilation's

quicksand, their pride and assurance disappeared, too. The dominant emotional tone among American Jews became the one that characterized German Jews, *tsitterdikness*. . . . For when the Germans set off for the United States, they brought with them a tradition, a mindset, of accommodating Jewishness to the prevailing level of German anti-Semitism. After all, in the past century, they had lived neither isolated with other Jews in primitive *shtetlach,* as had the East European Jews, nor in the atmosphere of religious and political freedom enjoyed by the Sephardim, but in German communities, out in the open, exposed, convenient targets for their Christian countrymen. And since Germany always held anti-Semitic sentiment—sometimes strong, sometimes in abeyance—German Jews for self-preservation kept a vigilant eye on the barometer of irrationality and employed the necessary degree of pacification accordingly. Understandably, the strain of maintaining this fine balance made them *tsitterdik*. Thus, whether a German Jew was the proprietor of a dry-goods store in Richmond, Virginia, or, like Oscar Straus, American minister to Turkey, the *tsitterdik* syndrome operated not far below the surface.

For this malady, wealth had ameliorative powers. In 1860 American millionaires could be counted on the fingers of one hand; twenty-one years later the number had increased beyond finger counting. In 1887 the New York *Mail Express* listed forty-one Jewish millionaires in New York alone. Such wealth, obviously, offered many advantages. For Jews, one of the greatest was protection—or at least the feeling of protection. Consequently, in addition to the usual incentives for amassing a fortune, German Jewish millionaires had been highly motivated by their *tsitterdik* condition. This was true not only of those who traded in astronomical sums on Wall street—relaxed in the *gemütlichkeit* of the Harmonie Gesellschaft (from whose windows, looking south over Reservoir Park, its 400 members could see the Union League Club)—and who built their stone palaces along Fifth Avenue, but of German Jews who blazed new trails all over the country. There were the Gimbels and Brentanos in Vincennes, Indiana; Adolph Gluck of Dodge City, Kansas; the Rosenwalds of Chicago; the Rosewaters of Omaha, Nebraska; the Michaelsons of Virginia City, Nevada; the Spiegelbergs of Santa Fe, New Mexico; the Seasongoods of Cincinnati, Ohio. . . .

In California, a former prospector, Levi Strauss, began a fortune—and initiated a classic fashion—with a wagonload of denim canvas he brought to San Francisco to be sold as tent material. When a miner advised Strauss that durable pants were needed far more than tent material, Strauss had the denim made into pants. ("Look at those pants of Levi's. Doggone, if a man ever had pants as strong as these before.") After Strauss began making pants out of blue denim, a tailor suggested the pants pockets—which often sagged with tools and rocks—be secured with copper rivets. And so levis became an American institution; their creator a millionaire. In 1865, A. Goodman in Philadelphia met another need by setting up a matzo-making machine and turning out the flat ritual Passover bread—following the rule for machine-made matzo laid down by England's chief rabbi, Nathan Adler: No more than nine minutes should elapse before the dough was placed in the oven. A decade later Goodman moved to New York, where his firm, A. Goodman & Sons, expanded into noodle-making. When he originally began making matzos, Goodman declared, "I had no idea except to make such as might be sold to Jews at the Passover season. It was found, however, that year by year the demand for them grew, so that at all seasons our factory is busy. . . ." ("Matzoth for Passover in the middle of winter!" exclaimed a character in a Sholem Aleichem story, who had just landed in New York. "It is obviously a Jewish town.")

In direct counterpoint to the Goodman fortune made on unleavened bread was that acquired by Charles Fleischmann —an emigrant to Cincinnati—out of his recipe for producing compressed yeast cakes from froth that was a by-product in the brewing of liquor. After an extremely effective exhibit at the Philadelphia Centennial Exposition in 1876, in which awed spectators saw Fleishmann's yeast made, dough set, and bread baked, then served to them at an adjoining restaurant, Fleischmann's fortune was made. And before long Charles Fleischmann attained an $80,000 yacht, a *Schloss* at Fleischmanns in the Catskills, a collection of French art, and the reputation for giving away $100 a day to charity. All these, no doubt, calmed whatever *tsitterdikness* he may have had.

As the nineteenth century swung into its last decades, American Jews had already produced not only millionaires, but individuals whose accomplishments had brought them esteem from the country as a whole: from Rebecca Gratz, an aristocratic beauty, famed as the model for *Ivanhoe*'s Rebecca,* who started the first Jewish Sunday schools, to Ernestine Rose, a formidable suffragate, who helped women in Wyoming get the vote; from David de Leon, a doctor who established the first drugstore in the United States, to Abraham Jacobi, its first pediatrician; from Solomon N. Carvalho, an artist-explorer who accompanied General John C. Fremont across the Rockies and was the first official photographer of a scientific expedition, to Commander Uriah Phillips Levy, a naval officer who helped abolish flogging in the United States Navy;† from David Kaufman, a politician who was Texas' first Congressman and for whom Kaufman County was named, to Mordecai Manuel Noah, a Tammany Hall leader and journalist who was also sheriff of New York County (to an objection that he, a Jewish sheriff, might have to hang Christians. Noah retorted, "Pretty Christians to require hanging"), a playwright and visionary who set out—in vain—to establish a Jewish city, which he named Ararat, on an island off Buffalo.**

All these diverse individuals had been part of the United States during its first hundred years. By 1881 the Promised Land to which Russian Jews' hopes were directing their lives had added twenty-five more states to the original thirteen. Scattered throughout these thirty-eight states were 250,000 of the "Hebrew Persuasion," most of whom had achieved re-

---

* Washington Irving had described Miss Gratz's beauty with a passionate lyricism to Walter Scott. It was rumored that she'd refused to marry Washington Irving because he wasn't Jewish. However, if this rumor were true and had Miss Gratz known the use Washington Irving would serve tens of thousands of Russian Jewish parents a hundred years or so later, she conceivably might have relented. All those immigrant parents who wished to call a son after deceased relatives named Isaac, Isidore, or Israel, but wanted a name less Jewish-sounding, chose Irving because rationalization required that the name selected at least begin with the same letter as that of the departed ancestor. Washington Irving, moreover, was a distinguished literary figure, and his surname had a fine dignified ring to it.

† Commander Levy was also called the "American Dreyfus," having been subjected to six court-martial hearings and constant harassment from his fellow officers. Some of his collateral descendants claimed that these troubles didn't stem from anti-Semitism in the Navy, but from his fierce temper. But on the other hand, the fierceness of his temper was undoubtedly exacerbated by anti-Semitism in the Navy.

** Alas, Noah was also, in addition to his many other interests, an advocate of slavery, leading Horace Greeley to exclaim, "There's a Hebrew with the heart of an Egyptian."

spectable positions and the security Russian Jews had never had. Yet had those quarter million Hebrews known then that the days of being called "Hebrew," a designation laden with grave dignity, or even "Israelite," which resounded with Biblical grandeur, were numbered and that with the arrival of their East European co-religionists, American Hebrews and Israelites would be indiscriminantly lumped together with the new arrivals and referred to as "Jews" (just one gloomy example of how their cherished refinement would decline) *tsitterdik* rumblings would have sounded earlier than they had. When General Grant issued his notorious Order No. 11 in 1862, which directed the expulsion of "all Jews" from the military area designated as the Department of Tennessee, the New York *Herald* reported the most insulting aspect of General Grant's act to be that he used the word "Jew" rather than "Hebrew" or "Israelite."

At the time of the East European immigrants' arrival, states and territories in the Far West already had small Jewish populations—with a Jewish police commissioner in Portland, Oregon, and a B'nai B'rith chapter already launched in San Francisco. There was also a Jewish Sewing Circle in Cheyenne, Wyoming, and an annual Purim Ball in Leadville, Colorado, and when the territorial governor attended a Jewish wedding in Virginia City, he kept his hat on.

As for the East Coast, the New York *Herald* declared approvingly that "socially the New York Jew stands well. He is not a dude and he keeps out of the alleged exclusive set which produces this element of social life. . . . Among themselves the Jews are very social. Innumerable social gatherings, balls and parties are given. These are attended by whole families, the object being for the members of one family to become acquainted with those of another, or as a leading Israelite tersely puts it, 'that the young ladies may become acquainted with the young gentlemen.' "

Having prospered, German Jews, who were to be known collectively by East European Jews as *Yahudim,* developed a passionate, religious devotion to their adopted country. (A reference to Zionism and the possibility of a Jewish state drew a sharp denunciation from Dr. Isaac Mayer Wise. "We want no Jewish princes or government," he wrote. He then went on to make the kind of *Yahudim*-like remark Russian Jews love to deride: "We prefer President Hayes to a Jewish prince.")

For those who didn't have the enormous wealth of Schiffs, Seligmans, Strauses, Strausses, or Fleischmanns and therefore

a passport to upper-class status, there was comfortable affluence and a desire to achieve conformity with the American
middle class. Consequently, when Oscar Straus sought Dr.
Keyserling's scholarship to uncover a link between the Jewish
people and the discovery of America, he expressed his reason
with unequivocal honesty: to shore up the security of American Jews in advance of an avalanche of Russian Jews.

6

"Blows Passed in a
Certain Synagogue"

The avalanche actually imperiled the lifework of a formidable
personality. He was only five feet eight, but his immense, distinctive head was suitable for a man a foot taller. Gray hair
hung over the back of his collar like the hair of a frontiers-
man, and his muttonchop whiskers debouched into a smoothly flowing mustache worthy of a railroad president. No ritually prescribed beard covered his chin. Steel-rimmed spectacles
customarily perched on his brow. He even wore them under
his hat. A cigar in his mouth, a cane in his hand, he had an
opinion on everything: table tilting, prizefighting in Great
Britain, the phenomenon of sunstroke, how to preserve a
piano, and the flaws of Darwinism. And for most of the more
than eighty years of his life, Dr. Isaac Mayer Wise directed
his prodigious energies—he often worked eighteen hours a
day—and his high enthusiasms into shaping, unifying, and,
inadvertently, occasionally dividing American Judaism. In
these endeavors his greatest obstacles were the attitudes, customs, and orthodoxy of the East European Jewish immigrants.

Yet even before their arrival, he regarded himself as the
savior of Judaism in America. And no means of advancing
the cause of Reform Judaism were too arcane or far afield.

63

Since novels might conceivably serve as a vehicle for his purpose, Dr. Wise turned out sixteen in German and eleven in English, though, as his East European co-religionists might say in their vernacular, a Sholem Aleichem he wasn't. (On one occasion, he had two girls fall in love with the same man and then didn't know how to get rid of one of them. "I had no experience in such things," he said plaintively, "and yet I wanted to dispose of her decently, romantically and effectively. I therefore had the poor thing become insane, and the unhappy creature jump from a window during the conflagration of the Ghetto of Frankfurt and thus meet her death." But "the most serious feature of the whole matter," he complained, was that Mrs. Wise "made sport of me.") He compiled an American ritual prayer book, *Minhag America,* with both German and English translations. He and his brother-in-law, Edward Bloch, formed a publishing house dealing in books of Jewish interest. He edited *Die Deborah,* a German-language weekly, and an English-language weekly, the *American Israelite,* whose circulation was larger than the aggregate readership of "all the Jewish papers published between the Atlantic Coast and the Rocky Mountains." (Of course, the *Israelite* in its palmiest days never reached the circulation figures and level of influence of the newspaper published by Dr. Wise's daughter Effie's husband, Adolph S. Ochs.)

"On that commonplace twenty-third of July," Wise wrote, "in that commonplace year, 1846," when he landed in New York "with wife and child and two dollars in my pocket,"* a Jewish population of 50,000 had established fifty congregations. Three were Reform; the rest, nominally Orthodox, had members who were less and less disposed to inconveniencing themselves for devout purposes. They ate pork during the week and said kaddish on the Sabbath. Because no organization bound the scattered congregations together, each functioned in isolation and independently. Fights during services over ritual and prerogative weren't uncommon. "Blows passed in a certain synagogue in New York on Kol Nidre evening, because one party insisted that at the close of the service the *adon olam* be sung first, and then the *yigdol,* while the other insisted on the opposite." In New Orleans, when a member of

---

* By the end of his life, Dr. Wise had augmented his family: two wives and fourteen children. His material wealth didn't increase proportionately, for he never made more than $6,000 a year. When at the end of his life it was suggested that he make a will, he declared, "I have nothing to bequeath. The world will laugh at me if I leave a will."

the congregation questioned the right of Dr. Roley Marks—chazan, part-time actor, and captain of the fire engine—to lead them in prayer, Dr. Marks exclaimed irately, "By Jesus, I will *daven* and no one will dare to stop me."

A basic cause of this turmoil was the absence of a theological seminary in which to train American rabbis. In the entire country, of the sixty men serving as rabbis before 1850, only three—including Isaac Mayer Wise—were known to have been ordained. (And there were those who gleefully cast doubts on *his* having received proper ordination.) The others were mere chazanim. Their duties, Dr. Wise wrote scornfully, encompassed everything from reading "Shiur for the departed sinners" to playing cards "with the living." And "among all the *chazanim* whom I learned to know at that time," he recalled, "there was not one who had a common school education or possessed any Hebrew learning." At the first service Wise attended in New York, he noted with displeasure that "the cantor had on a Christian gown, trilled like a mock nightingale, and leaped about like a hooked fish." Irony was implicit: Judaism, which had withstood century after century of assault, seemed destined to disintegrate in an atmosphere of complete religious freedom. Native Jews, Wise declared, "were tinged with Christian thought . . . there were Episcopal Jews in New York, Quaker Jews in Charleston, and so on, everywhere according to the prevailing sect." So American Judaism—in disarray, and with few leaders who had any Hebrew education—appeared slated for extinction. But then, after mid-century, it was revitalized by the Reform movement.

Reform Judaism wasn't an American innovation; it had its genesis in Germany, where its originator, Israel Jacobsen, had been, not a rabbinical scholar, but, more appropriately in the view of Orthodox Jews, a rich German Jewish banker. In 1801 he established a non-sectarian boarding school in Seesen, a small southern German town, and began holding services there in German rather than Hebrew. Gradually, he introduced other changes: a choir; weekly sermons rather than the usual two or three a year; an organ; a shortened service. It wasn't until seventeen years after this initial wedge that a Reform synagogue, the first in the world, was built in Hamburg.

Acrimony, scathing denunciation, polemical dissertations on the Talmud—pro and con—and sheer unscholarly wrangling swept through Jewish community life in Germany and England in the wake of the reform movement. (Orthodox leaders in London excommunicated an entire congregation for the apostasy of turning to Reform.) However, European efforts to institute changes in Judaic ritual were frustrating at best, futile at worst. Its most significant move occurred just before mid-century, when newly ordained proponents of Reform Judaism emigrated to the United States, where a prevailing liberal spirit was conducive to reform of all kinds. Many of those fervent young rabbis became prominent American Reform advocates. But only Isaac Mayer Wise maintained—and, indeed, he may have been right—that he saved Judaism from extinction in the United States by organizing, structuring, and securing a firm base for American Reform. Otherwise, "it would not have been strong enough," Wise asserted, "to outlive the end of the 19th century."

At his first post—Congregation Beth El in Albany, New York—Dr. Wise began to eliminate those exotic customs of Orthodox Jewish ritual which he felt would discomfit native Jews who did not want to feel that their religious observance separated them from their countrymen.

To accomplish this, Dr. Wise performed extensive surgery on ritual—in two congregations in Albany and for forty-six years in one congregation in Cincinnati. It was necessary, Wise felt, to save the life of the patient. But his opponents viewed his treatment as radical, involving transplants from Christian services. He replaced certain long Hebrew prayers with English and German hymns sung by a choir, not only unorthodox, but dissonant. ("In all of Albany," Wise complained sadly, "there was not one person who could sing with the exception of two bassos.") When his small daughter died of cholera, Wise refused to permit the Orthodox ritual of rending his and his wife's garments, nor would he sit *shivah*— sit on the floor or on low stools, for the seven-day mourning period. He abolished the women's gallery in the synagogue; the idea of banishing women to a distant spot, so their sexual attractions would be unable to reach men at prayer and distract them, did not fit his idea of culture and progress.

Half the Orthodox body in Albany rejected Dr. Wise's "Christian" transplants and brought him up on heresy charges: He had publicly ridiculed the *mikveh,* the women's ritual bath; he had been seen writing—considered work and therefore profane on *erev* (the eve of) Rosh Hashonah in an Odd Fellows Lodge; and he had been seen in Mineral Springs Garden on the Sabbath, swinging on a swing—*geshwungen in a schwing.* . . .

And so, at the Rosh Hashonah service that year, when Rabbi Wise stepped up before the ark to take out the scrolls, the president of the congregation "without saying a word," Wise indignantly recorded, "smites me with his fist so that my cap falls from my head."

Since this sort of incident obviously went beyond ordinary congregational dissension, Dr. Wise led his faction to more tranquil pastures. Eventually they settled in a former Baptist church, where the family pews had been left intact, and the custom of men and women sitting together during services was instituted.

In 1854, Wise accepted a call to Cincinnati's Bene Jeshurun. There, through the years, one Orthodox tradition after another was sheared away: observance of the second day of holy days; worshiping with covered head; some ritual prayers dating from the Middle Ages; dietary laws. . . . While these alterations in Orthodoxy made Bene Jeshurun the leading Reform congregation in the United States, it was Wise's phenomenal genius at organization that transformed the invigorated American Judaism. By 1873 he had taken care of one weakness by organizing twenty-eight synagogues into the Union of American Hebrew Congregations; two years later he eradicated an even more basic flaw by founding the Hebrew Union College in Cincinnati, the first successful American rabbinical seminary.

Thus, by 1881, the year the Russian pogroms began, Isaac Mayer Wise had set up a Reform establishment of formidable potential. And through all his years of controversy and battle, he had developed the Reform movement into the dominant sect of American Judaism; in the process, Orthodoxy had lost adherents and grown weaker. For American Orthodox Jews did not have Reform's unity. A left-wing group, who would eventually form the Conservative movement, wanted to modify Judaism rather than change it. Up to the year of the pogroms, Dr. Wise's major opponents, for the most part, had been members of this group—leaders of Western European Sephardic Orthodoxy. (Employing that vital rise and fall of inflection so necessary to Yiddish expression for change of emphasis—though Sephardic Jews were Orthodox, East European Jews were *Orthodox*.)

Everything in East European Orthodoxy ran counter to an element which both Reform and Conservative Jews believed essential to modern Judaism—propriety, decorum. "There is a lack of refinement and true spirituality," declared a Conserva-

tive paper, "despite the exactness with which they adhere to
their traditional habits." *Davening*—the singsong chanting of
prayers in the Orthodox service, which few of the worshipers
understood because they were in Hebrew—was done by the
congregation at each person's individual pace and accompanied by his singular style of swaying back and forth for con-
centration. The overall impression was of a prayer race, the
devout achieving a paradoxically sacred babel. But this approach to prayer simply reflected the East European's peasant
relationship with God. Their everyday *shtetl* closeness to Him
made for a boisterous uninhibited heartiness. God was one of
them; in His presence no esthetic airs were needed. Similarly,
Reform Jews saw God in the image they sought to project, a
genteel American image (with just a slight German accent);
therefore, their service, of necessity, had to equal in refinement that of the American Prostestant.

When those masses of Russian Jews began disembarking—
threatening Dr. Wise's edifice of Reform with the zeal of
Orthodoxy—Dr. Wise was sixty-two and firm in the belief
that he'd elevated the status of Jews in the United States.
"Those who now say with just pride, I am an Israelite, where
some years ago they carefully concealed the fact," he wrote,
"are not aware of the bitter struggles in the combat against
friend and foe which this change has cost, and most likely
never will appreciate it."

To Wise, the torrent of crude, unworldly Russian Jews presented the only major obstacle to his fifty-year goal of Americanizing Judaism, for they were steeped in "medieval rubbish"
and flooding city slums during the last two decades of his life.
"Count Ignatiev," he wrote feelingly in 1882, after Ignatiev's
May Laws sent steerageload after steerageload of Jews to the
United States, "ought to be hanged."

In their estimate of Wise, Russian Jews were no less vehement. To them, he appeared the quintessence of the *Amerikanishe Deitche Yahudim*—the arrogant, opinionated, American German Jew—and hardly a spiritual leader. Nor could
they take the leaders of the less radical Conservative movement seriously. Those who followed Halakah—traditional
Jewish law—viewed the distinctions between Reform and
Conservative as minor or nonexistent. "There is no difference
at all between the Conservatives and the Radicals," wrote an
Orthodox scholar, "except that the former are soft-hearted
like babes who hide themselves beneath their mother's petti-
coats and dread stating their opinions publicly."

So at the time of the immigrants' arrival, a furious upheaval had created a schism in the American Jewish community. To the incoming orthodox Russian Jews, changing any aspect of Jewish law was out of the question. Native Jews, however, agreed on the necessity of change—evolution—but they differed on the degree Judaism should be altered to conform to American society. The moderately Orthodox—the Conservatives—wanted only a minimum of change. This meant altering, rather than discarding. But Dr. Wise viewed many Orthodox traditions as accretions of a medieval age to be thrown out as superstitions. The Ten Commandments, he believed, were the basis of Judaism. He therefore held that "Religion is a set of principles and not a system of observances or a mode of belief or worship."

Thus, viewed objectively, American Jews—of predominantly German origin and conflicting estimates on the extent to which they should modernize their faith—had nothing in common with East European Jews but their religion, a bond that would generate the widest divisions between them. Still, according to genial metaphor, Judaism was a vast umbrella under which Jews of all theological shadings could stand protected from the world's inclemencies. But in the final two decades of the last century, while American Reform and Conservative Jews stood sheltered, it was only the arrival of the Russian Jews that prevented a waning Orthodox Judaism from being left out in the rain.

They came, too, just when Judaism appeared to be approaching a full integration with American life. Reform temples were being built throughout the country and attended by decorous, refined congregations who had abandoned "slavish imitations of meaningless observances." And Dr. Wise's conviction that "Jew" was "an improper and unbecoming appellation for the children of Israel" had found acceptance by the properly designated Israelites or Hebrews and also by Christians. It was at this hapless moment in history that those who inelegantly referred to themselves as *Yiden*—Jews—arrived to provide a cultural shock to their American co-religionists and trigger a severe epidemic of *tsitterdikness*. Nevertheless, a crisis of identity, that intermittent Jewish malaise, afflicted neither American Reform Jews nor immigrant Russian Orthodox Jews. Each knew its identity and the identity of the other group. "They are Jews," declared Dr. Isaac Mayer Wise. "We are Israelites." And the Russian Jews said with equal assurance, "We are Jews. They are goyim."

7

"Multipeds and Bivalves" and "Men of Purely Jewish Stomach"

Because of all the alarms and apprehensions making up the *tsitterdik* syndrome, American Jews wished to avoid an unseemly, embarrassing fight over ritual with the Orthodox that would make Judaism appear "a hybrid before the world," although Jewish theological arguments were hardly a novelty—Dr. Wise and the native Orthodox rabbis had clashed incessantly over the years—and theological interdenominational wrangles were also common in Christianity. But their fear of public dispute had validity, for their own character and that of the immigrants made a battle inevitable.

"The nature of this country," Haym Salomon, one of the early East European immigrants, wrote sadly, "[is] *wenig Yiddishkeit.*" Upon their arrival about a hundred years later, Salomon's *landsleit* were also struck forcibly with not only the lack of *Yiddishkayt,* but with the abandonment of traditional ritual. It stunned Russian Jews to come, as they did, to Rochester, New York, to Easton, Pennsylvania, to Denver, Colorado, and elsewhere and find their American co-religionists preparing to remove their headgear during services and men and women sitting side by side in family pews; the Talmud had fallen into disrepute; Hebrew prayers had, in many cases, been forsaken for English translations; and American Jews did not observe the second day of holidays. (One Orthodox young man in Easton, heading for shul on the second day of Rosh Hashonah, passed the shuttered Reform temple and mischievously hung a sign on its doorknob that read, "Closed on Account of Holiday.")

No sooner did the Russians arrive than they began rounding up minyans and renting any available meeting room or lodge hall to serve as a shul. Could so much religion, shocked American Jews wondered, be proper? Moreover, Orthodox synagogues reproduced with a speed that suggested parthenogenesis. In New York City, by 1900, there were 200 Orthodox shuls. Frequently, a shul's membership would be made up entirely of the former residents of one *shtetl*. This even occurred in cities with much smaller Jewish populations.

In some cultures, ten men gathered together might constitute a new political party; among Orthodox Russian Jews, it was a minyan—enough to start a shul. If the ten grew to twenty or twenty-five or more and cross words were exchanged over pilpulistic minutiae, they split into two shuls—three, four. As a consequence, small synagogues were not only very numerous, but highly individualistic. Indeed, in Denver, one man, Israel Chatz, established his own synagogue known as "Chotsky's shul," into which, his neighbors claimed, he lured congregants with promises of whiskey.

Yet, in spite of all this Orthodox hyperactivity and the uneasiness of native Jews, the Reform movement, whose membership included the richest, most powerful Jews in the United States, appeared secure in its eminent place in American Judaism. From this lofty position, Reform Jews lectured the Orthodox on the need to leave their "superstitions" behind them, declaring they must "teach these newcomers to distinguish between the Judaism of an Isaiah and of an obscure cabbalistical Maggid" and maintaining that "until the old Orthodox notions they have brought with them from Russia have been modified or eliminated, there is little to be expected even from the children."

"From a religious point of view," an anonymous New York Jew stated to a *New York Times* reporter, "the Russian Jew is further from the American Jew than the American Jew is from a Christian or an infidel." A story—"an amusing incident"—reported by a gentleman, Mr. A. B. G. in New Haven, Connecticut, to the *American Israelite,* indicated that this may not have been overstatement. A Russian Jew who worried about having to work on the Sabbath was told by an American Jew "that there is a twenty-four-hour difference in time, so that when it is Saturday here it is Friday in Russia, and those who work on the Sabbath commit no sin provided they rest on Sunday."

Optimistic opinion among American Jews predicted that though pious Russian Jews would continue in their contrary fashion to follow their "impractical, outlandish and medieval beliefs and customs," some of their children could be encouraged to attend Hebrew Union College to study for the rabbinate. Eventually—so the thinking went—they, as Reform rabbis, would influence a whole generation and, in fifty years, Orthodox Judaism would be extinct. However, within four years after mass immigration started, two events shook Reform to its very foundations—upsetting the delicate balance of radical and conservative opinion in Reform theology and rallying Orthodoxy to new strength.

The first of these incidents took place at the time of the Hebrew Union College's first graduation, held in conjunction with the tenth annual meeting of the Union of American Hebrew Congregations. "The fourteenth of July, 1883 will ever stand out as epochal in American religious life," David Philipson, one of the four graduates,* wrote of the event. Yet the banquet, to honor those graduates and delegates of the Union of American Hebrew Congregations held three days earlier, may have been every bit "as epochal in American religious life." ("The Cincinnati *Enquirer* with goyish innocence called the banquet "a Jewish Jollification.") A banquet committee composed of local wealthy German Jews had engaged the caterer who served the Cincinnati Jewish social club. The committee members maintained and continued to maintain—though it was as to a stone wall—that the caterers had been firmly instructed to observe kashrut—the dietary laws—for those guests Dr. Wise called "kitchen Jews."†

The banquet took place in Highland House—a new, monstrous palace of entertainment. In keeping with its name, it was located on top of Mount Adams, one of the hills sur-

---

* At HUC's inception the first class contained one girl and "fourteen noisy boys," most of whom, according to Dr. Wise, "had come only to kill time and at the command of their parents. Four of them wanted to study; ten wanted to make noise."

† Dr. Wise's sentiments on kashrut were simple: "It is not religion," he said, "it is sanitary advice." Nevertheless, he objected to eating pork. It was, he felt, a health hazard, and he pounced gleefully on cases of trichinosis as proof of its impurity.

rounding Cincinnati. Two towers lent distinction to the two-story frame building's exterior; bronzed fountains served the interior's show of opulence. No single aid to conviviality had been overlooked: two ballrooms; a billiard room; a bowling alley; a wine cellar; a beer vault; and, on the second floor, a large dining room.

"The great banqueting hall was brilliantly lighted," Philipson recalled. Among those seated at the gorgeously appointed tables were eminent Jewish and Christian citizens of Cincinnati and representatives of 114 congregations, "the largest body of representative Israelites from all parts of the country ever assembled on this Western continent." Following the invocation by one of the guest rabbis, "the waiters served the first course," placing before all assembled, including "the men of purely Jewish stomach," Little Neck clams—small, raw, on the half shell—and forbidden by the Almighty. In a word, *tref!*

"Terrific excitement ensued when two rabbis rose from their seats and rushed from the room." Had they—and those similarly offended who followed them—stayed, they would have been served increasingly outrageous trefa dishes: soft-shell crabs, shrimp salad, creamed frogs' legs. In addition, French delicacies added a note of decadence via gluttony: *filet de boeuf aux champignons, sweetbreads à la Monglas, poulets à la Viennoise, vol au vents de pigeons à la Tyrolienne.* Naturally, one could not expect the magisterial *Deitche Yahudim* to sanction the serving of those ubiquitous features of present-day Jewish banquets—contributions of Russian Jews to *Gastronomique*—a mound of chopped chicken liver atop a lettuce leaf and garnished with crumbled egg yolk, or a weighty portion of *gefilte kishke*, but a dish such as *carpe à la juive* (carp, Jewish style) could have been served without destroying the French ambience while at the same time preserving a certain relevancy. And had those outraged Orthodox rabbis remained at the banquet board, they would have been served four wines, Roman punch (lemon ice with rum poured over it) champagne, and cognac, which had the potential, at least, of blurring the hard, straight, divine line between tref and kosher.

No wines could have calmed the emotional weeks following the trefa banquet; wrathful screams grew in intensity. "The Orthodox Eastern press rang the changes on the *terefa* banquet week in week out," Philipson wrote in disgust. As far away as St. Petersburg, a Russian Jewish newspaper regarded that infamous seafood as indicative of "an ever-swelling break in the wall of religion which destroys its foundations." In Hartford, Boston, New York, and Philadelphia, congregations withdrew from Dr. Wise's Union of American Hebrew Congregations and from support of the Hebrew Union College. Indeed, the very mention of Wise's name among Eastern Orthodox leaders of both left and right wings, native and immigrant, evoked eye-flashing, beard-bristling unspirituality among the former and all the possible colorful invective of Yiddish among the latter. Furious exchanges took place between rabbis of the Reform and Conservative movements. The *American Hebrew*—a Conservative paper—and Dr. Wise's *American Israelite* lashed out with fulminations for and against "multipeds and bivalves" and against each other. Dr. Wise wrote reams in explanation, then in justification, and finally in defiance. Such expressions as "ignorant fanatics," "kitchen Judaism," "ridiculous, Lilliputian, demeaning" were flung out angrily. And he propounded what might be called Wise's Law: "There is a law which stands higher than all dietary laws, and that is 'Be no fanatic,' which translated in our vulgar language would sound like this: 'Be intelligent and allow your reason to govern your passions, propensities and superstitions.' " His opponents fought back with the kindest criticism aimed at his "low tone" and voiced "general alarm concerning the example set to its [HUC's] students for the ministry."

Two years later, the move to clarify Reform's position—by means of the Pittsburgh Platform—set off an even more heated battle. The platform reinforced the split between Conservative and Reform and indicated their respective distances from Orthodoxy.

When the nineteen Reform rabbis emerged from Rodef Shalom Synagogue on Pittsburgh's Fifth Avenue in mid-November, 1885, they had formulated an eight-point platform which would be the basis for American Reform Judaism for half a century. Rejecting those Mosaic and rabbinical laws regarding diet, dress, belief in bodily resurrections, and heaven and hell as antiquated products of a medieval age, Reform also cast aside the goal of a national restoration in Palestine (so much for the burgeoning Zionist movement, which Dr. Wise would scornfully dismiss as that "Russian-Polish hobby"). In declaring science and Judaism to be compatible, Reform discarded "miraculous narratives" of the Bible as reflections of the "the primitive ideas of its own age." And before any theological clamor could be raised, the Pittsburgh

Platform put itself on record as upholding a belief in God; at the same time, it struck a blow at Felix Adler's Ethical Culture Society which had subsituted social justice for divine belief. ("There is no God," Dr. Wise wrote with sardonic glee, "and Felix Adler is his prophet.") But Reform Judaism proclaimed not only its devotion to God, but dedication to social justice. Furthermore, the platform maintained that Sunday services were not contrary to Judaism's tenets. ("A congregation which holds Sunday services," retorted Rabbi Benjamin Szold in Baltimore, "may be compared to a bigamist who still clings to his first wife and loves both spouses. . . .")

The Pittsburgh Platform loomed as a radical document—so radical that certain of its most controversial points have since been moderated. The cries of rage from Conservative and traditionally Orthodox leaders rose to a crescendo that soared beyond their reaction to the trefa banquet. Choleric sermons —even at funerals—inflammable newspaper articles, and face-to-face encounters contributed to the division of American Judaism. Amid the raging battle, one goal set by American Jews was briefly neglected: that of "the moral elevation of millions among our co-religionists who do need refining influences and a soul-inspiring example." For clearly, if Judaism could not serve as a unifying force between American Jews, it most assuredly would not be a means of communication between them and the East European immigrants whose *shtetl* Orthodoxy was unfathomable to most American Jews.

The *mikveh,* vividly, concretely, illustrated the impasse. This ritual bath, in which Orthodox Jewish women immersed themselves after each menstrual period, and sometimes oftener, was an object of distaste to members of Reform. The arduous lengths to which the Orthodox would go to perform such a ritual simply defied their understanding. In Central City, Colorado, for example, Jewish women traveled fifteen miles to the mineral baths at Idaho Springs every week, over a hairpin-curved narrow mountain road, whose sheer drops had terrified even Ulysses S. Grant.* While at his first pulpit in Baltimore in 1888, Reform Rabbi David Philipson recorded in shocked astonishment:

Another piece of barbarism to be revived! My God, is it

* General Grant was merely passing through; he was *not* on his way to the *mikveh.* There is, after all, a limit to expiation—even for issuing Order No. 11.

possible in this late day such a custom should be revived? The Orthodox element here is soliciting money to build a mikveh!!! In this age of bathrooms, public and private!! Oh! The Shame of it. That even the most Orthodox man, if he were but a little enlightened should permit this much, much have I thought them capable of doing in their fanatic and ignorant zeal, but this never.

8

200 to 1

But of course, the differences in religious ideology between native Jews and Russian immigrants was only one factor in the American Jews' *tsitterdik* syndrome. The effect of a large immigration on the expanding national economy and on nativistic American public opinion caused even greater anxieties. In the late 1880's, in American Jewish homes all over the country, a single question was probed, fretted over, debated: How could these people transferred from the most medieval and autocratic of societies to the most modern and free adapt themselves to American life? Yet if a propitious time could have been chosen for their arrival in the United States, 1881 was in certain ways as good as some and better than most.

Until then, anti-Semitism scarcely tainted the United States. Indeed, a lady of Sephardic lineage pinpointed it even more precisely by remarking that until the arrival of the Russian Jews, she "had never heard the phrase, 'Jewish Question.'" Jewish dialect humor was indistinguishable from German, in the same way that German Jews often appeared facsimiles of German Christians. In the New York *Times,* the activities of Jewish clubs in New York were listed with German clubs; thus under a Teutonic Club heading was the B'nai B'rith. Whatever anti-Semitism did exist was diluted by a confusion of Jew and German. *Puck* and *Judge* and other American

humor magazines delighted in presenting full-page color car-
toons of men, women, and children with huge hooked noses,
gross lips, and crude manners who were labeled "Hebrews."
But in their columns, these cartoon figures spoke with a
vaudeville German accent. (So when *Puck* published an
imaginary interview with Moses, the founder of Judaism said,
"Uf you don't tell nobodies, I vas told you somedings. Der
faect is, I vas a Shoo myself. Foldks don't know it, un I don't
make no ostentations abouit it; aber I vas a Shoo. . . .")

However, a number of circumstances during the nine-
teenth-century crisis of currency which so agitated the Middle
West and South—and which on three occasions catapulted
William Jennings Bryan with indifferent aim toward the
White House—made Jews more than vaudeville comics: a villainous company of international Jewish financiers, "the
Israelites, the great money-getters of the world. . . ." Conceivably, the sudden appearance of hundreds of thousands of
Russian Jews might have proved instructive, informing Popu-
lists that in addition to the bloated, clawed stereotype they
had created, there were an immense number of very poor
Jews. One could have even argued that these Jews served, so-
ciologically, by filling a gap in American Jewry. The Sephardim were the upper class; the Germans, the middle class; and
now, with their arrival, the Russians were the lower class.

But alas, in actuality, the poverty of Russian Jews didn't
enhance their value at all. And their growing numbers—packing city streets and tenements—aggravated an apparently en-
demic prejudice. With curled lip, Henry James observed "the
Hebrew conquest of New York." The decline of rural population intensified the situation, for industry and boredom were
urbanizing the United States. But although Jews were inundating the slums, provoking not only expatriate novelists but
an assortment of individuals, they as a people had the unique
ability of adapting to urban life.

One man who exemplified the paranoid fears of Anglo-Saxon aristocracy was Henry Adams. To Adams, rich German
Jews epitomized the vulgar *nouveau riche;* poor Russian Jews,
the squalidly illiterate. Indeed, over the decades, as Adams sat
brooding in his Lafayette Square study, overlooking the White
House, Jews appeared to embody that vulgar material power
which excluded Adamses from the pinnacle of patrician
power which should have been theirs. And through the years,
he expressed grim forebodings for a world that had rejected
Adamses by investing Jews with uncommonly extensive

spheres of influence. They were everywhere: in Mayfair, on the Bois de Boulogne, in Wall Street. Adams believed they not only dominated the money centers, but were moving them to New York. "Westward the course of Jewry takes its way!" he wrote with a bitter lilt. They were conspiring successfully against the world: "The Jews have fixed the cards all around." Consequently, they assumed control over whole nations. "The German Jews now own France"; even more astonishing, "probably the Jews have bought Russia." God, Adams maintained, "tried drowning out the world once, but it did no kind of good and there are said to be four hundred and fifty thousand Jews now doing Kosher in New York alone. God Himself owned failure."

The incident that gave anti-Semitism social cachet occurred when a Saratoga hotel refused accommodation to the prominent Jewish banker Joseph Seligman.* And then in 1879, Austin Corbin, president of the Long Island Railroad and an ambitious real estate developer, had a dream—irresistible, poignant—to make Coney Island "the most fashionable and magnificent watering place in the world." But how, he pleaded rhetorically, could he "bring the highest social element" if "the Jews persist in coming"?

As though not to be outdone by the competition, other resorts advertised: "No Jews Accepted," even "No Jews or Dogs Admitted Here." The basic reasons were purely commercial—exclusivity would, in all likelihood, have enhanced the Black Hole of Calcutta. The stated reasons: Jews had no social refinement; they wore patent leather boots, showy trousers, and conspicuously vulgar jewelry. Ignorant of drawing-room courtesies, they also showed disrespect for the Christian Sabbath by playing cards in their rooms with the doors ajar,

---

* Judge Henry Hilton, who managed the Grand Union Hotel, maintained that while he admired "Hebrews," he disliked "Jews." Presumably, Seligman was a Jew. Some years after he wrote "The Outcast of Poker Flat," Bret Harte, whose grandfather had been Bernard Harte, a prominent Jewish merchant, amused himself with the Outcast of the Grand Union Hotel and Judge Hilton's distinctions "twixt 'Ebrew and Jew." "You may give to John Morrissey supper and wine/ and Madame N. N. to your care I resign,/ You will see that those Jenkins from Missouri Flat/ Are properly cared for, but recollect that/ Never a Jew/ Who's not a 'Ebrew,/ Shall take up his lodgings/ Here at the Grand U./ You'll allow Miss McFlimsey her diamond to wear,/ You'll permit the Van Dams at the waiter to swear,/ You'll allow Miss Decollete to flirt on the stair,/ But, as to an Israelite, pray have a care/ For, between me and you/ Though the doctrine is new,/ There's a business distinction Twixt 'Ebrew and Jew."

apparently to madden God-fearing Christians with the tempting sight of a deck of cards in use. Another vicious proclivity —this one ascribed to Jews by bartenders—was their failure to spend enough money at the bar. As a general overall criticism, resort owners declared that Jews swarmed everywhere—not an easy task either, for the ratio of Christian to Jew in the United States was 200 to 1.

It was all most unfair! Why shouldn't vulgar Jewish millionaires and their ill-bred pushy wives be permitted to enjoy the bloom of ostentation with the same impunity as vulgar Christian millionaires and their equally unpalatable wives? Soon enough, the children of both would be turning to simple black dresses, polo, and understatement.*

As a result of these pernicious forces, American Jews in the fall of 1881 felt one particular anxiety which alone could account for their aversion to a surging influx of East European Jews. So many Jews, they reasoned, especially ones with an alien outlandish appearance, would only inflame a rising anti-Semitism. (As James Thurber was to recount in his *New Yorker* series on radio soap opera, a Jewish character was deleted from one serial because, as the sponsor's representative explained, "We don't want to antagonize the anti-Semites.")

Another sinister idea was in the air. The whole alien influx to America from Eastern and Southern Europe—Jews, Slavs, Poles, and Italians: "brachycephalic, small in stature, dark-eyed and dark-haired"—popularized the spurious German-imported science of race superiority. ("What Shall We Do About the Dago?" an article in *Popular Science Monthly* inquired.) According to its axioms, only those nationalities of Northern Europe, "dolichocephalic, tall, blue-eyed and fair-haired," possessed the highest intelligence, noble features, exemplary morals, innate gentlemanliness, and, of course, the discernment to recognize these characteristics in themselves. How else than through the ennobling powers of pure Anglo-Saxon blood could one explain the ability to dine without spilling food unduly or to speak in moderate tone without gesturing?

In 1894, as a consequence, the Immigration Restriction League of Boston began to work assiduously for federal legis-

---

* Years later Maud Nathan wrote in a revealing flush of indignation: "Proprietors of fashionable resort hotels and of New York apartment houses frankly advertise that they exclude all Jewish patrons, using no discrimination between Jewish families who have had generations of culture and refinement and those who lack such a background."

lation to restrict immigration from Southeastern European countries. The league's members, gentlemen of New England and New York, were mildly affluent, but extraordinarily well fixed when it came to Anglo-Saxon lineage; still, inexplicably, they had little national influence. Only one conclusion could be drawn: The country was sliding downhill because of racial deterioration. The unrestricted "invasion" of Jews, Italians, and Slavs, "the beaten members of beaten breeds," would eventually outbreed their superiors and become the "Master Race."

In 1916 the league's vice-president, Madison Grant, published a mélange of racist ideology, *The Passing of the Great Race,* which asserted that the Nordic was "being literally driven off the streets of New York City by the swarm of Polish Jews" and urged wide extension of the miscegenation laws "if the higher races are to be maintained." In preparing his immigration restriction bill, Congressman Albert Johnson consulted Grant. The final version of his legislation, enacted in 1924 provided ethnic quotas, virtually wiping out significant immigration from Southeastern Europe and ending the mass migration of East European Jews into the United States.

Yet despite growing anti-Semitism among certain classes of American society, which eventually led to the 1924 immigration restriction, discrimination, prior to that time, had never been part of any federal or state policy, and the Russian Jews could not have come to a country more different from Russia —in religious, social, and economic freedom. An incident that occurred a year before their arrival revealed precisely how vast a gulf lay between the United States and Russia in the relationship of Jews to their government. The issuance of Thanksgiving proclamations had always been a source of irritation to Jews because of their references to the United States as a "Christian country." When Governor Henry Hoyt of Pennsylvania issued the Thanksgiving Proclamation for 1880 and alluded to "the power of a free Christian Commonwealth," he received a letter of protest from William B. Hackenburg, a Jewish silk manufacturer and philanthropist in Philadelphia. In response, Governor Hoyt agreed the phrase "might be obnoxious" and said it had therefore been changed to "a commonwealth of freemen." The governor explained that he had merely used the word "Christian" to denote "civilized."

In spite of the disparity between Russia and the United States, at the time of the arrival of the Russian Jews, a curious coincidence, linking their old homeland and their new, had taken place. The assassination of Alexander II by a nihilist, Alexander III's accession, and the onset of the pogroms occurred in March, 1881. On the following July 2, in Washington's Pennsylvania Station, President James A. Garfield was shot—not by a nihilist, but by a type more appropriate to a democracy: a disappointed office seeker. Garfield lingered in this world until mid-September. And his funeral took place on the day the National Line steamer *Egypt,* carrying one of the first cargoes of Russian Jews, docked in New York, where shopwindows were draped in funereal black.

In Cincinnati the Plum Street Temple recited kaddish for Garfield. Several weeks later, there occurred in that city a blessed event which surely must have cheered all those dour pessimists who predicted the impossibility of East European Jews' adjusting to the United States. The wife of Joseph Loomawitz, one of a number of immigrants passing through Cincinnati on the way to Sicily Island, Catahoula Parish, Louisiana, to redeem their souls through farming, gave birth to a boy, "supposed to be the first Russian born in this city." The infant was named Moses Garfield Loomawitz. And William Stix, of a prominent Jewish family, "ever ready for a mitsvah" acted as godfather and paid all the expenses involved in the baby's birth.

Stix's family had arrived in the United States about a half century earlier, so a gentleman of goodwill like Mr. Stix could still summon up a tenuous sort of relationship with Jewish immigrants. But no such affinity related Sephardim, the first Jewish settlers in America, and Russians, the last. Even their shared religion differed at almost every point: liturgy, ritual, the pronunciation of Hebrew, and fidelity to traditional observances. Indeed, when Sephardim first arrived in America, legend had it the Marrano ancestors of some of them, accustomed in Catholic Spain to concealing their worship as Jews, were unable to say Hebrew prayers without telling them on rosary beads.

Despite this gulf between Sephardim and East Europeans, had Jewish immigrants been presented with the opportunity of doing a mitzvah for Emma Lazarus, a thirty-two-year-old spinster of Sephardic descent, they wouldn't have hesitated a moment. They would have found her a husband. As it turned out, their mitzvah for Miss Lazarus was inadvertent—and less practical. They gave her immortality.

9

The Liberation of Emma Lazarus

"Handsome, clever and rich," she was, overprotected and with a father fixation, too. But unlike Jane Austen's Emma Woodhouse, after whom she had been named, Emma Lazarus was a hypersensitive, highly intellectual, literarily precocious young woman, inspired by Hellenistic themes and subject to melancholy. She belonged to the Nathan-Seixas family axis; the Lazaruses were one of the best-known and oldest Sephardic families in New York City, directly descended from a Portuguese Jew who had been expelled during the Inquisition.

If anyone among Sephardic aristocracy epitomized the totally accepted, quasi-assimilated, semi-un-Jewish individual, it was Emma Lazarus. To associate her in any way with the Jews of the *shtetlach* was far-fetched, indeed. So little Jewish atmosphere permeated the Lazarus home that Philip Cowen, editor of the *American Hebrew*, once heard himself referred to by Emma's sister, Anna, as "one of my sister's Jewish friends." Her adored father, Moses Lazarus—a far cry from the valetudinarian, dim-witted Mr. Woodhouse—had retired at fifty-two with a substantial fortune from the sugar-refining firm of Johnson and Lazarus. The life of Mr. Lazarus, a patrician upper-class New Yorker, whose ancestors had arrived in America just a step or two behind the Pilgrims, met the exacting standards of Victorian respectability—even though he was of the "Hebrew Persuasion." He occasionally attended religious services at the Spanish Portuguese Synagogue—Congregation Shearith Israel—the oldest in New York, not for spiritual values, but as an example for the lower classes. A more intense devotion went to the Knickerbocker Club, which he'd helped found, and to the Union Club, to which he also belonged. So close, so dependent upon him were his family that when he left home for only twenty-four hours, his daughters wept. Of his six daughters—one less than Tevya the dairyman, and it's doubtful whether he would have appreciated the comparison—Moses Lazarus' favorite was Emma. She was not an ordinary girl, slim, dark-haired, and with a "slightly Jewish" nose. "Emma had beautiful eyes," her cousin Annie Nathan Meyer, a founder of Barnard College, recalled, "but large features and a skin that was always, the few times I saw her, unappetizing." Rebecca Kohut, wife of Conservative Rabbi Alexander Kohut, regarded her as "so reserved and timid that she almost gave the impression of actually being afraid." Even in later years, when she was fairly well known, she cringed at publicity, which she regarded as an invasion of privacy. "I hear," she wrote angrily to Philip Cowen, "that my name is being advertised in connection with the *American Hebrew* at the advertising illumination on the corner of 23rd Street and Broadway. If you have any knowledge of or any connection with this advertisement, I request that it be discontinued forthwith. I cannot understand how you could adopt this rather peculiar mode of advertising without first consulting my wishes & shall await impatiently for assurances that a stop has been put to it." In order to protect her from the harsh realities of Mrs. Ogden Hoffman's School, she was tutored at home.

At nineteen, Emma began a correspondence with Ralph Waldo Emerson that lasted until shortly before his death. Emerson's advice, his criticism, alternately encouraged and discouraged her; his inexplicable omission of her work in his poetry anthology *Parnassus* cast her into a state of depression that lasted for years. Early in their exchange of letters, Emerson suggested that instead of dwelling on classic themes—"the old world of Memory"—Emma might direct her verse to the "despised Present." In spite of a few efforts in this direction, the present or its near vicinity was still not a period that inspired her.

Similarly, whatever interest she had in Jews and Jewish life prior to 1881 was tenuous, literary, and detached. If she touched on this subject in her verse, the reference was clearly to Jews who had lived in medieval Spain. "Nor," her sister Josephine was to recall, "had she any great enthusiasm for her own people." Though she attended synagogue as a child, she didn't as an adult, rejecting the rites of Sephardic Orthodoxy as obsolete. "Judaism was a dead letter to her." Consequently, when Dr. Gustave Gottheil, the genial rabbi imported a few years earlier from Manchester, England, by Temple Emanu-El (so universally popular that he was considered "the best rabbi which the Christians of New York ever had"), approached her for help in modernizing a prayer book, Emma displayed little interest. She couldn't, she told him, write to order. Moreover, she declared, "I shall always be loyal to my race, but I feel no religious fervor in my soul. . . ."

The blend of intellectuality, romanticism, a temperamental incompatibility with the nineteenth century, her unrequited love for her cousin the "wild and extravagant" Washington Nathan (extraordinarily handsome, though "anything but an intellectual")—to say nothing of her living only three blocks from Washington Square—gave Emma the somewhat ethereal quality of a Henry James heroine. Subject to spells of despondency, she complained to a friend that despite all her literary efforts, she "had accomplished nothing to stir, nothing to awaken, to teach or to suggest that the world would not equally well do without." When this friend suggested Jewish tradition as a source of inspiration, she replied that "although proud of her blood and lineage, the Hebrew ideals did not appeal to her." In a similar attempt to sway Emma toward a literary interest in her people, John Burroughs told her that Hebraic influence had inspired Walt Whitman, but she remained unmoved by this information.

In late summer of 1881, however, incessant, abrasive reports of Russian pogroms filtered through Europe, crossed the Atlantic, and caused a startling alteration in Emma's feelings. On the arm of Dr. Gottheil, she walked through Wards Island and beheld the Jewish immigrants huddled there. "I saw her face," Dr. Gottheil recalled, "now aglow with scorn, now suffused with compassion."

But it wasn't a sight that evoked compassion in all. "Candidly speaking," bristled the New York correspondent for the *American Israelite,* after his visit to Wards Island, "they looked exactly like Polish riff-raff of which most European cities are only too familiar. . . . Their appearance is certainly against them. And what is said by those who know of their personal characteristics is not calculated to increase the sympathy which we are all bound to feel for them." Unquestionably, for those who preferred their Russian pogrom victims to look like neat Germans who knew their proper station in life, Russian Jews could not help being an immense disappointment.

Just as Yiddish stirred no racial memories in Emma, the sight of immigrants failed to set off the *tsitterdik* syndrome; she didn't regard Russian Jews as a threat to her status. But observing those whom Secretary Manuel Kursheedt of the Russian Emigrant Relief Fund was disposed to call "these unfortunate creatures" with their "peculiar traits" shocked Emma out of her preoccupation with the Middle Ages. On a practical level she persuaded De Witt Seligman to begin organizing relief for the immigrants, but, in her writing, she still could deal with their condition only on a heroic, romantic basis. Turning a degree away from the *shtetl* dwellers, Emma wrote a long poem—"The Banner of the Jew"—invoking with fiery apostrophe the grandeur and triumphs of Judah Maccabee: "Wake, Israel, wake! Recall today the glorious Maccabean rage. . . ." Several months later, an article she had written on Disraeli appeared in the *Century;* it proudly asserted that Disraeli "knew himself to be the descendant, not of pariahs and pawnbrokers, but of princes, statesmen, poets and philosophers." An apologia for the pogroms by a Madame Z. Ragozin appeared in the same issue. Emma was appalled.

The Ragozin article had evidently been written to silence the cries of denunciation that arose in Europe and America. In February, 1882, in London's Mansion House, in New York's Chickering Hall, and in large cities all over the United States, huge assemblages of Jews and non-Jews gathered to express their sympathy and collect funds for the pogrom victims. Thus, on behalf of the autocratic image, it was thought to be necessary to defend Russia in the only way such indefensible acts are defended—by blaming the victims. Yes, Jews were being treated harshly in Russia, but the fault lay not with Russia, but with the Jews themselves.

Madame Ragozin set about her task with the heavy predictable hand of an imperial trusty. After a brief nod toward the regrettability of what she called "the popular outbreaks against the Jews," Madame Ragozin found valid reasons for these "spontaneous occurrences." Then, untroubled by any dedication to accuracy, she went on to list ethnic shortcom-

ings, with a profundity that can be gauged by her assertion
that there were two kinds of Jews: "The Jews who followed
Jesus and those who crucified him." Jews were despised "not
because they are of different blood, not because they dress
differently, eat peculiar foods," and not even because they
herded together "in unutterable filth and squalor." Surprisingly, even their being "a loathsome and really dangerous element—a standing institution for the propagation of all kinds
of horrible diseases and contagions" hadn't put the Russians
off. According to Madame Ragozin, autocratic Russian anti-
Semitism arose simply because of the victims' refusal "to
stand up for themselves and manfully resent insult or oppose
vexation but will take any amount of it if they can thereby
turn a penny, will smirk and cringe. . . ."

Outraged and disgusted, Emma wrote a stinging reply, giving a point-by-point sardonic rebuttal. It appeared in *Century*
the following month: "Russian Christianity Versus Modern
Judaism." It was obvious, Emma declared, that in Madame
Ragozin's mind, the fallacy that Christians have been persecuting Jews has been forever demolished and there had been
"established in its stead the conspicuous fact the Jews have
been always and still are, persecuting Christians, especially in
Russia." To the madame's two-kinds-of-Jews statement,
Emma retorted, "The dualism of the Jews is the dualism of
humanity; they are made up of the good and the bad. May
not Christians be divided up between those Christians who
denounce such outrages as we are considering and those who
commit or apologize for them?"

And while Emma did her best to counter Madame Ragozin's astute detection of a fatal Jewish flaw—abject subservi-
ence—the immigrants on Wards Island, whose condition had
inspired Emma to write yearningly of "the glorious Maccabean rage," proved by their action, that there were, at least,
exceptions to the stereotype. "Oh deem not dead the martial
fire," Emma had exclaimed in "The Banner of the Jew." "Say
not that mystic flame is spent." And, indeed, it wasn't, for in
mid-October, Wards Island was rocked by an uprising: the
Tzimes Revolt.

Although revolts are alien to committees, acrimonious correspondence isn't. No exception, the Russian Emigrant Relief
Committee functioned just long enough to have its own sta-
tionery printed on which to accuse English relief agencies of

poor judgment in their choice of those who were being sent to the United States. Send only young bachelors and skilled mechanics, the committee piteously reiterated; but the *zaydes* and the *bobbehs* came, and so did the families of seven and eight and even more—occasionally whole *shtetlach*. And none had the skills American Jews were willing to recognize.

Financially, organizationally, temperamentally, the RERC couldn't cope with long-range assistance. Such aid called for a more substantial, permanent body. So in late November, 1881, more than 200 prominent American Jews gathered to consider the matter—appropriately, considering their objective, in the Hebrew Orphan Asylum at Seventy-seventh Street and Third Avenue. At this meeting, Jacob Schiff, Judge Meyer Isaacs, and Julian Bien, a well-known mapmaker and lithographer, wrangled over the need for such an organization, which Schiff complained smacked "of sectarianism." To Schiff's defiant query whether any other race or nationality had such an agency, someone snapped, "Plenty of them." Then Judge Isaacs contended that the emigration from Eastern Europe was a temporary phenomenon. Of this airy view, Bien scornfully inquired, "Who is going to Castle Garden tomorrow morning to look after those 500 Russian Jews there?" As answer, an agency later incorporated as the Hebrew Emigrant Aid Society was formed. (One fairly reliable device for distinguishing between the agencies created by American Jews and those self-help organizations established by Russian Jews merely called for checking the spelling of "immigrant." American Jews used "emigrant," as if the individuals to whom it referred still resided outside the country; the Russian Jews' "immigrant" made it clear they were right in the United States, as they certainly were.)

Throughout the hot summer of 1882, in a dingy basement office at 15 State Street, the HEAS committee fought off the importunity of the desperate immigrants who thronged the streets and milled about the doors of their office. Although guarded by two tall policemen "whose function was to cut the air or the heads of the immigrants with their long clubs," the committee grew almost as frantic as the immigrants.

With only stopgap, ineffective semisolutions to the staggering problem of what to do with the thousands of men, women, and children lying in wait for them—and thousands more poured in every week—the beleaguered members of the committee couldn't help feeling that the recipients of their compassion were thwarting their determined efforts to comply with the noblest Judaic traditions concerning charity. During its single year of existence, HEAS had three presidents and four secretaries. This volatile executive turnover was understandable. In the suffocating heat of the HEAS office, to have to point out to immigrant mothers of small children "the need of the most elementary sanitary rules" wasn't everyone's idea of elevated leadership. "Emigrants arrive daily," HEAS cabled its representative in Europe. "Majority incapable of supporting themselves; will be permanent burden on the community. Our officers wearied through the intractability of refugees and lack of support . . . are daily resigning." But the sympathetic, perceptive Michael Heilprin—a journalist, scholar, editor of *Appleton's Cyclopedia*—proved more successful than the others. During a meeting, upon hearing Russian Jews referred to contemptuously as "Polacks," Heilprin rose with the unhurried poise of dignity. "I am a Polish Jew," he said quietly. "I belong to that despised race."

Heilprin not only had to make impassioned appeals to "the better feelings" of American Jews, but also had "to argue earnestly with the more impatient and obstreperous of the immigrants who could not or would not always understand that the land of liberty was . . . subject to laws and restrictions which must be obeyed."

In the spring of 1882 they loaded penniless immigrants who had no destination onto the 110th Street Ferry and transported them to Wards Island and the shelter of an old, unused insane asylum. The immigrants arrived in time to celebrate Purim with a repast, provided by Jacob Schiff, of cold meats, cake, and, perhaps with the dim hope that *mann ist vas mann esst,* genteel claret punch.

Although Jacob Schiff stubbornly insisted that charity ought to be strictly nonsectarian, he had a deep abiding feeling of responsibility for fellow Jews. The immigrants' obvious need therefore melted his intransigence. He contributed $10,000 to improve the Wards Island Refuge. Revamped, the shelter, consisting of four tar-covered barracks, was called the Schiff Refuge. The main building held 500 people and, it was pointed out pejoratively, looked "on the inside like a sukkah" —a symbolic makeshift structure which the Talmud specified need have no more than two complete walls.

An HEAS-appointed superintendent and his assistant administered the refuge: Superintendent Henry Blank—called by his charges the Father, with the same filial devotion Jews felt when they referred to the czar as the Little Father—and Assistant Superintendent Zadok.

In mid-October fifty more immigrants arrived at Wards Island; they'd been chosen because of their "calloused hands and healthy appearance," to dig ditches for water pipes. Among them was George Moses Price, an eighteen-year-old former *Realschule* student from Poltava, Russia. Having concluded that a "Jew has no future in Russia," young Price had arrived in New York in July, 1882, penniless, a striking figure in his *Realschule* uniform, long hair, pince-nez. Beneath this exterior churned excitement and expectations upon seeing "the magnificent shores of America" for the first time. But his experiences in the months that followed dimmed those initial luminous hopes. Confined to Castle Garden and then expelled, as more immigrants arrived, Price with thousands of others crowded the streets and parks around Castle Garden. They had neither a means of livelihood nor a remote prospect of employment. Then, briefly, he and a number of fellow immigrants* were hired as longshoremen at $1.75 a day ("Just think $1.75—these are three and a half roubles—this is wealth!") until the regular longshoremen—on strike, demanding $2 a day—stoned them and "threatened to knock out our European soul." Finally, Price found himself on Wards Island, working with crowbar, shovel, and spade.

"The Father" and his assistants treated Price and the rest of the inmates of the Schiff Refuge with arrogant disdain, and the HEAS committee members, on their periodic visits, wouldn't even listen to complaints. According to a reporter from the New York *Times,* the food at the refuge was "wholesome, well-cooked and is supplied in liberal quantities." But the immigrants, who ate that food, found it consisted of soft half-baked bread; a mysterious muddy liquid, presumably coffee; watery soup "in which very often instead of grains of cereal there floated worms," and smelly meat. On holidays, a fruit dish was added, "which they called tzimes† of a somewhat suspicious quality."

To George Price—in whose future there would be a notable career of medical service and under whose leadership of

---

* One of them was nineteen-year-old Alexander Harkavy, who, in ten years, would begin compiling the first Yiddish-English dictionary, a work of distinction and genuine scholarship.

† A compote whose ingredients may be either mixed dried fruit or, more popularly, carrots and potatoes.

the Garment Center's Joint Board of Sanitary Control the roller towel and the common drinking cup would be abolished —the idea of wormy soup and dubious *tzimes* could "serve as an immediate cause of the inflammation of the passions."

On the morning of October 14 a mood of brooding uneasiness, of impending disaster, permeated the Schiff Refuge. More than 400 inmates ate their breakfast in extraordinary silence, with not even the usual derisive remarks about "the Committee's coffee," though, to be sure, they drank it and "with an indignant expression." And ostensibly, the inexplicable quiet affected the children, for they "did not shatter the air with the customary unbearable shrieking, crying and wailing."

Following breakfast, a delegation confronted Superintendent Blank with complaints about his assistant, Zadok, and received only incivilities in reply. At dinner that night when a waiter ladled out the *tzimes*, he deliberately bypassed Jacob Rabota, a young man with whom he had previously had trouble. Rabota protested. Summoned, Zadok began threatening Rabota, who grabbed a bowl of *tzimes* and threw it in Zadok's face.

A free-for-all broke out: Zadok and kitchen staff versus Rabota and his fellow immigrants. Superintendent Blank called the police; they arrived from the Harlem precinct a half hour later and arrested Rabota and those who'd championed his cause. According to George Price's irate observation, "When the policemen with raised clubs began to swing them right and to the left without regard for the children and women, the crowd retreated. Within a short time, however, stones came flying at the police." Men also used sticks as weapons against the police and kitchen staff, while women and children bit them—carrying out literally a frequent accusation of their benefactors that they bit the hand that fed them. "Shouts, wailing, cursing and moaning, children's crying, the whistling of police, the groans of the wounded—all blended into a horrible uproar."

When "the Father" sent for reinforcements, the infuriated immigrants stoned the buildings in which the staff lived, and enraged women searched for the superintendent himself. In George Price's opinion, "they would have torn him to pieces had he not fled through the window, jumped into the bay and swum to the opposite shore where he was rescued by the police." By the time a larger detachment of police arrived the Jewish barracks had become a bloody battlefield, and the fury of the immigrants had subsided sufficiently for them to ap-

point "a provisional government consisting of ten notable immigrants."

Although the HEAS committee admired the abstract poetic
concept of a "glorious Maccabean rage,"* to have that rage
actually directed at *them* was, understandably, aggravating.
Ironically, they failed to appreciate the possibility that these
immigrants—victims of lifelong oppression and whom they
themselves had criticized as having "a slave psychol-
ogy"—were by their spirit of protest already responding to
the climate of individual freedom in the United States. The
next day, when the committee came out to investigate, it listened to the immigrants' demand for unspoiled food and hu-
mane treatment. Though the committee dismissed "Father"
Blank and Zadok, it, nonetheless, felt the whole agitation had
simply arisen out of idleness. "Last Sunday," wrote an
angered reporter in the *American Israelite,* "our Russian
brethren, save the mark, varied the monotony of their existence—is it not monotonous to eat, drink and do nothing—by
a little riot." (If American Jews had had a familiarity with
Yiddish, they could have disposed of the riot in one disparag-
ing expression, *a gantsen tzimes*—a great fuss over nothing.)

Still, a public outcry arose over the mismanagement of the
refuge. Emma Lazarus, in a long letter to the *American Hebrew,* set out in crisp unromantic terms the defects of the
Wards Island administration and facilities: not enough soap
and water to keep the habitants clean, not enough work to
preserve their character, not any system of education for "the
swarms of children that infest the place [and who] literally
run wild in every stage of dirt and raggedness." She stated
bluntly that charity was not a pastime for dilettantes, "no
longer a moral luxury to be safely indulged in according to
the chance inspiration of the benevolent, it is recognized by
modern thinkers as a difficult science only to be properly applied by carefully trained minds and skilled hands."

Emma had, in fact, descended so far from her remote literary heights that she'd learned Yiddish to be better able, on
Sunday afternoons, to teach English to Russian Jewish girls
and to write a series of sixteen articles for the *American
Hebrew*—"Epistles to the Hebrews." In these articles, she

---

* The Maccabees, indeed, became all the rage. Some years later
New York Police Commissioner Theodore Roosevelt, while looking for
Jewish candidates for the police force, decided "it would be a particularly good thing for men of the Jewish race to develop that side of them
which I might call the Maccabee or fighting Jewish type."

urged a united Jewish effort to rescue East European Jews, and for those already in the United States she advised that a technical education be provided for their children. (Booker T. Washington had made the same recommendation for the redemption of Southern blacks.)

Emma's appeal for work for the Wards Island refugees had, as the *American Hebrew* playfully pointed out, "borne excellent fruit." A fruit-canning factory in Ravenswood "had offered employment to all the women and larger children in the settlement on Wards Island." Each morning a tugboat picked up all women and children able to peel and clean apples and transported them to Ravenswood, Queens, where they received five cents for each pail of apples they processed. In the evening a tugboat took them back to Wards Island. Thus idle hands were set to work, and presumably the character of the immigrants was strengthened accordingly. This was just as well, for they "learned that they were being exploited and paid less than half" by the benevolent gentlemen who employed them. "And although they were only new arrivals in the land of strikes and labor disputes," George Price pointed out, "they acquired very quickly this trait of American laborers and decided to demand the American wage for American work." Their demands were met. However, the committee was irritated by those they considered ignorant troublemakers, "a class of people," as one indignant correspondent of the *American Israelite* declared, "for whom the softest sentimentalist would find it difficult to entertain very much sympathy . . . a dirty discontented and ungrateful set."

Finally, the immigrants left the Schiff Refuge, struck out on their own—with the help of *landsleit* and relatives. Early in 1883 HEAS believed the crisis to be over and, with a collective sigh of relief, suspended operations entirely.*

In late November of that year William Evarts, chairman of the Pedestal Art Loan Exhibition, approached Emma Lazarus concerning an attempt to raise money for a pedestal on which to place the huge statue of "Liberty Enlightening the

* Literally an incalculable number of *Yahudim*-initiated-societies were organized specifically for the relief of Russian immigrants. For example, agencies called Hebrew Emigrant Aid Societies sprang up all over the United States—Albany, Boston, Louisville, Charleston, Cincinnati, Chicago, New Orleans, Milwaukee, St. Louis—and each of them, like the one in New York City, was ephemeral. As each new emergency arose—another huge influx of immigrants—the same *Yahudim* would once again meet, elect a committee, and form a new organization—probably bearing the name Hebrew Emigrant Aid Society.

World" that France wished to bestow upon the United States. He requested a manuscript from her which could be auctioned off, along with manuscripts by Mark Twain, Bret Harte, Walt Whitman, and Henry Wadsworth Longfellow. Emma's obsessive distaste for writing to order led her to refuse, but she continued to think about it—and inevitably associated the concept of a Statue of Liberty in New York Harbor with the immigrants on Wards Island. Two days later she sent Evarts "The New Colossus," a fourteen-line sonnet, which, on the first night of the auction, brought $1,500 toward the cost of the pedestal.

Four years after the *Tzimes* Revolt at Wards Island, after many of the immigrants involved had long since begun working in the garment trades and after George Moses Price was a city sanitation inspector and beginning his long steady climb to graduation from the New York Medical School and a noteworthy medical career, the Statue of Liberty was dedicated. But the words of "The New Colossus" weren't engraved on the pedestal until 1903, when Emma Lazarus already lay in Union Fields Cemetery, overlooking Jamaica Bay. "After a long and very painful illness . . ." the New York *Times* reported on November 19, 1887, "there died yesterday a young writer of New York." She died of cancer at the age of thirty-eight, with no idea that her compassion for those "tired," those "poor," "the huddled masses yearning to breathe free," all that "wretched refuse"* would serve to perpetuate her name and her work.

Publicity-shy, posthumous honor was not one of Emma Lazarus' objectives; a poet, she knew compassion must be pure compassion and not an alloy of sincere feeling and ulterior motive. Her fellow American Jews, however, sought to relieve their *tsitterdikness* by transforming the immigrants into the only acceptable image they knew—their own likeness. But what was to be molded wasn't malleable. One immigrant expressed a typical reaction:

When I first put my feet on the soil of Chicago, I was so disgusted that I wished I had stayed at home in Russia. I left the

---

* In the International Arrival Building at Kennedy Airport, a marble plaque with a raised torch and displaying four lines of "The New Colossus" greets all air passengers entering the United States. However, the line referring to "wretched refuse" was omitted, presumably because for present-day new arrivals, with their matched luggage and Polaroid cameras, the reference may seem inappropriate.

Old Country because you couldn't be a Jew over there and still live, but I would rather be dead than be the kind of German Jew that brings the Jewish name into disgrace by being a Goy. That's what hurts: They parade around as Jews, and down deep in their hearts they are worse than Goyim, they are *meshumads* [apostates].

PART III

FIRST YOU STAND,
THEN YOU SALUTE

The man who has been only three weeks in this country hates few things so much as to be called a greenhorn. . . . In the old country he never appeared in a short coat; that would be enough to stamp him as a free thinker. But when he comes to New York and his coat is worn out, he is unable to find any garment long enough. The best he can do is to buy a cutaway, or a Prince Albert, which he often calls a Prince Isaac. As soon as he imbibes the fear of being called a greenhorn, he assumes the Prince Isaac with less regret. Many of the old women, without diminution of piety, discard their wigs, which are strictly required by the Orthodox in Russia, and go even to the synagogue with nothing on their heads but their natural locks.

> —HUTCHINS HAPGOOD: *The Spirit of the Ghetto*

> Yankee Doodle went to town
> Ariding on a *ferdil*
> *Er ferht arein* in barber shop
> *Un shert zich op dos berdl.*
>
> (Yankee Doodle went to town
> Ariding on a pony
> He went into a barber shop
> And cut off his beard.)
> —*New York City street rhyme*

10

"How Can We Americanize Them?"

It was to be expected that young Rabbi David Philipson—a Hoosier from Terre Haute—who had been outraged by the Orthodox reaction to the trefa banquet in 1883 would in 1888 not only be anguished my *mikveh* building in Baltimore but would also be highly sensitive to "one of the great questions which we must solve in the near future . . . how can we Americanize them?"

Twenty-four years later, Mary Antin, one of "them," asked rhetorically in her best-selling book of 1912, *The Promised Land*, "How long would you say, dear reader, it takes to make an American?"

A derisive answer to this question was supplied by Keidansky, the "oracle of Division Street," a Jewish counterpart of Finley Peter Dunne's Mr. Dooley and the creation of journalist Bernard G. Richards. According to Keidansky, "the business of making Americans" was becoming "one of the largest industries of the lower East Side":

It will soon be as extensive as that of making sausages and wurst. And I understand that some of the same machinery will be employed. At the same end of the machine where the cow or ox will be thrown in, the newly arrived immigrant will now enter and out the other end they will emerge, not only a new-born American citizen, but an alderman-elect from the 8th District. . . . Various new suggestions are being made . . . that will ultimately turn an immigrant into a full-fledged American in three minutes and six seconds. There are those who say it will be possible to make an American of an immigrant before he even thinks of leaving his old home. . . .

But Americanization's most vociferous champions, the *Deitche Yahudim*, weren't laughing. To them the problem of Americanizing East European Jews overshadowed every other for almost a half century. Americanization was more than acculturation, more than adjustment to a new environment; it possessed ennobling—even spiritual—powers. It also had the capacity to effect a miracle cure for the disease of being alien, a disease with blatant symptoms: outlandish clothes, earlocks or *shaitels* (wigs), inelegant Orthodox Judaism or radical politics, and a hybrid language. Indeed, the revival meeting oratory which urged Americanization upon immigrants both elevated it to a holy creed and reduced it to a patent medicine panacea. The aim of Americanization, declaimed a speaker with artless candor at a B'nai B'rith meeting, was to transform "the poor down-trodden Russian, Roumanian, or Galician Jew into a free and patriotic well-to-do American citizen."

In the process of Americanization, the immigrant would shed every aspect of his background and ancestry, and thus become a nondescript tree upon which could be grafted those virtues *Yahudim* conceived as American: politeness, inconspicuousness, obedience, and the verbatim knowledge of "a few patriotic songs." However, to the Jewish immigrants—especially the older ones—being an American simply meant being able to live as they had in the *shtetl*, but without the brutal attentions of a hostile government. And by reverse implication, Americanization signified to them that their own culture was not only dangerous, but worthless. It can't have escaped some individuals that in the United States, "to Jew down" was a pejorative verb, while "to Americanize" was an act of improvement.

Irreconcilable as were the views of most native and immigrant Jews, many immigrants—especially the younger ones—wanted fervently to drop their alien customs. One of the most lyrical was Mary Antin. At thirteen, bearing the un-Americanized name Mashke, she had arrived in Boston from Polotsk, a *shtetl* in the Pale. One of the "green children" in Chelsea, she skyrocketed from first grade to sixth in a half year. Impressed, Barrett Wendell, professor of English at Harvard, proclaimed her "a miraculously precocious child" and gave her a reader's ticket to the Athenaeum and its 200,000 books.

Mary's father had preceded his family to America. On the eve of his wife's departure, he wrote her that "progressive Jews in America did not spend their days in praying; and he urged that she leave her wig in Polotzk, as a first step of progress." And in his daughter Mary, née Mashke, the Americanization concept of those "progressive" American Jews would reach its apotheosis.

From the time when the strains of a neighboring class singing "The Star-Spangled Banner" sent "delicious tremors" up and down her spine, rendering her "faint with suppressed enthusiasm," to her acclaim as a literary celebrity—three books, short stories, and cross-country lecture tours—Mary Antin played, as she was to recall, "homely but passionate variations on one master theme, the spiritual meaning of America. . . ."

American Jews found her ecstatic reaction to the United States gratifying, yet this running dive into the sea of American culture and the supposition that rhapsodic expression of patriotism placed her on a level with Christians who traced their ancestry to the Pilgrims were not as pleasing to those Christians as might be supposed. For one, Dr. Barrett Wendell, Mary's erstwhile patron, grew waspish, complaining of an "irritating habit" she had developed, "of describing herself and her people as Americans, in distinction from such folks as Edith and me who have been here for three hundred years."

Actually, at the beginning of the mass Jewish immigration, most American gentiles had a clinically detached attitude toward the Jewish immigrants from East Europe. In the eyes of those in the middle and upper class, the Russian Jews appeared so bizarre, so outside their experience, it was as if they had dropped from *The Golden Bough*. These staid Americans viewed them through a haze of guileless sociological and anthropological observations: "The two most important characteristics of the Russian Jews are their short stature and their contracted flat chests." America investigated the immigrant's folklore, tribal rites, and exotic foods. Magazines filled their pages with pitiful attempts to come to grips with such esoterica as *shmaltz*—"a rich thick grease"—and *gribenes*—"bits of crackling . . . when they are on the menu of a Kosher restaurant the fact is announced by a placard in the window, as planked shad or soft-shell crabs are advertised in other eating houses." The Russian habit of drinking tea through a lump of sugar—an Oriental osmosis—was remarked on and puzzled over. But only clairvoyance could have revealed the inordinate number of dentists that would be produced by those sugar-sucking tea drinkers. They even kissed differently, or so it appeared to a reporter attending a wedding: "The lips were pressed together again and again with a long deep and almost solemn emotion; such kisses as English-speaking people exchange only at moments of direct tragedy or the most passionate exaltation. These kisses are, I think, peculiar to Russian Jews."

The low rate of alcoholism among Jews was noted with appropriately awed commentary. (Sociologists somehow missed a segment of Jewish men who drank excessively—"pale-faced, hollow-chested, listless and brutified" New York bakers, dehydrated by the heat of the ovens. And in 1887 the bakeries on the Lower East Side in which they worked were described by Morris Hillquit, then a young union worker, as "deep and dark subcellars, without ventilation or any hygienic accommodations. The walls and ceiling were moist and moldy. The shops were infested with rats and reeked with dirt. The air was pestilential. The work was all done by hand." Consequently, the bakers spent whatever leisure time they had in a saloon on the corner of Ludlow and Hester streets, which "provided the only romance in their drab lives." The attempt of the United Hebrew Trades to unionize the bakers included establishing their headquarters in a saloon on Orchard Street; this caused a split in the ranks—those who supported the Ludlow Street saloon and those who supported the Orchard Street saloon. "To the Jewish bakery workers of that period," Hillquit wrote, "the class struggle assumed the form of a fight between two rival beer saloons." Eventually, unionization redeemed the bakers and protected the consumer from wretchedly unsanitary conditions.)

For several decades, magazines offered provocative articles on the Jewish psyche. In a six-year period, interrogating and declarative titles enticed readers: "Are the Jews a Pure Race?" "Are the Jews an Inferior Race?" "Will the Jews Ever Lose Their Racial Identity?" "Is There Room for the Jews?" "What It Means to Love a Jew." "What It Means to Be a Jew." "I Am a Jew." "Jews: Nation or People." "Jews Are Not Aliens." And, inevitably, "Why the Jew Is Too Neurotic."

Friendly observers ascribed not only keen intelligence and a law-abiding nature to the Russian Jewish immigrants, but often conferred even higher compliments: "The Hebrew cast of countenance was not as marked as we expected."

Conveniently, for those so disposed, the stereotype of the money-hungry Jew could account for everything from the East Side popularity of the thick solid novels of Charles Dickens—"The inherent Jewish trait of getting their money's worth"—to their purported preference for tenement living—"their in-born love of money-making leads them to crowd into the smallest quarters." An expert also maintained with learned gravity: "Most Hebrews commit their crimes for gain." And a school principal assured non-Jews that the progress of Jews "in studies is simply another manifestation of their acquisitiveness."

Examples of "inherent Jewish traits" and "in-born characteristics" proliferated, and alert sociological observers—eager to extend the boundaries of knowledge—pounced on them. Thus, the fact that "some chiefs of police will not tolerate a Jewish prostitute in their city because they find it impossible to subject her to regulations" revealed to the sociologist the stubborn contentiousness of Jews and, to those who probed even more deeply, a covetousness which led Jewish prostitutes to refuse to pay police graft.

Even statistics favorable to Jewish immigrants could be explained by "race traits." Their low crime rate, for example, might simply be due to an unresponsiveness to American environmental influences. "No Jew," *World's Work* reported in 1904, "has ever been tried for rape in the state of Ohio, which has a Jewish population of 150,000." But surely even this seemingly laudable record could merely reflect the notorious Jewish dislike of struggle, of good hard physical labor. Few writers felt themselves unequal to the task of recounting "the peculiarities of the race." The activities of "a strange Jewish sect," the Hassidim, aroused consternation in, of all people, the German novelist and perversion innovator Leopold von Sacher-Masoch.

Such caricatured generalizations spread alarm among American Jews, and the *tsitterdik* syndrome flared up like autumn leaves to a match. "Let me assure you," wrote Congressman Isidor Straus in 1895, by which time more than 800,000 East European Jews had entered the United States, "that in case nothing is done to eradicate the innate principles [one version said "natural inclinations"] of these people, they will, by their superior numbers, in time bring so much injury to our children that I shudder to think of it."*

By 1903 well over 1,000,000 immigrant Jews had settled in the United States, and Rabbi William Friedman of Denver declared at a New Orleans meeting of the Council of Jewish Women:

> We, who are the cultured and refined, constitute the minority . . . shall be judged by the majority, by the Russian Jews, by the children of the Ghetto. . . . What a powerful weapon your influence can become in a Jewish community, in lifting up and educating and civilizing the Russian Jews. . . . Their children will far outnumber your children and your children, though educated, cultured, refined, wealthy, will find themselves in the minority and judged by the Russian Jews.

Thus driven by concern for their status, the fate of their children, and in no small measure by the Judaic tradition of compassion,† American Jews organized committees, collected funds, and distributed pamphlets on etiquette. "A declination of a Jew to serve upon a committee," the *American Israelite* pointed out in a period before Freud, "is justly looked upon as a reproach upon his manhood." I. M. Rubinow, who had emigrated from Poland at eighteen and was to become the "father of Social Security," defined the situation from the immigrant's point of view:

> The wealthy Jew who suffers a great deal from social ostracism tries his best to erase his individuality and to compel the public to forget that he is a Jew. And when he imagines that he has succeeded, his Russian cousin shatters this idyll by the outward appearance of the latter. This prompts him to exclaim in despair, "Let us Americanize him as quickly as possible."

The frenetic urgency—and, of course, the Americanization

---

* Shortly after Straus' letter had gone the rounds on the East Side, the *Jewish Gazette* reported that a certain Samuel Hamburger was arrested for stealing jewelry from the brother-in-law of Nathan Straus. And Hamburger, it said, was the son of German parents, who had "no natural inclinations" to endanger Mr. Isidor Straus' children.

† Rabbi David Philipson observed in 1890, "Whatever may be said of the lack of culture, the ignorance, the superstition, the filth, the laziness of the Russian Jews, yet all this does not alter the pitiful aspect of the problem."

objective—generated bitter resentment among those whom the *Yahudim* aimed to uplift. How could American Jews have offered aid so that it wouldn't have been resented? Attempting to convey affability through humor—somewhat Teutonic in weight—had certainly not been successful. "As usually happens," reported the *Jewish Gazette* sardonically, on the annual ball of the Russian-American Hebrew Association, "when the German benefactors come to tell the Russians how much they sacrifice for them, so at this ball, the Russians present were insulted by their German friends. Lawyer Greenbaum, the German Jew who is active in many charities, honored the ball with his presence and, naturally, with his speech. At the beginning he said: 'Who would have believed that this is a gathering of Russian Jews? Why, everybody here looks human!' " (At a similar Russian-Jewish social gathering, a Russian non-Jew exclaimed in wonder, "And these are our Russian Jews? It is wonderful! What have become of their bent backs, of the fearful look in their faces! See how they walk in an upright manner.")

This situation produced lofty philanthropy and acrimonious acceptance. "Rich Jewish Aristocratic Women from uptown," reported the *Forward* scathingly, "will shower favors upon and seek remedies for downtown Jews." It was the *Forward*'s expressed opinion that these ladies of the National Council of Jewish Women tossed out pennies "with their bediamonded hands more to show their delicate alabaster fingers with well-manicured nails than really to save the unfortunates."

In Chicago, German Jewish debutantes held great charity balls for the benefit of the thousands of Russian Jews huddled together on the West Side, but no Russian Jew ever received an invitation. In New York's Mount Sinai Hospital (whose name was changed in 1866, from Jews Hospital in an ingenuous attempt to indicate its nonsectarian policy), most of the patients were East European Jews, but no doctor of East European origin could grace the staff. Many chapters of B'nai B'rith found "them" too vulgar and too uncivilized for membership; the Phoenix and the Eureka clubs—both of Rochester, New York—excluded them; and the Harmonie Club—the most elite German Jewish men's club in the United States—stated its position with oblique clarity: "more polish and less Polish."

Yet exclusion was defense, not solution. And the pressing need to shape up unwilling immigrants and make them presentable could not depend on charity drives, vehement lectures, didactic editorials, or even an inspirational poem by Minnie D. Louis,* which specified "What it is to be a Jew." (It was *not*, Mrs. Louis expressly pointed out, "To have an Oriental cast/in hair eyes and nose/To find a joy in wealth amassed . . .")

The transformation of the immigrant was work for a new breed of *shtadlonim*—American *shtadlonim*. And from 52 William Street and 20 Broad Street Jacob Schiff and Louis Marshall emerged, as philanthropic as Baron de Hirsch and less *tsitterdik* than Baron de Gunzburg.

* Mrs. Louis' labors on behalf of Russian Jews went beyond the mere poetic. After an episode in which, as she described it, "the offensive behavior of an ignorant Jewish family" had caused them to be expelled from Coney Island, Mrs. Louis hadn't spared herself in her campaign "for the improvement of this class." In 1884, she started the Louis Downtown Sabbath School which grew into the Hebrew Technical School for Girls. Presumably, a Jewish girl armed with a technical education was acceptable to Coney Island.

11

The Schiff Era and Marshall Law

Jacob Schiff and Louis Marshall! In the early years of the twentieth century, Schiff and Marshall went together in the thoughts of their East European co-religionists like lox and bagel. The two of them—first Schiff, then Schiff and Marshall, and, finally, Marshall alone—dominated native and immigrant Jews for just short of fifty years. It was a period in philanthropic time known as the Schiff era, during which, despite rebellion and indignation, Jews in America were brought under the authority of what was mockingly called Marshall Law.

Indeed, rebellion, indignation, and mockery directed at their benefactors flowered among the East European immigrants. "They take upon themselves the right to be our mentors, our guides, our critics and chastisers," Jacob Gordin wrote in the socialist paper *Die Zukunft*. "They want to control every branch of our life, our politics, our education, our press. How did they come to achieve such prerogatives? They are our representatives and patrons! How is this coming to them?"

How, indeed, did one become a *shtadlan* in the United States? One received the impression from the *shtadlonim* themselves that they arrived at their position through some elusive, ineffable grace.

"Of course," a reporter said to Louis Marshall, "you speak in the name of American Jewry. You are *the* Jewish leader. . . ."

"Not at all," Marshall denied quickly. "Not at all! You mustn't say that. No one is elected to that throne."

"Jews do not elect their leaders," remarked Jacob Schiff, who was sitting nearby, "one becomes a leader among them."

"And how does that come about?"

"One needs to have God in his heart," Schiff answered. "An ethical figure before whom the people stand in awe and to whom they will listen with deference even though they may not like what he has to say—such a person is naturally a leader. . . ."

Just over five feet, with a ramrod posture and the mien of a prophet, Jacob Schiff might very well have been describing himself. However, he neglected to mention one other essential in *shtadlonimdom,* which he also possessed: great wealth. Nowhere was it written that one have so vast a sum as $50,000,000, but such abundance did no harm. Coincidentally, the Schiff era began in 1881, the same year as the Jewish exodus from Russia. In that year, thirty-four-year-old Jacob Schiff, who had been an American citizen only for a little more than a decade, assumed virtual control of Kuhn, Loeb & Company, whose address, 52 William Street, became among American Jews "a euphemism like the White House and 10 Downing Street and the Quai d'Orsay . . . or even if you will, the Vatican." Following this elevation, a variety of committeeships, trusteeships, and, above all, contributorships to Jewish and non-Jewish causes descended on him as knighthood would on Ernest Cassel, his good friend in England. At first Schiff complied to requests for strictly Jewish causes with reluctance, if at all. When he was asked to contribute to a fund for a flag for Jewish veterans of the Spanish-American War, he refused, saying, "We are all Americans, especially those who have fought under the flag, and I am not in favor of dividing ourselves into classes."

To Jacob Schiff, being a Jew was not only a private matter, but purely a matter of religion. He regarded the distinctions of separate cultures as irrelevant. And he found East European *Yiddishkayt* not only alien, but distasteful. He was not, he said, a "race" Jew, but a "faith" Jew, and he expressed his faith in an Orthodox kind of Reform and a Reform kind of Orthodoxy. He observed the Sabbath and the dietary laws, but he belonged to that citadel of Reform, Temple Emanu-El.

Shabbas licht were blessed at the Schiff Fifth Avenue home, but the master of the house also talked business after Friday-night dinner.

Yet for all his assertions that philanthropy should be secular, he could not cling to that principle in the face of the Russian Jewish immigrants' needs. He was simply unable to overcome his feeling of responsibility for them. So he and members of the other great *Yahudim* families—Lehman, Seligman, Straus, Sulzberger—who sometimes seemed to have been born not only with a silver spoon in their mouths, but with a gavel and the minutes of the last meeting in their hands—headed committees that poured thousands of dollars into strictly Jewish causes: settlement houses, YMHA, immigrant refuges, yeshivas, Talmud Torahs, Free Loan Society. . . . And the Schiff name at the head of a donors' list had a magic effect.

(When money was needed, everyone flocked to Schiff. An immigrant mother appeared at the Henry Street Settlement on a day Schiff was visiting and requested an audience with the financier. When asked why she wanted to see him, she said, "I'd like him to buy my daughter a piano." "Is she talented?" "How would I know?" the mother shot back indignantly. "She doesn't have a piano.")

Jacob Schiff appeared so remote and austere, "nobody except his family or his senior business associates ever called him by his first name." But in between their bouts of hostility toward him, Russian Jews regarded Schiff with warmth, because of the personal interest he had often shown in them. (Once in order to help Julius Butensky, an immigrant sculptor, Schiff went down to Butensky's East Fourteenth Street tenement, only to find that the sculptor had been evicted. After a week of searching, Schiff finally found Butensky and commissioned him to do a statue—Isaiah beating his sword into a plow—which eventually was exhibited at the Metropolitan Museum.) They detected under Schiff's dispassion a sympathy to which they responded with affection. When he attended a Zionist meeting—although he did not approve of the movement—Zvi Masliansky, the Yiddish orator, turned to him and exclaimed affectionately, *"Yankele, Yankele, du bist doch unser Yankele."* ("Jakie, Jakie, you are after all, our Jakie.")

Louis Marshall, equally respected and admired, was admittedly not equally endearing to the immigrants; none, for example, called him "our Louie." To American Jews, Schiff represented the power of wealth, while Louis Marshall gave that power trenchant articulation. "He was chosen by God Almighty to lead the children of Israel." Autocratic, dictatorial, Marshall "liked to lay down the law." And no individual could do that more competently than he. As a constitutional and corporation lawyer Marshall was one of the most successful—despite his somewhat pompous attitude in court which made it appear "the judges were definitely there to learn," to garner "wisdom and experience." (Once when arguing a case before the Supreme Court, Marshall continued beyond his allotted time. Chief Justice Edward White leaned over, and said apologetically, "Mr. Marshall, one of the most unpleasant duties presented to the head of this Court is that he sometimes is obliged to shut off the light.") Marshall's air of sowing edification also prevailed in the committee rooms of all the Jewish organizations he led. And toward those expounding anti-Semitic doctrine, he presented an unflinching posture—not in the least *tsitterdik*—a refreshing change in American Jewish history.

A native of Syracuse, New York, Marshall's parents had emigrated from Germany: his father in 1849, his mother five years later. He waggishly claimed that his father, whose name was spelled "Marschall," had been seasick for the entire fifty days of the voyage and, therefore, upon arriving in the United States, had dropped the "c" from his name. With the encouragement of Judge Mayer Sulzberger and Sulzberger's friend Randolph Guggenheimer, thirty-eight-year-old Louis Marshall left his well-established law practice in upstate New York for Manhattan and a partnership in the prominent law firm of Guggenheimer & Untermeyer, which became Guggenheimer, Untermeyer & Marshall.

"Now, Louis," Judge Sulzberger, an ingrained bachelor, cautioned him, "if you stick to your work and don't marry one of those damned society women in New York, you'll have a great career ahead of you." Barely a year later, Marshall married Florence Lowenstein, of a socially prominent New York family. They settled down at 47 East Seventy-second Street, just a few blocks from the 932 Fifth Avenue home of Jacob Schiff.

But family life and law did not delimit Marshall's interests. He wrote poetry—none of which was published. He had a profound concern for conservation and worked tirelessly for the preservation of the Adirondacks, and he collected American and French landscape paintings. But his primary activity, outside his legal practice, centered on "defending the rights of Jews wherever these rights were assailed."

Before Marshall's stocky, rotund frame appeared on the scene, hostile references to Jews merely stirred up a cautious apologetic protest, accompanied by painstakingly documented proof that Jews had a right to exist. But Marshall's approach —often sardonic brilliance—placed anti-Semites on the defensive. When an official of the Union League Club in New York City, which excluded Jews, asked Marshall to lend the club a number of paintings for exhibition (evidently one need not be Jewish to have *chutzpah*), Marshall replied with ill-concealed enjoyment:

> Under ordinary circumstances I would be greatly pleased to do so; but I can scarcely reconcile myself to the incongruity of finding my property welcome where I would be excluded. Your invitation, while a great tribute to the universality of Art, does not, however, modify the regret with which I regard the manifestation of the narrowness and intolerance of man, as disclosed by the records of your organization.

Since the old Jewish policy of circumspection had come to be expected by the public, even non-Jews, presumably not anti-Semitic, resented the Marshall way of confronting racism. An episode, "this Dewey matter," which occurred in 1905, exemplified this reaction. It involved Melvil Dewey (really Melville, but he championed simplified spelling) who was the librarian of the State of New York and organizer of a residential resort, the Lake Placid Club, which presented in a brochure such prestigious features as barring anyone as a member or guest "against whom there is physical, moral or race objection or who would be unwelcome to even a small minority. This excludes absolutely all consumptives or rather invalids, whose presence might injure health or modify others' freedom or enjoyment. This invariable rule is rigidly enforced; it is found that it is impracticable to make exception to Jews or others excluded, even when of unusual personal qualifications." The brochure also pointedly mentioned that "Mr. Melvil Dewey, the president of our company, is Librarian of the State of New York."

Indeed, Mr. Dewey had many exemplary achievements to his credit. "A tall, loosely jointed man, built along generous lines," though apparently not always acting on them, Dewey vigorously supported woman's suffrage. He founded the

American Library Association, the *Library Journal,* and the first training school for librarians, and he evolved the Dewey system of decimal classification of books, used in most libraries (through Dewey's ingenuity anti-Semitism became 301.451 924).

At the end of 1904, Louis Marshall and a number of other eminent *Yahudim* of New York sent a petition to the Regents of the University of the State of New York objecting to Mr. Dewey's Lake Placid Club brochure. A month or so later while the Board of Regents were still considering the matter, the Reverend I. K. Funk—whose family's firm, Funk and Wagnalls, had just published the ten-volume *Jewish Encyclopedia*—wrote Marshall that he disapproved of the petition. Feeling that Marshall's protest stirred up anti-Semitism, he presented his proof. During the previous week, at a dinner attended by seventy-five New York clergymen, the Reverend Mr. Funk asserted that "this Dewey matter was talked over and much feeling was expressed. Old stories against Jews were resurrected, and I heard more talk of this kind, at that meeting, than I heard in the previous ten years of clergymen's meetings which I have attended."

After remarking that "the old stories" the Reverend Mr. Funk mentioned couldn't have been the stories of Hebrew prophets, poets, moralists and philosophers in the *Jewish Encyclopedia*, "of which you are justly proud," Marshall wrote more incisively:

> You may tell your theological friends that while we are shocked at your disclosure, we are not dismayed; that while we grieve at such a manifestation of what is sometimes termed an unChristian spirit, it is not a new experience with us. . . . You ask us to be magnanimous and once more to assume our wonted attitudes. From Mr. Dewey there has been no word of regret for the wrong that has been done; no apology, no recantation, nothing but patronizing and nauseating slobber. We must kiss the hand that strikes the blow; we must exercise self-restraint; while your clerical friends stand by and raise not one word of protest, of indignation, or of admonition, but on the contrary, voice the gospel of hate, of intolerence, and of bigotry. No; the petition will not be withdrawn. If there has ever been any doubt as to the course to be pursued, your letter has solved it effectually.

The Board of Regents censured Dewey; shortly after, he resigned as state librarian. And, as it turned out, Dewey and his Lake Placid Club merely served as a preparatory skirmish for the long battle, sixteen years later, that Marshall waged successfully against Henry Ford and his Dearborn *Independent*.

"Short and round," James Marshall said in describing his father, "he virtually rolled when he laughed." But laughter did not characterize this quick-tempered man. "His capacity for invective was astounding but there were limits to this, too, and in situations in which most men might reflect on the maternal ancestry of the offender, or when ladies or children were present, he would splutter, 'He's a, he's a—' So in the family, quite a number of persons became known as 'Heezas.'" Marshall's political philosophy embraced a resolute conservative Republicanism, and, as head of Temple Emanu-El, he ran a taut temple. Consequently, two prominent "heezas" were men who refused to abide by the conventions of each of those institutions: Theodore Roosevelt and Stephen S. Wise.

Though staunchly conservative, Marshall and Schiff in 1911 clashed with President William Howard Taft, another Republican conservative and one for whom they had a high regard.

12

A Recipe for Buttering Parsnips

The conflict between Schiff, Marshall, and the Taft administration—the first important episode in which American *shtadlonim* showed their muscle—arose over the Russo-American
Treaty of 1832, a trade compact with the government of Nicholas I, which had been negotiated by James Buchanan, then
American minister to Russia. During the next half century,
leisurely restrained exchanges took place between the Russian
imperial government and the U.S. State Department over one
of its clauses. According to Russian interpretation, the clause
stating that foreigners visiting Russia were free to enjoy "the
same security and protection as natives of the country" meant
that when American Jews visited Russia, they were to be
treated like Russian Jews. The United States, on the other
hand, maintained that all American citizens should be treated
equally. However, during those fifty years, no position was
changed, no policies were moderated; Russia continued her
arbitrary treatment of visiting American Jews.

In the early 1800's an American Jewish circus performer
traveling through Russia with a troupe was threatened with
expulsion because of his religion. However, he was permitted
to remain when he artfully explained that he "was not one of
those Talmud Jews," but that he belonged to a sect—Reform
Judaism—whose tenets only "closely approached those of Ju-

daism." (In the immortal words of Jonathan Miller, he wasn't a Jew exactly, just "Jew-ish.") A decade later Russian diplomats invited Oscar Straus, American minister to Turkey, to stop off in Russia on his way home and offered him a permit by which "The Jew, Oscar Straus, is permitted to enter Russia for three months." Mr. Straus chose to come home through the Balkans.

The case of John Ginzberg illustrated the workings of the treaty for a Jew with less agility or status. In the early 1890's Glasgow, Montana, on the Milk River in Valley County, had a courthouse, a bank, a building two and a half stories high, a reputation as a rowdy cow town, and one Jew—John Ginzberg, formerly of Loguiston, Russia. (Several other Montana towns had sizable Jewish populations. Helena possessed a Hebrew Benevolent Association and a Reform temple. But the closest co-religionist Ginzberg had in the state was Jew Jake, a Landusky saloonkeeper, who had a leg shot off by a sheriff and used a Winchester rifle as a crutch.)

In Glasgow, Ginzberg led a blameless life. As he himself wrote, "I tried to set a good example in Glasgow. . . . I was very faithful to my employer . . . and once swam the Milk River to save his horse Billy."

Also an exemplar of a good Jewish son, twenty-nine-year-old Ginzberg left Glasgow in 1894 to visit his parents in Russia. After he had been gone about six months, Robert M. Lewis—who with his brother, John M. Lewis, were Lewis Brothers, Glasgow shippers—received a letter from Ginzberg, a former employee. Addressed to "my High educated Friend," Ginzberg wrote with the anguished apostrophe of Jeremiah:

. . . Weep and cry all ye inhabitants of Glasgow, Montana, for your friend John Ginzberg. Indeed, trouble, trouble, and gnashing of teeth are upon me, and understand my cause in Valley County . . . I fell into the hands of the Russian rulers last fall and I am still under arrest; all because I became a citizen of the United States. With an American passport I have tried to go back to my old homeland to visit my parents and see my friends. I crossed Germany peacefully but was arrested when I crossed into Russia near Prostken. I have not only been arrested unlawfully but they have also taken my clothes away from me, even my shirt and have sold them. They carried me to many jails but finally they took me to Pinsk, Russia, where they have taken my American papers away from me. I don't know what they intend to do with me but I did hear it said that my case had been taken directly to St. Petersburg. . . .

The charge against Ginzberg that he had "escaped military service in 1886," merely moved the American minister in St. Petersburg to make a casual diplomatic plea for leniency. But Robert Lewis ("I tell you the truth," Ginzberg wrote him, "when I say I have not another friend in the world like you") dispatched letters to Clifton R. Breckinridge, the American minister in Russia, to Governor J. E. Richards of Montana, and to the State Department in Washington. Governor Richards, in turn, also sent off a letter to the State Department, urging action in Ginzberg's case and including an affidavit that proved Ginzberg's American citizenship.

This intercession by prominent citizens accelerated the State Department's actions to a pace that might be mistaken for genuine concern. But Breckinridge pointed out in a letter to Ginzberg: "This legation will continue to do all it can for you; but the laws of Russia and the laws of the United States are exactly opposite to each other upon the subject of your arrest; and we must depend upon the circumstances of the case . . ."

Hardly comforting words to a man sitting in a Russian prison without any clothes. The circumstances to which Breckinridge alluded were these: Though the charge of evading military service was patently absurd—since Ginzberg had left Russia when he was fourteen years old, four years before he would be subject to military service—nonetheless, the Russians held him accountable. The desertion charge stemmed from his having become an American citizen, for Russia did not recognize the right of its subjects to become citizens of another country. So while American citizenship expressly demanded that former Russian subjects renounce their allegiance to the czar of Russia, the State Department appeared uncertain about the means to protect them once they had done so.

During the next two years, Russia and the United States occupied themselves with diplomatic exchanges over the case. And Ginzberg's spirits, as revealed in his correspondence with Robert Lewis, sank lower and lower. "My heart melts like wax before the fire every day, every hour and every moment because of my distress. . . . With eyes full of tears and the gnashing of teeth, I have been as forgetful as a dead man." And in his letters to Lewis, he continually summoned up nos-

talgic memories of Glasgow and its inhabitants. "Tell your
brother Mr. John M. Lewis and all the boys in the store about
me. I am only waiting and living from day to day like Jay
Bush did in Glasgow. . . ."

Indeed, had it not been for Ginzberg's friends back home,
it's highly unlikely that he would ever have been able to return "to the United States of America, my only and lovely
home." After a trial in which he was "convicted of the crime
of changing his nationality without the consent of the Imperial government" and sentenced to deprivation of civil rights
and banishment from the empire, he lacked the money to
leave Russia. The edict from St. Petersburg stated that unless
his friends furnished funds "to pay for his passage through
the Empire and through Germany . . . he will be sent to Siberia."

Immediately upon receiving this information, Robert Lewis
collected $50—95 rubles—from nineteen Glasgow citizens and
sent it to Breckenridge at the American ministry in St. Petersburg. And by the spring of 1897 John Ginzberg was on
his way back to Glasgow.

Ten years later, in 1907, the State Department sent out an
official circular:

> Jews, whether they were formerly Russian subjects or not,
> are not admitted to Russia unless they obtain special permis-
> sion in advance from the Russian Government, and this Depart-
> ment will not issue passports to former Russian subjects or to
> Jews who intend going to Russian territory, unless it has the
> assurance that the Russian Government will consent to their
> admission. . . .

This calm statement, virtually a sanction of Russia's dis-
criminatory practices, had an explosive effect on Schiff and
Marshall. A year earlier they and other prominent New York
Jews had founded the American Jewish Committee, whose
avowed purpose was to protect the rights of Jews anywhere in
the world. Marshall, as spokesman for the AJC, shot off a letter of protest to Secretary of State Elihu Root, who then privately informed Marshall that the circular had been recalled
and implied it would be nice to forget the whole episode. In
Root's acerbic view, the whole matter was ridiculous. Why in
the world would Jews want to go to Russia anyway? But as
Root undoubtedly knew, that wasn't the point. Very few
American Jews *did* want to go to Russia; those who did went

to visit parents or other relatives. However, by refusing to honor the passports of American Jews and having this policy accepted by the United States, Russia made American Jews second-class citizens of their own country.

On January 19, 1911, Louis Marshall began a campaign to have the United States abrogate the entire treaty. Speaking before the Council of American Hebrew Congregations on "Russia and the American Passport," he declared that an American Jew could "suffer in silence as his ancestors did for centuries. But he is more than a Jew—he is also an American citizen, and the hand that smites him inflicts a strain on his citizenship. It is not the Jew who is insulted; it is the American people. And the finding of a proper remedy against this degradation is not a Jewish, but an American question." Nevertheless, this was not a view shared by Philander Knox, Taft's Secretary of State, and his department. A blind spot existed in the minds of many Americans in government in regard to Jews: Matters affecting the rights of Jewish citizens, they thought, were a purely Jewish matter. Abrogation of the Treaty of 1832, therefore, appeared to Knox to satisfy only "the interests of the Jewish population of the United States." Consequently, many in the Taft administration believed that by supporting abrogation it would be surrendering to the political pressure of a vocal minority.

To the *shtadlonim*—those proponents of Americanization —it was vital that American Jews—native and naturalized—be recognized as part of the whole. That, after all, equaled Americanization.

A month after Marshall's speech the President invited the leaders of AJC and several other organizations to the White House for lunch. Included among those invited were Louis Marshall, Jacob Schiff, Judge Mayer Sulzberger, and Simon Wolf, a tireless communal leader, a former president of the B'nai B'rith and a former consul general in Egypt, who had, during his residence there, formed a B'nai B'rith chapter in Cairo. An estimable gentleman in many ways, Mr. Wolf had a weakness for trying to please those in power; consequently, he was not Marshall and Schiff's kind of *shtadlan*. And so several days before the White House lunch, Marshall wrote Schiff:

. . . The great danger will be that some of these gentlemen will feel so flattered by the invitation that they will readily concede that everything has been done that can be done . . . it would be just exactly in line with Mr. Wolf's ordinary policy to say "Amen" to anything that the governmental authorities may suggest. . . . The time is past when sweet words will butter our parsnips. . . .

At the meeting President Taft gave his guests no opportunity to present their views; instead, he revealed his conclusions, which were disheartening. Although the treaty ran counter to "our constitutional principle of equality for every one . . . and no distinction as to religion," the treaty was an old one, and the United States had permitted the offensive provisions to continue for many years. It would be awkward suddenly to abrogate the treaty. Moreover, American commercial interests—International Harvester, Singer Sewing Machine, and Westinghouse—had investments in Russia, amounting to $60,000,000, that would be endangered by abrogation. Even if those investments were to be sacrificed, Taft was convinced it would be an unwise gesture, for Russian Jews would be made to suffer renewed pogroms.

Jacob Schiff exploded. ("When Mr. Schiff grew indignant," a friend commented, "he had a way of expressing himself clearly and forcefully.") After stating categorically, "Mr. President, you have failed us, and there is nothing left to us now, but to put our case before the American people directly . . ." he stamped out. (Simon Wolf reported seeing the President the next day, and, "in the most good humored way," Mr. Taft said, "Wasn't Mr. Schiff angry yesterday?")

Throughout 1911 public opinion was mobilized—or perhaps "marshalled" might be a more apt word. Thirty-two thousand copies of Marshall's speech, "Russia and the American Passport," went to opinion-makers in Congress, newspapers and magazines, and clergymen and judges. The issue was debated on the forum and in print. Though Marshall never made his appeals for abrogation on a partisan basis ("Taft is a very obstinate man and will be more apt to become actively hostile, if he feels we are attacking him . . ."), Congressional Democrats seized on the issue—autocratic Russia's insult to American citizens—to use it against the administration. Jewish and non-Jewish Americans flooded members of Congress with petitions for abrogation. In one day, Senator Henry Cabot Lodge received seventy from Massachusetts groups.

Finally, on December 17, 1911, two days short of a year after Marshall's opening blast for abrogation, President Taft announced the abrogation of the Treaty of 1832.

The successful abrogation battle was a superb object lesson in Americanization for Russian Jews—displaying the means open to individuals in a democracy in achieving desired ends. But Russian Jews, so quick to resent authority, so sensitive to any suggestion of condescension, found it impossible to be a passive admiring audience. Forthright and fearless, Louis Marshall appeared to believe that only leaders should have these qualities; the immigrants were to be quiet, well behaved, and content to be led by the *shtadlonim*, who would handle everything. Although realistic, Marshall never failed to be shocked and astonished when they responded differently.

13

Centers of Sweetness and Light

Schiff and Marshall found it easier to deal with President Taft, with whom they had much in common, than with their constituency, the East European Jews. After all, the three men were orthodox Republicans, and two, Marshall and Taft, worshiped law. Conversely, the *shtadlonim* observed that immigrant Orthodox Jews viewed the Republican Party, if they noticed it at all, as at best an ephemeral institution and regarded man-made national law as clearly inferior to the Divine Word.

But Tammany Hall dominated Democratic politics in New York and appealed to all immigrants, for it courted them with concern and small favors. And since Marshall regarded Tammany as a sink of corruption, the immigrant Jews flocking to the Tammany Tiger's benign embrace filled him with horror.

Even worse, the younger generation of immigrants, religious in a semiradical way, were socialists, and those devoutly irreligious became anarchists. Obviously neither group was an auspicious candidate for the Grand Old Party. And the alarming activities in union organization of both factions caused great agitation uptown.

From the beginning, Americanization efforts floundered. So many areas of danger and avenues of error beckoned to immigrants that no one knew quite where to attack. Should they aim to redeem adults or salvage children? Men, who had to go out and earn a living, became more worldly, more secular—Americanized faster—than women, who stayed home and clung to religious tradition. This was a curious reversal. Often, in the *shtetl*, the woman went to the marketplace and worked while her husband stayed home and studied the Talmud. And it wasn't only American Jewish leaders who felt concern; the Daughters of the American Revolution, or *Techter fun der Amerikanishe Revolution,* as their name appeared in the Yiddish guidebooks they sponsored for immigrants, fired a broadside of advice for the whole immigrant family. Their suggestions ranged from proclaiming *Amerika uber Alles* to urging the Brotherhood of the Workingman. ("Give up all prejudices and remember that all workmen are brothers, it matters not in what nation of the world they were born.") They counseled caution in a variety of situations:

A person, who having a husband or a wife living, marries another person, is guilty of the crime of bigamy. Maximum penalty five years in prison. THE FACT THAT THE FIRST WIFE LIVES IN EUROPE AND HAS NEVER BEEN TO THIS COUNTRY MAKES NO DIFFERENCE.

Avoid strong drink. Strong drink makes weak men.

Do not buy bread and cake at dirty bakeries. Are your grocery and butcher cleanly in person? Are their clerks cleanly?

GIRLS AND YOUNG WOMEN SHOULD BEWARE of strange men who offer them well-paid positions or who propose marriage to them. They should know the character and position of men who insist upon having money as a condition of marriage. Such men are often swindlers, take the money and disappear.

The Jew like any other foreigner is appreciated when he lives the American social life. Until then he counts for nothing. Join American clubs, read American papers. Try to adapt yourself to the manners and customs and habits of the American people. Have your name placed on the roll of the league or union of your trade. . . . Become an American citizen as soon as you can. It is an excellent thing for a Jew to join a military company, a regiment of the National Guard. . . . Membership gives social advantage, and the opportunity of healthful exercise in athletic games and drills is very important to a man who lives in a great city.

MOTHERS! The home should be made a happy place to

which the young people will bring their friends. Encourage your daughter to introduce to you all her men friends. Win her confidence by sympathy with her desire for proper amusement and pretty clothes. Do not prevent her attending dances held in respectable halls, but insist upon her returning home early. Be sure you know the conditions of your daughters' employment. Do not take your children to Court for commitment to an institution.

One of the DAR's Yiddish guidebooks struck an inventive note in the Americanizing process. It presented patriotism as a religion. Under a picture of the Capitol Building, for example, the caption identified the edifice as "the *Kedisha Kedoshum*—the Holy of Holies—*fun der Americana nation.*"

Indeed, the existence of such a large body of non-Christians on their very doorstep proved a challenge Protestant church leaders could not resist. They responded by directing a missionary campaign toward the young who were tempted toward atheism and socialism and the malleable very young still in school. A circular of the Emanu-El Brotherhood heatedly condemned "the mendacious activity of numerous missionaries who employ various seductive methods to evangelize Jewish children." Oblivious to such criticism, missions sprang up in old stores on the East Side—Houston Street was one location, in particular, "where anti-Jewish designs are most marked." Many bore somewhat deceptive names—the American Hebrew Athletic Club—and flaunted the presence of a newly created Christian who invariably bore a clearly unChristian name, like Isidore Cohen. So deceptive were many of these missions that an old Hebrew teacher, Adolph Benjamin, assumed the duty of unmasking sewing schools and recreational clubs as conversion agencies. And so zealous was Mr. Benjamin in his pursuit of apostates and missionaries that he impoverished himself for the cause, haunted Jewish newspaper offices to point out yet another camouflaged conversion mill in language that "could not always find favor." To the chagrin of American Jews, many East European Jewish parents could not distinguish between some missions and Americanization agencies organized by *Yahudim*. Thus, on occasion, it actually happened that Jewish children attended *chedar* on Friday afternoon, shul on Saturday morning, and Christian Sunday school on Sunday morning.

In 1893, the Hebrew-Christian Mission of the Allen Presbyterian Church had been in operation for one year. (The clergyman in charge of the missionary work was a former rabbi from Poughkeepsie, a convert to Christianity with the provocative name, Reverend Herman Paul Faust.) The mission's workers visited 1,225 Jewish families, distributed 10,065 tracts and pamphlets, and made 51 conversions. In the same year the Reverend Dr. Schauffler of the Presbyterian City Missionary Society suggested that "the truths of Christianity might and should be presented" to the Jews of New York City "in such special manner as was necessary in the case of a peculiar people." On December 13, 1896, the Reverend Dr. John Hall of the Fifth Avenue Presbyterian Church baptized fifteen Jews: eight men, three women, two boys, one little girl, and one infant. Occasionally wealthy Christian spinsters even diverted their financial support from efforts to clothe South Sea Islanders. "Miss Sarah Burr, a wealthy and pious lady of New York City, recently deceased," reported the Philadelphia *Dispatch,* "bequeathed ten thousand dollars toward the work of converting Jews." Miss Mabel B. Atwater of New York devoted her entire time to the work of Christianizing Jewish women and girls. "I am not so much concerned about whether my little girls are Christians or Jews," she said. "All I want them to be is good little girls and I try to help them by teaching them the Church is their friend. If I do that they will be Christians when their judgment shall be matured." Understandably, ladies like Miss Atwater and missionaries like the Reverend Drs. Hall and Schauffler drove old Mr. Benjamin into a perfect frenzy in which he shot off letters to the editors of every newspaper within range.

Often even when no intention to convert, overt or otherwise, existed, that impression remained. For example, when Henry Booth House, a settlement house in Chicago's "Russian Jew quarter," opened a kindergarten for Jewish children, in the center of the room there was a painting of the Sistine Madonna. "I little realized," one of the workers remarked ingenuously, "that a feeling had been aroused over the Madonna."

The threat of conversion may have loomed ominously, but apart from a few religious transients, its menace faded after a brief period. One Christian minister concluded glumly that Christianity was being Judaized rather than the reverse, because of modern Protestant theology's endeavors "to deprive Christ of his divine character and dignity and to make him merely a brilliant Jew." Perhaps Christianity's lack of success with Jews might be ascribed, as it was by the renowned sociologist Edward Alsworth Ross, to a reprehensible racial trait. "In their religious ideas," he noted, "our Jewish immigrants are so stubborn that the Protestant churches despair of making proselytes among them."

Nevertheless, the threat remained. "Until the Jews of New York realize their religious responsibility toward their brethren on the East Side," Grace Dodge, YWCA president, declared sternly to Rebecca Kohut, her Jewish co-worker among the immigrants, "and as long as any unchurched man or woman of any faith knocks at our doors, we shall greet them lovingly in the name of Christ."

So American Jews took steps to stabilize the East European Jewish immigrants in a religious posture neither Orthodox nor Christian and to predispose them toward the Republican rather than Socialist Party by establishing a temple of Americanization, "a center of sweetness and light, an oasis in the desert of degradation and despair," the Educational Alliance.

The concept of the settlement house to alleviate conditions in city slums originated in England in 1884. Toynbee House, started by an Anglican clergyman, Samuel A. Barnett, was staffed for the most part by resident workers who were students from Oxford and Cambridge, searching with the desperation of youth for a purpose in life. Among the many similar institutions and associations that followed was a semimilitary group of Jewish boys from London's slums. The British army officer, Colonel Albert Edward Williamson Goldsmid, who organized it, sprang from an eminent Anglo-Jewish family—and was supposedly the model for the hero of George Eliot's novel *Daniel Deronda*.* The name of Colonel Goldsmid's group, while weak on *Yiddishkayt,* was beguilingly British: The Jewish Lads Brigade.

Almost immediately, American social reformers set about establishing settlement houses: University Settlement House and Henry Street Settlement in New York City, Maxwell Street Settlement in Chicago, and Touro Hall in Philadelphia. By 1897 seventy-four settlement houses existed in the United States.

---

* Colonel Goldsmid, a very romantic figure, hadn't been brought up as a Jew, and it wasn't until he was twenty-four that he formally entered the Jewish community—in Poona, India, where he was posted. He became a devoted Zionist. His daughter, Carmel, was exceedingly religious. When she visited Bialystok in 1906, to investigate the pogroms, she refused to eat in a home until she received absolute assurance that it was kosher.

Of all of them, the Hebrew Institute—known among its sponsors as "the Palace of Immigrants" and under its new name, Educational Alliance—became the most famous and far-reaching for the East European Jews. From the minute immigrant children came under its supervision, the alliance maintained "that a decided improvement was noted in their demeanor, cleanliness and general appearance." Was some miraculous metamorphosis expected when Eddie Cantor, a small scrawny thirteen-year-old, appeared on the alliance stage in a blond wig as Little Lord Fauntleroy? If so, it wasn't completely far-fetched. After all, another poor Jewish boy, Jacob Epstein, from a Polish *shtetl*, received his first art lessons at the alliance—at 3 cents a week—and eventually became Sir Jacob Epstein. Yet another, Lewis Sterling, born to impoverished immigrant Jewish parents on Orchard Street, who attended classes at the alliance when it was still the Hebrew Institute, went to England, became head of the vast Educational and Musical Industries combine *and* Sir Lewis Sterling.* And barely a dozen years after young David Sarnoff, formerly of Uzlian, in Minsk gubernia, learned English at Educational Alliance classes, he wrote a memo to his employers, the Marconi Company, suggesting:

> I have in mind a plan of development which would make radio a "household utility" in the same sense as the piano or phonograph. The idea is to bring music into the home by wireless.
>
> While this has been tried in the past by wires, it has been a failure because wires do not lend themselves to this scheme. With radio, however, it would be entirely feasible. . . .

Yet the air of condescension that all too often accompanied the Educational Alliance's declared purpose—"of an Americanizing, educational, social and humanizing character—for the moral and intellectual improvement of the inhabitants of the East Side"—provoked a sour reception from the beneficiaries. (The administration of many settlement houses suffered from this same chronic patronizing attitude. In its early years, the Maxwell Street Settlement House in Chicago, for

---

* A generously philanthropic man, Sir Lewis gave away more than 1,000,000 pounds ($2,800,000) before he died in 1958. During World War II, he established a refuge for bombed-out East End mothers and children on a Surrey estate, with the slogan "East Siders for East Enders."

example, was far more popular with the aspiring Lady Boun-
tifuls among Chicago's Jewish debutantes than it was with the
immigrants. If an immigrant used all its facilities but ignored
English classes or preparations for naturalization, he "was
looked upon as a pauper, begging for alms and was treated as
such." A more congenial atmosphere prevailed next door at
Leo Porges' drugstore, where a group of Russian Jewish immigrants would meet every night behind the prescription
counter for the kind of discussion and debate frowned on at
the settlement house.)

It had been to shed sectarian implication that the name Hebrew Institute became Educational Alliance. "At first blush
our work may seem sectarian," Alliance President Isidor
Straus explained carefully, "it is nothing of that sort. It is educational, humanitarian, philanthropic and patriotic in the
broadest sense." And in a rationalization that couldn't bear
too close scrutiny, he added, "It is true that we have reached
chiefly Jews, but this is due to the fact that the neighborhood
in which the Alliance is situated is inhabited principally by
Jews."

Playing down any Jewish associations may have pleased
Mr. Straus' uptown friends, but the downtowners objected
strenuously to the ban on speaking, reading, or writing Yiddish. They also received, with frank hostility, importunities
that they remove children from *chedar* and send them instead
to the Educational Alliance's English classes. "The German
Jew," a young immigrant wrote, "accepted axiomatically the
fact that the Russian Jew was incapable of transporting his
cultural treasures with him to his new environment."

In the Educational Alliance's substantial five-story red-
brick building on the southeast corner of Jefferson Street and
East Broadway uptown and downtown Jew met; on this bat-
tleground, each found grave shortcomings in the other. For
the immigrant, "in that institution there prevailed a feeling of
haughtiness, of contempt and of animosity." And *Yahudim*
felt they had to administer huge doses to the immigrants of
English classes, American history sessions, and lectures on hygiene, morals, sports, marriage, civic responsibility, and the
Republican Party.

They quickly despaired of the older generation of immigrants, made alien by beard or *shaitel*, and preoccupied with
kashrut. Nor did they hold any hope for the young intellectuals—socialist and anarchist—characterized by high fore-
heads, introspective eyes, celluloid collars, and dirty white

neckties. Therefore, the Educational Alliance directed its attentions to the unaffiliated young. The appointment of David Blaustein, a young Russian Jew with a Harvard degree, as director and his subsequent reinstatement of Yiddish as a permissible language helped relieve some downtown hostility toward the alliance. Yiddish papers appeared in the alliance reading rooms. Yiddish lectures were sponsored and Yiddish societies were permitted to meet in alliance rooms, where they were once "considered dangerous to the welfare. . . ."

Though Dr. Blaustein convinced the alliance board of directors that Yiddish could be a tool of Americanization, their strongest faith lay in external displays of patriotism—and often, according to the *Daily Forward*, "at the expense of the Greener Jews." The *Forward* sardonically described a holiday ceremony at the alliance on the eve of Thanksgiving, 1900:

> He [Dr. Blaustein] gathered over fifty *green* children, put them on the stage, gave each one an American flag and paraded them on the stage like monkeys. . . . Blaustein told the greeners to raise their heads toward the flag on the stage and repeat a declaration of loyalty. The *Greeners* then marched on the stage several times, and Blaustein explained to them the significance of Thanksgiving Day and called on them to observe it in every detail, even up to the eating of turkeys which they have not got.

H. G. Wells, accustomed to more extraterrestrial subjects, found that the sight of "a big class of bright-eyed Jewish children, boys and girls, each waving two little American flags to the measure of the song they sang, singing to the accompaniment of the piano on the platform beside us . . . the most touching thing I had seen in America."

But over and above acquiring "the simpler elements of patriotism ("no more," Wells said, "than an emotional attitude toward the flag"), the social graces—the civilities—had to be cultivated. By what means could they moderate those loud, Yiddish-accented voices, eliminate those gestures? How could a layer of silken refinement be superimposed over their rough manners? Printed signs and instructions were not effective. At an alliance meeting, someone suggested that forming a dance class "would tend to keep the young men away from evil resorts" and "would give them very necessary schooling in etiquette," but the social committee "did not feel justified to accept the responsibility connected with mixed dancing in the building." Some years later the proscription was lifted, with considerable consequence to generations of dancing America. An extremely tall, awkward adolescent named Murray Teichman learned to dance at the alliance with such gratifying results that he made it his profession, a decision that eventually transformed Murray Teichman into Arthur Murray.

Dr. Blaustein's aspirations went beyond those who could be refined by dancing. He hoped to develop the Educational Alliance into an institution to attract all the diverse elements of the East Side, and this would require not only the permission of the *Yahudim*, but the cooperation of the fiery young downtown intellectuals. Not only did he fail to win over these radicals, but in 1901, led by the Russian Jewish playwright Jacob Gordin, they organized their own settlement house, the Educational League, in protest against the "retrogressive" politics of the Educational Alliance. The student body consisted of teen-age boys and girls, bearded men, and middle-aged women, "former Gymnasium students from Russia and semi-illiterates from Galicia." But, as an Educational League student reported with disappointment:

> Its fine liberal spirit tended to degenerate into a mere absence of system and order. . . . [T]eachers and students alike were too interested in the lectures and discussions on literary and social matters to give much attention to the exercises in orthography. By the latter part of September, I took an inventory of my added stock of knowledge, and found that I had learned the names of fourscore new books and authors as well as the difference in meaning between the English words "county" and "country" and "excellent" and "surpassing" of which latter I was far from certain.

The most popular of the Educational League's offerings, however, was a new one-act play, written especially for a league ball by Jacob Gordin. Entitled *The Benefactors of the East Side*, the play parodied the *Yahudim* and their attitudes. A wildly enthusiastic crowd of 2,000 easily recognized who Gordin had intended the characters to represent: philanthropist Ashley Jefferson Yoshke was Jacob Schiff; rich lawyer Moses Herring, Louis Marshall; and a supercilious rabbi, the Reverend Dr. Knobel, the new head of the Jewish Theological Seminary. Yoshke, whose wealth is exceeded only by his patriotism, refers redundantly to Russian Jews as "schnorrers and beggars," and asserts that in uplifting the Russian

Jews on the East Side, they will be following in the footsteps
of Lincoln. "Of course," he says, "the East Side is not black,
but they are Roumanian. True they are not Ethiopians, but
they are Russians. . . ." Lawyer Herring recommends physical
culture to stop crime on the East Side, which he believes is
caused by flabby muscles. Dr. Knobel advises Russian Jews to
conceal "their extraction because German Jews despise poor
Russian Jews." The cast of characters also include several uptown lady types who urge cookbooks and baths as the solution
to ghetto problems. The only character who doesn't have a
burlesque name like Herring or Knobel, or a pretentious one
like Ashley Jefferson Yoshke, is the hero—a "celebrated agitator and friend of labor" and a broad precursor of a Clifford
Odets hero. His name is a good, plain Everyman's name:
Morris Goldberg.

But satisfying as the Gordin play was to East Siders, those
at whom its sarcasm was leveled ignored it and continued the
task of uplift. As founders of the Educational Alliance, Schiff
and Marshall aimed at the goal of secularizing Judaism—
de-emphasizing religion. This would, they believed, lead directly to Americanization of the immigrants. Another organization supported by Schiff and Marshall, the Temple Emanu-El
Brotherhood, chose to achieve Americanization by *emphasiz-
ing* religion; thus they covered all bases. The brotherhood established a model Reform service in their settlement house—a
few rooms on East Fifth Street—but they specified "it is to be
constantly kept in mind that the work of Reform, as contem-
plated by the projectors of this organization must proceed
with delicate caution, no hint of our purpose to be given lest
they, whom we are to reach, elude our quest. . . . The service
itself, it has been recommended, should be strongly conservative so as not to repel the elders, who might desire to join the
young worshippers, and to obviate, so far as possible, the suspicion that the 'Brotherhood' is an instrument of Reform."

Covert Reform service or not, the Emanu-El Brotherhood
failed, as had the Educational Alliance, to attract "the elders."
Even more distressing, the brotherhood had little effect on the
young.

Yet despite routine controversy over approach and an ambience of condescension, settlement houses as a whole deeply
influenced young East Siders, if for no other reason than because of their physical facilities—libraries, lecture halls, concerts. (The Educational Alliance even had a roof garden.)

One episode, however, "the Cinderella story of the decade," had an almost intoxicating effect on young Jewish girls.

In 1903 the University Settlement House at Eldridge and Rivington streets had among its resident workers a number of very idealistic young men from wealthy, upper-class Christian families. The most prestigious was James Graham Phelps Stokes—one of nine children of banker Anson Phelps Stokes —thirty-one years old, unmarried, over six feet tall, with deepset dark eyes, a cleft chin, and the profile of an Arrow collar man. "A descendant of families prominent in the Colonial history of New England who had chosen to forsake the Stokes mansion at 299 Madison Avenue to live at the settlement house," Graham Phelps Stokes had other assets. He was a millionaire. He was president of the State Bank of Nevada. He was a railroad president (his Nevada Central Railroad ran only 92.3 miles between Battle Mountain and Austin, Nevada, with only three locomotives and one passenger car, but a railroad is a railroad). He had a medical degree from Columbia's College of Physicians and Surgeons. (He never practiced, but a doctor is still a doctor.) He was also a socialist.

Late in 1903, Rose Pastor, a brown-eyed, flaxen-haired, slim, pretty twenty-four-year-old reporter from the *Tageblatt*, came to the settlement house to interview Phelps Stokes. Regarded among her peers on the East Side as "very interesting, very sincere, but somewhat of a dreamer," she had been born into an extremely poor family in a Suwalki *shtetl* in the Polish Pale. In 1881, when she was two, her family emigrated to London. Ten years later they came to the United States and settled in Cleveland. Rose worked for eleven years in a cigar factory, where her only education consisted of constant reading. She began sending poems to the *Tageblatt* in New York. After it bought a few, she came East and was hired by the paper—at $15 a week—to write a lovelorn column for its English page and to do an occasional interview.

If her interview with Phelps Stokes seemed somewhat incoherent, that might simply have been a result of that emotion she later described as "love at first sight":

> Mr. Stokes is a deep thinker . . . his youthful face takes by virtue of its fresh earnest and kind expression. One glance at his face and you feel that he has sown his black young curls with the bleaching cares of half a million men. . . . Mr. Stokes is very tall and I believe, six feet of thorough democracy. A

thorough-bred gentleman, a scholar and a son of a millionaire, he is a man of the common people, even as Lincoln was. . . .

"Rose," said her editor when she turned the story in, "if I thought as much of Mr. Stokes as you seem to do, I would take care not to let anybody know it."

Which showed how little *he* knew. After Stokes read the two-column story Rose had written, he invited her to dinner. Soon she began helping him with the work of the settlement house. In early April, 1905, a headline on the front page of the New York *Times* announced:

J. G. PHELPS STOKES
TO WED YOUNG JEWESS
Flattering Article by Miss Pastor
As Reporter, May Have Brought
About The Engagement

They were married on her twenty-sixth birthday in July, 1905, at the Stokes summer residence in Noroton, Connecticut, and the ceremony was performed by the groom's younger brother, the Reverend Anson Phelps Stokes, Jr., rector of St. Paul's Episcopal Church in New Haven. The couple honeymooned in Europe, including in their itinerary a visit to the *shtetl* in which Rose had been born. On their return they settled down in a six-room one-bath $38-a-month apartment on the top floor of a seven-story building on the corner of Grand and Norfolk streets. In the fall of 1906, *Harper's Bazaar* diverted its readers with an article called "Mrs. J. G. Phelps Stokes At Home." Since Mrs. Stokes, "whose ancestors were of the Jewish race" and who "might have been the model for Rossetti's Beatrice or for the quiet and dreamy maidens in Burne-Jones' drawings," had taken up helping her husband improve the lives of tenement dwellers, she practiced shortcut housekeeping. (Because "nice napery amounts to quite an item in household expenses," Mrs. Stokes used no table linen and substituted disposable Japanese napkins—100/20¢.) A different version of the home life of the Phelps Stokeses was implied by Anzia Yezierska, author of popular romances of the East Side. In 1923 she wrote *Salome of the Tenements,* a thinly disguised fictional account of the Rose Pastor-Phelps Stokes romance and marriage, in which Graham Phelps Stokes' fictional counterpart is John Manning, a cold, sexually repressed, self-righteous do-gooder, who, on his honeymoon

with "my beautiful maddening Jewess," reads the *Atlantic
Monthly*. Sonya, the heroine (Rose), is a darkly passionate,
even smoldering girl ("Russian Jewesses are always fascinating to men," declares one of Manning's bitchy cousins. "They
are mere creatures of sex.") To Sonya, the *Atlantic Monthly*
becomes "an offense." "Gesticulating hands betray her racial
origins," although her origins can't have been too mystifying
since she also has a habit of exclaiming *"Oi Weh!"* at inappropriate moments. When she finally leaves Manning, she hurls
the ultimate insult by calling him an "all-*rightnik."*

By the time Rose and Graham Phelps Stokes were divorced
in 1925, Rose Pastor Stokes was a well-known writer, an outright Communist, as well as an advocate of birth control and
other unpopular causes. Graham Phelps Stokes left the Socialist Party and, with age, grew more conservative. But despite
its eventual dissolution, the Pastor-Stokes marriage lent an
aura of fabulous romance to the halls of the University Settlement. For years afterward, to all the yearning sweatshop girls
who came there to study English, letter writing, dancing, par-
liamentary procedure, gymnastics, the works of Emerson and
Tolstoy, art history, and other areas of self-improvement, the
legend of a poor Jewish girl from the East Side who had
"caught" a handsome socialite millionaire socialist—who was
also a doctor—proved that at such institutions *anything* was
possible.

14

Red, White, and Blue Liturgy

Even before the establishment of the Educational Alliance and the Rose Pastor-Graham Phelps Stokes marriage, Orthodox Jews on the East Side had become alarmed at evidence that the bonds of religion had loosened on their children and had acted boldly without seeking help or advice from *shtadlonim*.

In early July, 1888, great excitement exhilarated East Side Orthodox Russian Jews, for their newly designated chief rabbi, Jacob Joseph, arrived in Hoboken on the German steamer *Aller*. The boat docked on a Saturday morning, and the rabbi stayed aboard while his welcomers waited impatiently onshore until sundown. On that hot July evening, thousands of other Jews swarmed around 263 Henry Street, where the chief rabbi and his family were to live. They were eager to see the figure who would establish them as equals of the *Yahudim*—not in a monetary sense, of course, but as a people in command of their own future.

Jacob Joseph epitomized scholarly Orthodoxy. A Vilna admirer described him accurately as "both brilliant and unusually pious," qualities which unfortunately rarely accompany a youthful appearance. Only forty years old, Rabbi Joseph could have been mistaken for sixty. Short and slight, the chief

rabbi had a graying, curly, divided beard and dressed properly
in a long black caftan and velvet-trimmed shtreimel.

The importation of Jacob Joseph as chief rabbi had ended a
series of involved, often frustrating negotiations by the Association of American Hebrew Orthodox Congregations—eighteen New York Orthodox congregations. The largest and oldest congregation among them was the thirty-five-year-old
Beth Hamidrash Hagidol on Norfolk Street. Upon its formation it had appointed Abraham Ash as its rabbi—though he
was not ordained, simply a *chazan*. Ash received $2 a week
and criticism for being a little too Hassidic and for not giving
his congregation his undivided attention. True, he manufactured hoopskirts on the side, but he contributed much of the
$10,000 profit he made from this venture to his congregation.
He resigned in order to attempt another business coup, im-
porting kosher wine from California. But the day of the con-
vivial drink made up of one part ginger ale to two parts sacra-
mental wine and a twist of lemon peel had not yet come, and
when Ash failed, he returned to Beth Hamidrash, whose
membership had increased to such an extent because of the
new immigration that he now received $200 a year.

Very shortly after Rabbi Ash's death, in early 1887, Beth
Hamidrash joined with many of the smaller Orthodox congregations in the city to establish the Association of American
Hebrew Orthodox Congregations. One of their immediate
goals was to "seek out ways and means of bringing a Chief
Rabbi for New York." The status of England's chief rabbi,
whose authority was respected by English Jews and recognized by the English government, served as inspiration. But
England also had a state church, which predisposed the entire
population to a central religious authority. Conditions for
such an office in the United States were inauspicious: No state
church existed, and even the federal government in Washington aroused distrust.

Nevertheless, for the Russian Orthodox immigrants, the
concept of a chief rabbi, invested with authority and dignity,
had therapeutic as well as religious values. In Russia, when
they had been the prey of *pogromschiks* and the imperial government, ritual Orthodoxy had cushioned the unrelenting persecutions. Now, in the United States, while still among the lowest on the social scale, they couldn't convince their children
that Rivington Street was an isolated *shtetl*, for the American
ghetto, unlike the Pale, offered numerous opportunities. A
young man or woman could obtain a secular education and go

into a profession, or work hard and start a business, or become a criminal; any of these avenues could provide a means of becoming "a somebody." And just as their economic and social condition no longer remained fixed, their Orthodoxy also eroded. "Our Russian brethren," pointed out one of their uptown* critics, ". . . jump almost without transition from extreme orthodoxy to agnosticism." Indeed, the constant harping of Dr. Wise's Reform *American Israelite* and the Isaac family's Conservative *Jewish Messenger* on the need of East Europeans to adjust to American ways and drop their superstitions—confused with piety—only evoked furious indignation. On observing "the charged atmosphere" between Chicago philanthropists and immigrants who had met to organize a settlement house, Jane Addams remarked, "It seems to me there is more ill feeling between Reform and Orthodox Jews than there is between Jew and Gentile."

What Orthodox Jews wanted was someone who would combine the prestige and authority of an Orthodox Hebrew scholar with a degree of sophistication sufficient to impress the *Yahudim* and the organizational genius of Isaac M. Wise. This combination of characteristics proved difficult to find: The leaders of the Orthodox group spent six months searching, by means of correspondence with European scholars in Lithuania, Poland, and Russia.

But America appeared a strange, terrifying land to these scholars, for there neither those who spent their lives studying the Talmud nor the Talmud itself was respected. After all, the Hebrew press in Russia had dwelt at great length on the iniquities of American Reform Judaism, pointing out that religious schools "attached to the rich synagogues in the upper part of the city" closed for the summer; that the Michael Reese Hospital, which Reform Jews had established in Chicago, served no kosher food and discriminated against Russian Jews; that to qualify as an American rabbi one need only be able to speak loudly and clearly and read Hebrew.

Isaac Elhanon Spektor of Kovno and Jacob Joseph of Vilna were among the eminent rabbis to whom letters were

---

* The exchange of derisive names between American German Jews and Russian Jewish immigrants was extensive. To the Russian Jews, American Jews were *"Deitchen,"* "Uptowners," *"Yahudim,"* "the 400," "our magnets," "our benefactors," "our so-called benefactors," "our philanthropists." To American Jews, the immigrants were "those wild Russians," "Orientals," "Asiatics," "Downtowners," "that element," *"shnorrers."*

written. They and the others sent cautious replies. Then a letter arrived from the secretary of Rabbi Isaac Elhanon, reporting that European rabbis had met and determined that the position of chief rabbi of New York City should be offered to Zvi Hirsh, son of Isaac Elhanon, who, though a young man, had the reputation of a scholar. Soon, letters endorsing the choice of Zvi Hirsh poured in from all European rabbis. But Russian Jews in America had already become less submissive to religious authority, and to be so imperiously directed to choose Zvi Hirsh didn't sit well with them. Consequently, when they learned that Zvi Hirsh had not only a scholarly reputation, but also a great many debts and an insane wife from whom he was separated, they felt justified in rejecting him. Now an air of desperation colored their search. After futile negotiations with a Polish rabbinical scholar, they settled on the one man who seemed reasonably eager to come: Rabbi Jacob Joseph, the highly respected spiritual leader of Vilna.

The Orthodox Jews of New York—those, at any rate, who brought him over—expected Rabbi Joseph to prevent the young from falling away from Orthodoxy and to elevate the East European Jews in the eyes of all America, especially in those of the *Yahudim*. However, the *American Israelite* had already stated dogmatically that "a man who can speak neither German nor English and whose vernacular is an unintelligible jargon [Yiddish] cannot be a fitting representative of Orthodox Judaism to the world at large." Orthodox leaders also expected Rabbi Joseph to correct "the abuses which have appeared in *kashrut, gitten* and *kiddushen*"—the dietary, divorce and marriage laws. But the Orthodox attitude toward these areas of jurisdiction profoundly disturbed Reform Jews. "The rabbi will find his uptown brethren eager to welcome him and to cooperate with him," the *Jewish Messenger* declared sternly, "providing he remembers that with all our interpretations that in marriages and divorces the courts of the State must be sought for redress, not the rabbinical court that he is reported to favor."

As for the kosher meat business, it was a jungle. From 1796, when a non-Jewish butcher named Nicholas Smart was charged with affixing false kosher seals on nonkosher meat, attempts to supervise and regulate ritual slaughter had been persistent, but unavailing.

Ritualistic complexity, human nature, passion, greed—all contributed to this dead end. Kashrut permitted only the forequarter of a steer to be eaten by Orthodox Jews. The fifth rib divided the kosher from the trefa, and the hindquarters of the cow was sold to butchers dealing in nonkosher meat. Kashrut also required that an animal be slaughtered according to precise rules: length of blade, sharpness of blade, the precision and rapidity of the cutting of the animal's throat. . . . So the slaughterhouses or butcher hired a shochet*—one trained to do ritual slaughter—then rabbis were employed to provide a religious stamp of approval. But no one standard existed to which all or even many adhered. Moreover, because of the greater demand for kosher meat as a result of the influx of immigrants—1,500 head of cattle a week were reserved for kosher slaughter—fierce competition led to outrageous irregularities. Thus, to provide a family on Houston Street with three-quarter pound of flanken, shochets, butchers, and rabbis denounced and slandered one another unremittingly. Charges of *trefa* rang throughout lower Manhattan with the shrill urgency of fire alarms. Fights among shochets and butchers and consumers occurred regularly in butcher shops; incidents in which pious women attacked a kosher butcher who'd been selling nonkosher meat became commonplace. And so kosher meat riots on the East Side became a staple news item for New York papers.† Indeed, it may be that in the production of that three-quarter pound of flanken, it was the cow from which it came who suffered the least.

The scholarly, compassionate, high-minded chief rabbi who arrived to bring order and enlightenment to this unsavory scene clearly had no gift for administration. The Association of American Hebrew Orthodox Congregations, which had imported Rabbi Joseph, was most eager to regularize the kosher meat business, but it also realized it had the opportunity to kill two birds with one stone—not by any means an approved ritual slaughter. It would place the entire supervision of kashrut under Chief Rabbi Joseph and levy an extra charge on kosher meat to pay the chief rabbi's salary and provide needed money for the organization. But Rabbi Joseph strongly opposed this arrangement. Finally, he persuaded the

---

* In their tireless attempts to clarify customs of Jews for Americans, a reporter explained that "shochats were rabbis or 'quasi-clergymen' employed exclusively as butchers. They dress differently from other members of their race, and in their speech and manners are a curious compound of clergyman and butcher."

† The trefa-kosher brouhaha wasn't limited to New York City; uncertainties existed in other localities. "When my mother saw Rabbi Genss use the meat cleaver just after the non-Jewish butcher had used it," recalled a Seattle lady, "she stopped buying kosher meat."

AAHOC not to charge extra for meat—considered the poor man's diet, for the affluent supposedly ate poultry. Consequently, the AAHOC insisted on fixing a charge of a penny on all poultry bearing the lead seal of the chief rabbi.

Disparate groups now rallied together in opposition to the chief rabbi, all shouting irately, *"Karobka!"* Karobka was the name of the tax the czar's government leveled on kosher meat, and the allusion to it was so close in memory and sensibility that its effect was impossible to overcome. Therefore, the butchers and shochets who opposed any supervision, the rabbis of the small *shtetl* congregations who were jealous of Rabbi Joseph's supposed power and status, the socialists and other antireligious radicals, the Galitzianers who resented the chief rabbi because he was a Litvak, and the militant *balabostas* who were indignant at the extra charge on poultry combined to bring down the chief rabbi in defeat.

Protest against his right to bear the title also came from all sides. A number of congregations banded together and proclaimed *their* rabbi *rav hakolel*—chief rabbi.* At the height of all of Rabbi Joseph's troubles, the famed Reform Rabbi Kaufmann Kohler dispatched a note to the New York *Evening Post* informing it that the title "Chief Rabbi" implied "no jurisdiction over other rabbis beyond his congregation or congregations." Several months later, he again pointed out, this time to the *Jewish Messenger*, that "it may be timely to remind the general press that Rabbi Jacob Joseph is not by any means the "chief rabbi of New York."

An incident that spotlighted the chief rabbi's failure in yet another vital area—inspiring the young to remain observant Jews—occurred on the eve of Yom Kippur, 1889. A group of young radicals, the Pioneers of Freedom, gave the first of what would become an annual sacrilegious event: a Yom Kippur Ball.† To desecrate a solemn holiday with frivolity was outrageous enough, but some of the excessively defiant young

---

* After an Hassidic rabbi emigrated from Moscow and assumed leadership of several congregations, he identified his position with a sign—"Chief Rabbi of America." When he was asked "Who made you chief rabbi?" he answered mischievously, "The sign painter."

† In years to come, the event would be more highly organized. An anarchist group, not usually known for their flippancy or, indeed, belief in organization, called themselves The Merrymakers of Yom Kippur in the interest of impiety and charged 15 cents for general admission, 30 cents for the press. A New York *Times* reporter noted, with obvious disappointment, that "the proceedings really were tame."

people also lingered in front of shuls on that fast day and ate ham sandwiches.

How could Rabbi Joseph have any effect on even the mildly disaffected young? He spoke no English and lived, as he had in Vilna, surrounded by young disciples in ringlets. In his sermons, he made awkward tries at reorienting himself by using American Yiddish. "Once," Abe Cahan wrote, "he used the word 'clean' for '*rein*,' and it was easy to see this was purposely done to show he was not a greenhorn."

A few doors down the street from the chief rabbi's office—and all its highly specialized, alien activities—was the School of Americanization of the Hebrew Education Society. But its indoctrination would no more have touched the *rav hakolel* personally than if the school had been located 2,000 miles away.

Though Rabbi Joseph continued to be chief rabbi, the title was an empty one. Disunity broke up the organization that had appointed him, and he had barely any income. The remainder of his life and its aftermath held the kind of tragedy beyond mere misfortune. His efforts to cope with life in America ended in a paralytic stroke which partially incapacitated him, and he died at the age of fifty-two, on July 28, 1902, exactly fourteen years and twenty-one days after he had disembarked at Hoboken.

"In spite of all that was said against the Rabbi during his lifetime," wrote the *Jewish Gazette*, "we all loved him because of his estimable qualities and the blameless life he led." This was the generally accepted feeling, for a procession estimated variously at 20,000 to 50,000, the largest gathering of this kind in East Side history, followed remorsefully and penitently behind 200 carriages and the hearse bearing the pine coffin. Away from Henry Street, the mass of mourners moved in and out of small stifling streets, through Grand Street toward the ferry-house and the ultimate destination, Cypress Hills Cemetery in Long Island.

As the hearse neared the Grand Street Ferry, those passing R. Hoe & Company, a printing press factory at the corner of Grand and Sheriff, were suddenly doused with water thrown from the window by Hoe employees. Then bolts, scraps of iron, and blocks of wood came showering down, accompanied by hoots and jeers. Outraged members of the procession dashed into the Hoe office, overturned furniture, and beat up a few workers.

Two hundred policemen arrived. "It was evident from the actions of the officers that they considered the mourners in the wrong. Slashing this way and that with their sticks, they waded through the dense crowd," injuring scores.

At the inevitable investigation (Louis Marshall was one of the five men appointed to the investigating committee by Mayor Seth Low), a commonly known fact was revealed—in such investigations all findings emerge as pristine information —that the East Side Irish, many of whom worked at Hoe, resented the enormous influx of Jews into the East Side.* Scores of incidents disclosing police brutality to Jews were recounted —clubbings, beatings, arrests, and fines for little or no reason. And a former labor leader, Meyer Schoenfeld (whose son Abe was to take part in a highly unorthodox crime-busting agency ten years later), pointed out that ". . . the police shut their eyes if the victim of the outrage happens to be a Jew."

Only in death did Rabbi Joseph touch the reality of the secular and the America outside his office.†

Louis Marshall and Jacob Schiff had observed the failure of Rabbi Joseph to command authority and influence among the children of the Orthodox Jews with no great surprise. Consequently, sometime before the chief rabbi's death, they had determined to import an East European Hebrew scholar of their own, one who would develop the faltering Jewish Theological Seminary (whose establishment in 1887, "for the perpetuation of Judaism in America," had been inspired in part as a result of the trefa banquet in Cincinnati) into a strong Conservative institution that would Americanize Russian Jewish Orthodoxy.

Their chief purpose in rehabilitating the Jewish Theological Seminary was unabashedly stated in the *American Hebrew* obituary of Leonard Lewisohn who left $50,000 to the JTS fund, which would afford "the surest and safest means of han-

---

* From across the street, Dr. G. Wonson Vandergrift had observed the riot. He testified at the investigation that "there had been a certain amount of race feeling in that locality for years." When asked what he meant by "race feeling," Dr. Vandergrift elaborated. "For instance," he said, "if a Hebrew with a tall hat passed along the street there would be trouble. His hat was generally a target for someone."

† By coming to the United States, Rabbi Joseph did, eventually, through his descendants participate in temporal American life. Lazarus Joseph, his grandson, became a New York state senator and city comptroller. And his great-grandson, Captain Jacob Joseph, at twenty-two, was the youngest officer of that rank in the Marine Corps and the first officer to die at Guadalcanal.

dling the downtown problems of Americanizing the foreign
element by sending among them trained and well-equipped
Rabbinized teachers. . . ."

To this end, in their customary *balabatish* way, Schiff and
Marshall raised a half million dollars. Jacob Schiff then
bought a piece of land on Morningside Heights and built a
three-story building. And their choice of a man to head this
institution was, like the late chief rabbi, bearded, a master of
Talmud, and a Litvak by ancestry, though Rumanian by birth.
However, when the *Yahudim* sought a bearded East European Talmudic scholar, they didn't seek him in a yeshiva in
Vilna; they went to Cambridge University in England.

For whatever it reveals about rich Jews, considerable evidence points to a curious fact. American Jewish *shtadlonim* in
the early twentieth century, when gathered in a group, could
not give business, politics, or sex the attention they deserved.
Instead, their eyes sparkled, their cheeks flushed, and their
voices dropped to confidential tones for only one subject:
philanthropy.

Inevitably then, one night in 1901, at an all-male gathering
in the upper Broadway residence of Isidor Straus, the subject
"of Jewish affairs in New York and particularly of Jewish education," came up. This led the conversation to the precarious
financial and organizational state of the Jewish Theological
Seminary. Jacob Schiff, "THE *Yahudi* of New York," was
present that night, and he quickly became convinced that re-
building the seminary was as much a sociological necessity as
a spiritual one, for a revitalized Jewish Theological Seminary
meant an institution that would train American rabbis in an
updated traditional Judaism, which would, in turn, check socialism and gangsterism among the children of the Russian
immigrants. As the *American Hebrew* pointed out, ". . . the
young men and women, English-speaking children of jargon-
speaking immigrants are entirely 'unchurched'!" So the *shtadlonim* determined to alter Orthodox Judaism through Americanization, for its rituals were, as Louis Marshall felt, "un-
congenial to a mind influenced by American culture."

Consequently, Schiff and Marshall immediately took steps
to reorganize the seminary and began negotiations to have Solomon Schechter, reader in rabbinics at Cambridge University, become its president and "Westernize" Orthodox Judaism.
Paradoxically, Dr. Schechter agreed to come to America so
his three children might have a more Jewish atmosphere than

they had in England, while Schiff and Marshall had engaged him to persuade the children of Russian-born Orthodox parents to accept a more secular Judaism.

Solomon Schechter wasn't an ordinary extraordinary Talmudic scholar, for he was sophisticated. At Cambridge, his closest friend was Sir James Frazer, author of *The Golden Bough*. Dr. Schechter had discovered and identified ancient Hebrew writings in a Cairo genizah and had mastered what he called "a kosher English." While he never lost his foreign accent, and though his pronunciation and spelling were erratic, he had a gift for the popularization of scholarly Judaic studies and had developed a felicitous English writing style. As a Civil War buff, with an idolatrous admiration for Abraham Lincoln, Dr. Schechter paraphrased Lincoln's farewell to his Springfield neighbors, when he left England for America. ". . . Here I have lived nearly twenty years and have passed from young man to old man. Here my children have been born. I now leave not knowing when, or whether even, I may return. . . ."

By the time he and his wife, Matilda,* and their two daughters and son had settled in their apartment on West Eighty-fourth Street in New York, Dr. Schechter had reached fifty-three, and his red hair and beard had turned auburn and gray. But his colorful personality had not faded. Women found him "handsome, dynamic," with "the most charming smile they had ever seen"—qualities more closely associated with Reform rabbis than with Conservative or Orthodox ones. For his part, Dr. Schechter regarded women with kindly patronization, because he "never accepted the idea of the equality of men and women." Indeed, so incisive was Schechter's intellect that, at times, it seemed he didn't fully accept the equality of other men either.

In addition to an imposing appearance—massive prophet-like head, with shaggy beard and piercing blue eyes—he had an impressive working knowledge of profanity complemented by a tendency to explode into sulfurous anger when presented with an opinion he found distasteful. Consequently, his presence at social gatherings often resulted in untoward incidents. "You are a fool, I beg your pardon," he was apt to observe wrathfully and in one breath to an astonished guest. "Please," he would say later, "never take things as hot as I dish them up

---

* Dr. Schechter's family-arranged first marriage in his youth had ended in divorce after one year. He remarried at thirty-seven.

in my excitement." At the seminary, the morning after such incidents, his secretary busily dispatched notes of apology from "that wild man of stupendous genius."

Under Schechter's leadership, Conservative Judaism developed into an influential movement, and the Jewish Theological Seminary became a strong supporting institution. But his goal differed from that of the *shtadlonim* who had imported him. Thirteen years after his arrival in the United States, he wrote Louis Marshall, "I must take it out of their [JTS board of directors] mind that I came into this country for the purpose of converting the downtown Jews to a more refined species of religion." (However, emotional eruptions did not alter the friendship of Schechter and Louis Marshall which included a shared interest in adventure novels. "My father was always worried when Schechter came to the house," James Marshall recalled, "because he would insist on borrowing *Midshipman Easy* or some such book and then forget to return it. When my father called on Schechter, he spent a considerable time browsing through Schechter's library in search of a book to be brought home and returned to his library shelves.") Both Marshall and Schiff found it impossible to tell the combustible Dr. Schechter that they really didn't care whether Russian Jews accepted Conservative or Reform Judaism, as long as they rejected socialism. And, according to their reasoning, there would be more chance of this if the downtown Jews were under the influence of "a more refined species of religion." The heart of their effort, therefore, was not to spread Conservative Judaism, as Dr. Schechter did, but to inculcate conservative Republicanism.

Far from unifying Judaism, Schechter's presence and personality made for hostility with Orthodox leaders, one of whom maintained that while Schechter's scholarship was inferior, "he did know how to get along with the leaders of the Seminary and with the men of wealth supporting it who were mostly *ame ha-arets*." Moreover, Dr. Schechter expressed his disdain for Reform "preachers" in derision. When a Reform rabbi refused a cigar, saying he didn't smoke, Dr. Schechter asked, "Then what do you do on the Sabbath?" He complained irately that certain Reform rabbis did "terrible mischief down town . . . ," that they cared little for Judaism, but that "their great aim [was] to smuggle in the Mission Prayer Book and other hellish things among the Russian and Roumanian Jews. . . . It is simply a farce to think that people whose whole Judaism consists in coming with their automobiles to listen to opera singers every Friday evening should now arrogate themselves the calling of proselitizers [*sic*]." And he had the most violent dislike for Kaufmann Kohler, Isaac Mayer Wise's successor as president of Hebrew Union College, whose radical Reform meant to Schechter "simply final conversion to Christianity." At a meeting of the Jewish Publication Society, Kohler, who was born in Fürth, Bavaria, remarked that prayers for the recovery of the mad prince regent were recited in every church and synagogue in Bavaria but Fürth. "Well," Dr. Schechter commented, "perhaps in Fürth, insanity is not a disease."

When Schechter resigned from the board of directors of the Educational Alliance at the end of 1912, saying, "the great question before the Jewish community at present is not so much Americanizing of the Russian Jew, as his Judaising [*sic*]." Marshall admitted philosophically in a letter to Schiff's son-in-law Felix Warburg that Schechter's influence among Russian Jews was not as great as it should have been. ". . . great as he is as a scholar," Marshall wrote, "and as a man, he nevertheless is impatient with the ordinary run of mankind, and treats them contemptuously so they are apt to resent it, and therefore not likely to permit him even if he desired to do so, to exercise any influence upon them."

However, the Conservative movement did, in a way, serve as a deradicalizing agent, but it did not, as it had been hoped, affect children of Orthodox parents. Rather, it checked the radical direction of the Reform movement whose leaders had imported Dr. Schechter. The steady drift to the left of Dr. Wise's Reform had resulted in a service that was increasingly criticized as too cold, dispassionate. Many of the young people at Temple Emanu-El grew disaffected and found Dr. Schechter's sophisticated traditional Judaism extremely appealing. One young man, in particular, Judah L. Magnes, the rabbi of Temple Emanu-El and Louis Marshall's brother-in-law, resigned his pulpit and joined the Conservative moment.

Instead of American Jews Americanizing immigrants, which in their opinion required making them less Jewish, immigrants were making American Jews more Jewish. In Sioux City, Iowa, American Jews had been almost totally assimilated—having joined the Unitarian Church. When the first East European Jews came and formed an Orthodox congregation, the American Jews withdrew from the Unitarian Church and organized a Reform congregation. Furthermore, the immigrants appeared to be affecting even the general population.

In Boston, at the early part of the century, three boys—Irish, Jewish, and Negro—were heard walking down the North Side arguing loudly . . . in Yiddish.

PART IV

THE MAN WITH THE HOE
COULD BE JEWISH TOO!

Send us funds and you will be astonished how fast we will settle on government land every able-bodied Russian emigrant. We think that the long deferred project of teaching people agricultural pursuits can now be speedily realized and the problem what to do with the Russian Jew can at once be solved.

—DR. ISAAC MAYER WISE, *American Israelite,* 1882

Our thought was to live in the open instead of being shut-ins who lived in artificial city life. We desired to be dependent for our living upon the elements of Father Sun and Mother Earth instead of depending upon the whims of others. We were not to be, at our farm vocation, jealous and envious one of another, but to live upon our own resources with the help only of nature. Our goal was to own a home and land as a means of earning a livelihood and to be true citizens of our adopted country.

—SIDNEY BAILEY, Alliance Colony, founded 1882

15

Destroying a Stereotype

Jews had an agrarian past, amply recorded in the Old Testament, but some 2,000 years had gone by in which much had happened. Czarist Russia, by imperial edict, forbade Jews from owning land. Russian Jews, therefore, could not, like their ancestors, be tillers of the soil, keepers of the flocks—except illegally, and furtive farming in the Pale had not a great deal to recommend it. Instead, many Jews lived in a rural-urban limbo, buying produce from Russian peasant farmers and peddling it, together with manufactured goods, in *shtetl*, town, and city. Usually, peddling of this sort provided a bare subsistence—at best, enough to welcome the *Shabbas* and celebrate Passover properly—but it held still another disadvantage, an intangible one. Nineteenth-century rationale maintained that such petty trading was to be contemptuously dismissed as "nonproductive." Agriculture, on the other hand, was an occupation invested with nobility, for it was "productive." And without the word "productive," rhetorical reference to agriculture would languish, lack completeness. From Jean Jacques Rousseau in the early part of the century to Count Leo Tolstoy in the latter part, social philosophers and intellectuals had elevated farming to a mystique. Tolstoy spelled it all out to Rabbi Joseph Krauskopf of Philadelphia in 1894 when he said, "Lead the tens of thousands of people

of your cities to your idle fertile lands and you will . . . spread
a good name for your people throughout the land; for all the
world honors and protects the bread producer and is eager to
welcome him. . . ." Thereupon, Rabbi Krauskopf went home
and started the National Farm School in Doylestown, Pennsylvania. For he, too, believed farming provided food for
mankind and spiritual fuel for its practitioners. And it would
also, he hoped, get the Jewish boys off the streets in Philadelphia.

This agricultural mystique obsessed Christian and Jew
alike. In Russia, particularly, intellectuals of both faiths were
transfixed with a veneration for the soil and the men who
worked it. But although Tolstoy and Turgenev and other non-
Jewish intellectuals could glorify the stalwart Russian peasant,
Jewish intellectuals had to create a romantic vision of a Jewish back-to-the-soil movement, complete with a larger-than-
life Jewish farmer illumined by an aura of rugged strength.
(There were, of course, a few genuine farmers among East
European immigrants. The family of Joseph and Ira Bregstone, for example, had a farm in the hills surrounding Ponie-
mon, a Lithuanian *shtetl*, where they were known as the Breg-
stones of the Mountains. When the Bregstone boys landed in
New York, they changed their name to Breakstone and started a retail milk business on the East Side.) Even hardheaded
Western European and American Jews indulged in the
"Dream." Since poverty-stricken Russian Jews were so sum-
marily classified as "nonproductive" (easily translated by
anti-Semites into "parasites"), it was, they thought, all the
more necessary that their regeneration be accomplished by
farming. In one stroke, this occupation would make for pro-
ductivity, an increase in income, and the pacification of anti-
Semites.

No other trade or profession could—or should—compete.
As Michael Heilprin, a scholar, sternly declared to Oscar
Straus, a politician, "We have too many artists, scholars, politicians, 'doctors' of every description, lawyers, writers. . . ."
Heilprin thought it would be far better to promote "the efforts of those whose object is to achieve a livelihood and respectable position among honest fellowmen by the diligent
and useful labor of their hands."

Indeed, the reverence with which Jewish philanthropist
Baron de Hirsch called attention and paid tribute to Jewish
farmers of Biblical times—"they drove their herds," "they
plowed the earth," they sowed, they harvested . . . —might

lead one to suppose that had not a malign fate made the baron a multimillionaire railroad magnate, he would have liked nothing better than to have become a farmer. Of course, he did indulge extensively in philanthropic farming. He sowed millions of dollars into the Jewish Colonization Association, the Baron de Hirsch Fund, and the Jewish Agricultural and Industrial Aid Society, hoping to harvest a healthy crop of self-sustaining Russian Jewish farmers in the Dakotas, Michigan, Wisconsin, Kansas, New York, and New Jersey.

The agricultural mystique had a universal appeal; its lyrical naïveté enthralled its eventual victims. "There are thousands of Russian immigrants who loathe peddling and all kindred occupations and nourish even an exaggerated view of the excellence of farming labor and farming life." Young Russian Jewish students, once convinced that Jews need only undergo complete Russification to achieve emancipation, reacted sharply to the pogroms by organizing the Self-Defense League in Odessa and by becoming imbued with the idea that the salvation of Jews lay "in the noble profession of agriculture which provides food for mankind. . . ."

Two organizations had this goal: Bilu, whose members emigrated to Palestine and formed two kibbutzim, and Am Olam (the Eternal People), whose members came to the United States. In Odessa, in Kiev, members signed up with Am Olam (which already had its own flag—Am Olam embroidered in gold letters, a plow, and a quote from Hillel, "If I am not for myself, who is for me?") and were given a copy of the constitution for proposed agricultural colonies. Characteristically, plans for education facilities were more detailed than those for crops. To the Orthodox, the constitution promised a shul, a shochet, and a *mikveh*. For "the progressive intellectuals there would be a library with books in several languages" and debating societies. But these paper arrangements weren't acceptable to everyone. "We were so sure of attaining this happiness [becoming farmers]," recalled one Am Olamite, "that some of us were already quarreling about the institutions we should establish . . . the kind of libraries we should found, whether or not we should have synagogues. . . ."

Bobbe-mysehs (grandmothers' stories) were told of Elizabetgrad Jews who had gone to America directly after the pogrom in that city "and become farmers in the United States—and how!" It was said "the American Government gave them free land; the American people met them with music; wealthy American farmers presented them with horses, cows and farm

implements, and now they were living in a veritable paradise.
. . ." If the Messiah had come, it could hardly have been better. Naturally, therefore, when the ship carrying one of the
groups hove into port, Am Olam members stood on deck ex-
pecting a warm welcome. "Our leaders unfurled our large
flag, so that the world might see and know who was coming
here. But no sooner had the flag begun to wave triumphantly
in the air . . . than a man ran over to us and ordered us to
lower the flag. We told him with an air of self-assurance that
this was a free country, whereupon he became furious,
snatched up the flag and hurled it straight into the sea."

Upon arriving in New York, amid dissension, some of the
members of Am Olam decided to remain there. And so while
one group went West to pursue their dream, another group,
including among them Abraham Cahan, started the Jewish
Labor Movement.

In late 1881 and 1882, there were not only clusters of Am
Olam chapters, but other groups, too, who were determined to
start farm colonies in the United States (or in Canada, where
five settlements blossomed and died; the largest was
Edenbridge—originally Yiddenbridge—in Saskatchewan).
And rumors of streets of gold notwithstanding, these immigrants arrived when a desperate urban crisis had already
created an American agricultural mystique. In passing from
rural economy to an industrial one, the United States had become a nation of cities, and in their proliferation and rapid
growth, crime and corruption flourished. Sin and city became
synonyms; rural life, viewed through the scrim of nostalgia,
was tranquil, innocent, healthful, even patriotic—the good
life.

During the nineteenth century, men who were always referred to as visionaries initiated many American farm colonies. And all of them were short-lived: Robert Owen's New
Harmony; Bronson Alcott's Fruitlands, where it was said the
colonists planned to "evolve orchards out of their inner consciousness"; the 192-acre transcendentalist Brook Farm in
West Roxbury, Massachusetts, "an institute of Agriculture
and Education" and whose aim was to combine "plain living
and high thinking." (Only John Humphrey Noyes' Perfec-
tionists of the Oneida Community in New York had any staying power, and their success was attributed not to the impon-
derables of the spirit, but to the manufacture of steel animal
traps, silver plate, and an enthusiastic practice of free love.)

Apart from these well-known experiments, American Jews

had similar visions: Major Mordecai M. Noah planned to settle Jews on an island to be called Ararat, near Niagara Falls;
Moses Levy, a rich Moroccan Jew who had made his money
from lumber in the West Indies, bought 60,000 acres in
northeastern Florida and on them settled seventy Jewish families from England and France. Despite his expenditures of
time and money, the colony lasted a bare three years. (Levy
was the father of David Yulee, the first Jewish Congressman
and the first Jewish Senator; one may also hope he was the
only Jewish member of either body who preferred to think,
and indeed, to circulate the story, that his father was a Moroccan prince and not a Jew at all.) The last utopian attempt
was made in 1837 by a group of New York Jews of German
and Dutch descent who bought 484 acres of miserably rocky,
infertile, virtually inaccessible mountainous land in Ulster
County, New York, and still had the courage or optimism of
whimsicality to name it Sholem. In spite of all their efforts to
subsidize their farming by the manufacture of goose quill
pens and fur hats, of peddling and tailoring, the last colonist
said shalom to Sholem in 1851.

Aside from these rare exceptions, very few American Jews
were farmers, nor did they aspire to the occupation except in
fanciful longing. (Though if owning a farm that lost money
made one a farmer, then Jacob Schiff with his prize herd of
cattle, grazing on his gentleman's farm near Red Bank, New
Jersey, was one. At a lunch, during which he provided both
great jugs of fresh milk and iced pails of French champagne,
Schiff ruefully admitted: "The milk costs me more than the
wine.") They were merchant princes—and some merely merchants—bankers, doctors, lawyers. They all were respectable
substantial citizens who needed no salvation. However, moved
by compassion for their pallid, stunted co-religionists and by
practicality, they viewed farming as a blessing, a panacea, a
chance for redemption, an opportunity "to elevate them to a
higher place. . . ." The *American Israelite* gave its facile, self-
assured prescription: "The Russian Jew first and foremost
needs physical restoration which they can find on the American prairies and forests. The atmosphere, the exercise, the
food and feelings of security and liberty to be found there will
restore and invigorate the immigrants."

While no one questioned the basic premise, the inherent
fruitfulness of "the American prairies and forests," one skep-
tic did cast doubt on the abilities of the Russian Jews to in-
duce them to yield anything. "These people are only fit for

"They were herded wide-eyed into Ellis Island and asked, 'Who are you? Where are you from? Where are you going?' and their eyes scrutinized for trachoma, the scourge of East European Jews."

Baron de Hirsch: "'His heavy long mustaches made him look more like an Austrian cavalry officer than a Jewish financier. . . .'"

American Jewish Historical Society

"Ship via Galveston": A group of immigrants en route to Galveston, photographed aboard the SS *Breslau* in Bremen, July, 1912.

"Lower Manhattan became a jungle of rickety pushcarts laden with cheap merchandise and fragrant and not so fragrant food. The sound backdrop to this scene, an incessant hubbub of clamorous Yiddish."

Julia Richman: "The pushcart controversy brought down the wrath of the entire East Side on her pompadoured head. . . ."

Emma Lazarus: "Had the Jewish immigrants been able to do a *mitzvah* for her, they would have found her a husband. Instead, they gave her immortality."

Jacob H. Schiff

"As philanthropic as Baron de Hirsch and less *tsitterdik* than Baron de Gunzberg, in the early years of the twentieth century Jacob H. Schiff and Louis Marshall went together in the thoughts of their East European co-religionists like lox and bagels."

Louis Marshall

From left to right: Simon, Samuel, Benjamin, Louis, Joseph and Morris Rosenfield, whose emigration from Warsaw to New York followed a typical pattern: Samuel brought Benjamin over; together they brought Morris; these three brought Simon, who then brought Louis and later Joseph. Then all six brought their mother and sisters. Five of the brothers were drawn to Minneapolis by the "Jewish Magnet"—relatives.

English class at the Educational Alliance: "It was 'an oasis in the desert of degradation and despair,' where huge doses of English, American history and lectures on hygiene, morals, sports, marriage, civic responsibility and the Republican Party were administered to immigrants."

"First you stand, then you salute": H. G. Wells found "a big class of bright-eyed Jewish children" saluting the flag "the most touching thing I have seen in America."

J. G. Phelps Stokes campaigning on the East Side, 1908: "He was a millionaire, the president of the State Bank of Nevada and a railroad president. He held a medical degree from Columbia . . . and he was a Socialist."

Rose Pastor Stokes: "And the bride, an East Side Russian Jewess of humble origin, who had spent years in a cigar factory. . . ."—*Harper's Bazaar,* September, 1906

Mrs. J. G. Phelps Stokes At Home
By Lillian Baynes Griffin

"When Johann Most [bottom] made the gallant gesture of presenting Emma Goldman [top right] with a large bouquet of violets, Sasha [Alexander Berkman, top left] exclaimed, 'Violets at the height of winter with thousands out of work and hungry?'"

photos courtesy YIVO

Solomon Schechter: "When the *Yahudim* sought a bearded East European Talmudic scholar, they didn't seek him in a Vilna yeshiva but at Cambridge University."

Isaac Mayer Wise: "A cigar in his mouth, a cane in his hand, he had an opinion on everything."

photos courtesy American Jewish Historical Society

Summer boarders, c. 1910: "To keep Russian Jewish boarders happy meant working to near hysteria. The owners of a farm dreaded the chill mornings when their first greeting might be, *'Nu,* I see it's raining... again.'"

photo courtesy Jennie Finkel

American Jewish Historical Society

The Woodbine community: "Its streets are clean, there are no saloons, no disorderly characters and no sweat shops. Reporters observed the town had neither a jail nor a house of prostitution."

A Woodbine family one year after their arrival: "Native Americans from surrounding villages observed curiously the singular behavior of these newcomers."

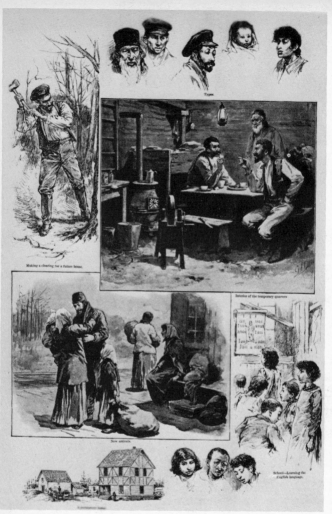

A page from *Leslie's Weekly* illustrating facets of rural Jewish immigrant life: "Writing about Woodbine, Jacob Riis rhapsodized, 'The cattle were lowing in the fields. The evening breathed peace. Down the sandy road came a creaking farm wagon and beside it walked a sunburned, bearded man with an axe on his shoulder.'"

Abraham Cahan: "His unique blend of socialism, pragmatism and *Yiddishkayt* led Jewish immigrants into twentieth-century America."

Judah L. Magnes: "By 1906 he had become the only idol American Jews had provided for young Russian immigrants."

photos courtesy American Jewish Historical Society

Shirtwaist Strike Gets Under Way

—*The World*

*Top, members of the strike committee; right, Clara Lemlich,
a strike leader; left, scene outside of Clinton Hall.*

courtesy ILGWU News-History

The Shirtwaist Strike, 1909: "By drawing a girl dressed
in a shirtwaist, Charles Dana Gibson created a generation's most popular fashion. But he also created real-life
'Gibson girls' like Clara Lemlich and 15,000 others who
worked fifty-six hours a week for as little as three dollars."

peddling or trading," he wrote to the paper, "or some other similar work, which they can easily obtain about cities and support themselves without trouble as they can live on a very small income and according to their own usage."

Nevertheless, rich men, men with rich relatives, rabbis with rich congregants, organization *kochleffls*, scholarly men who needed the vicarious experience of an outdoor life, men with social conscience, men who had never cleaned out a chicken house or been anchormen at the top of haylofts where the temperature was 108°—and who could therefore visualize the sheer poetry of rural life—were united in the belief that there was no better way to destroy the ignoble stereotype of the Jew as a peddler and petty tradesman than to make him a man of the soil.

This romantic concept of farm labor, however, was undergoing painful reexamination. "The Man with the Hoe," painted by Jean Français Millet, a French farmer's son, and first exhibited in 1863, created a storm of controversy over its "socialistic" implications. Reproduced in *Scribner's Magazine* some twenty years later, it was seen by Edwin Markham, a California schoolteacher. When he later saw the original painting in San Francisco, he became obsessed with "the slow but awful degradation of man through endless, hopeless and joyless labor." Markham's poem "The Man with the Hoe" caused even more uproar than the painting; it became the subject of conversation, debates, lectures, and sermons. Even the press "gave as much space to The Man with the Hoe as to prize fights and police stories."

> Bowed by the weight of the centuries he leans
> Upon his hoe and gazes on the ground,
> The emptiness of ages in his face,
> And on his back the burden of the world. . . .

Yet Millet's friend and biographer Alfred Sensier maintained that Millet hadn't intended to make so stark a commentary: "The forehead may recede, but the skeleton shows power and the limbs are well balanced and well proportioned. This being might labour contentedly for sixty years, for his instinct is to cultivate the ground and clear and fertilize all barren tracts."

And others, too, could look at the Millet canvas and see an entirely different vision from the one expressed by Markham: the salubrious open space in which the figure stands; an individual not hemmed in by ghetto life, one who has time to pause and reflect; a man leaning on his hoe—his support rather than his master. For them he would appear a symbol of patience, endurance, and stability.

And the Man with the Hoe, after all, could be Jewish, too!

16

A Plague of Failures

This hope that the stereotype of the Jew could be erased by his becoming a farmer was realized, but not, perhaps, in the way expected, desired or even recognized. For Jews, who have been accorded a reputation down through the ages for shrewd business dealings, devilishly acute insights, and inveterate—and offensive—achievements, revealed in their dozens of attempts at farm colonization instances—in the case of American Jewish leaders—of such poor judgment, such lack of shrewdness, and, in the case of colonists, such naïveté, improvidence, and an overwhelming propensity for *shlimazl-kayt*, as to make even the most ardent bigot lose faith in stereotypes.

If Jews were so accurate in their judgments, so artful in their dealings, how then could the committee of the Hebrew Emigrant Aid Society, among whose members were Judge Meyer S. Isaacs, Jacob Seligman, Frederic Nathan, Emil L. Boas, and Jacob H. Schiff, have so gravely miscalculated the possibilities of Sicily Island, the first Russian Jewish farm colony in the United States? Perhaps Sicily Island was chosen with the same kind of shaky deductive reasoning displayed by Charles Nathan, a locating agent for the Alliance committee. The climate in Calcasieu Parish in southwestern Louisiana, Mr. Nathan reported to the committee, was excellent "of which there is evidence in the bright appearance of the existing small population and the absence of Doctors. . . ." The 2,800 acres on Sicily Island, Catahoula Parish, Louisiana—"three hundred and fifty miles from New Orleans and seventy-five from Natchez, Mississippi. It can be reached by way of the Mississippi and Ouachita rivers"—was reported by the committee to have rich land, "not subject to overflow." In the spring of 1882, however, the Mississippi overflowed, ruining crops, tools, drowning livestock, inundating houses. "Catahoula," the report continued, "is regarded as healthy." Healthy? By whom was it so regarded? Well, possibly by the thick swarms of mosquitoes that fed voraciously off the colonists, who in turn suffered a severe malaria epidemic. Herman Rosenthal, the thirty-eight-year-old scholar and leader of the Am Olam group sent to Sicily Island, had wanted to go to Kansas or another western state, but the committee "wished to send us to Louisiana only." He wrote bitterly: "They called it a 'Paradise,' but we found nothing thereunto pertaining save some poisonous serpents, much however of Hell. A viler spot on God's Earth it would be hard to find and there our unfortunate, much tried co-religionists were to learn a love for agriculture." Many colonists simply walked away—to the closest city, where they could find factory work or a peddler's warehouse in which to be outfitted with a pack.

In late 1882 another group was dispatched to a dense forest in eastern Arkansas, where farming was utterly impossible. However, a lumber company offered to buy staves at a $20 a thousand rate, and there was an infinite number of trees. During the summer of 1883 the heat hovered fitfully between 105° and 108°. Snakes were ubiquitous. Torrential rainstorms followed one another, accompanied by lightning which struck trees and narrowly missed colonists. By early fall they had encountered mosquitoes, malaria, yellow fever, and floods. And the Arkansas colony went the way of Sicily Island . . . as did the eighteen colonies in North Dakota.

Cremieux in South Dakota—named for Adolphe Crémieux, founder of the Alliance Israelite Universelle—started out festively, with what in Yiddddish would be called *tam*—flavor. Its first members, the Greenbergs and the Samuelwitzes, arrived in Mitchell, South Dakota, and—precisely in the middle of the town's main street and under the astonished gaze of the one thousand citizens—brewed and drank Russian tea. Located twenty miles from Mitchell on a deserted Indian reservation, Cremieux was one of the few colonies that had dark, rich soil. But it ended, a victim of high mortgage interest, low market prices, and—"a reckless orgy of extravagant buying." For any reasonable observer, this should have expunged the stereotype of the sharp calculating Jewish businessman. Gingerbread lumber, highbred horses at $800 a team, and the first grand piano in prairie country! The subsequent realization that they had neglected to provide shelter and a water supply for the livestock made it necessary to have expensive—and inadequate—wells dug. Natural disasters weren't lacking either. A prairie fire which occurred *erev* Yom Kippur, as though it were God's considered judgment after the ten days of penitence, burned all their hay. A water shortage occurred the first year; the second year, a hailstorm wiped out their flax crop and the Hessian fly destroyed the wheat; the third drought burned out their crops and killed their cattle. True, the Almighty had visited plagues upon the Egyptians, but they were Egyptians. By 1889 Cremieux had been abandoned.

There was a pathetic sameness to the fate of most of the colonies in the West and Southwest. In a pair of them, however, unusual elements were involved. New Odessa, Oregon, was started by dedicated young intellectuals and Cotopaxi, Colorado, by a Jew unprincipled enough to please any but the most demanding anti-Semites.

A farm colony composed almost exclusively of young, militantly idealistic, cerebral Russian Jews who were determined to show "the world that Jews 'the Eternal People' can also have agricultural workers!" was a lofty but somber proposition. The satisfactions gained in arguing with one another every step of the way lightened their burden, but not their mood. In Douglas County, Oregon, twenty-five such young men and women solemnly vowed to live a communal life with both labor and earnings shared. For $4,800, they purchased 760 acres—600 of which were forest; the remainder, well-irrigated soil ready for cultivation and through which ran the Umpqua River, as thick with fish as a barrel with herring. They called the colony New Odessa. Before long, two dozen more Am Olamites joined them, and soon after that they raised a two-story frame building, with sleeping arrangements above and a kitchen, dining, and assembly hall below, where they gathered every night to debate passionately the philosophy of positivism, the ideology of communism, and the efficacy of vegetarianism.

According to one of the colonists, their week's activities went like this:

We work from six to 8:30 in the morning. From 8:30 to 9:45 we have our breakfast. Then, from ten to four in the afternoon there is again physical work. We have dinner from four to five, then rest, study, etc. Mondays, Tuesdays, Thursdays and Fridays, we have lessons in mathematics and English and Frey's lectures on positivist philosophy. On Wednesdays there are meetings on current events, and on Saturday questions on the inner life of the commune are taken up.

Sundays we are up at six and immediately there is noise and lively discussions. This week the woman question was taken up. At first the women demanded complete emancipation; they started working in the woods and the men had to take their place in the kitchen and in the laundry according to turn. However, the women were soon convinced that they were not as yet fit to work in the woods and they went back to their former places. Now they maintain they are much stronger. We spend our time in such discussions until breakfast. We all sit around the table and each receives rice, grits, cooked and raw apples, beans, potatoes, milk and bread. (We lead a vegetarian life.) . . . After dinner two men wash the dishes. The choir sings and the organ plays. . . . Seven o'clock begins the mutual criticism. Afterwards the chores for the entire week are distributed and the evening is finished.

The leader of the vegetarian positivists in New Odessa was William Frey; his followers weren't so much carried away by positivism as they were by him. "He was so friendly, so tolerant, so saintly, so respected, so well educated . . . besides he was a gentile and an aristocrat." In fact, he had been a Russian aristocrat and an army officer. A slim dark-haired man of medium height, with a soft full beard, Frey, as an idealistic communist, viewed both the revolutionary movement and the struggle to improve labor conditions as sinful. As a dedicated *Positivistik* he exalted humanity "as the object of worship to the throne of God." To ruin one's health destroyed an atom "of the great being humanity"; consequently, he chewed and swallowed his food in a prescribed way. Indeed, everything he did was "a holy undertaking; a mitsveh." But another group of colonists thought many of his views, particularly his opposition to the class struggle, were childish. And New Odessa's assembly hall rang with dissension between them and Frey and his followers.

But the problems of New Odessa went beyond mere "intellectual bickerings." Although the young colonists spoke of the glories of the rural life, of the spiritual elevation derived from a simple hardworking life, nevertheless such a life lacked intellectual stimulation. Then, too, there were problems of a more personal nature. Ostensibly, all the space in the commune belonged to all the colonists, though the few married couples among them were allotted a separate room each. However, if a couple wished to retire to their room for an hour or two, there was nothing to keep another colonist from marching in, book in hand, and settling down for a good read. Should they suggest he go elsewhere, he could proclaim his equal right to the room and refuse to leave on the grounds that it would "violate his sacred communist feelings and principles." Sex, in fact, created awesome difficulties in New Odessa. *"Es ungegungen freie liebe"* (There was free love).

Some years later, Prince Peter Kropotkin, the philosophical anarchist, and Emma Goldman argued heatedly about the place of "the sex problem in anarchist propaganda." Kropotkin believed more could be accomplished if less space was wasted "discussing sex." Finally, after agitated exchanges, Emma—twenty-seven years Kropotkin's junior—exclaimed, "All right, dear comrade, when I have reached your age, the sex question may no longer be of importance to me. But it is *now*, and it is a tremendous factor for thousands, millions even, of young people."

Kropotkin thought that over and then beamed at Emma. "Fancy," he said, "I didn't think of that. Perhaps you are right."

It was true, of course, that many factors contributed to the abandonment of New Odessa: Controversies raged over the merits of positivism, communism, socialism, anarchism and vegetarianism, raged so furiously that, after two years of verbal battle, Frey and his followers left. The remaining colonists carried on savage debates over the class struggle. This theorizing led, quite naturally, to smoldering, bitter resentments over who was actually working hardest. Then a fire razed their prize library. Devastating blow though this was, it lacked the incessant, aggravating power of yet another condition in the colony that illustrated the validity of Emma Goldman's thesis. It was a situation involving simple mathematics—there were thirty-two single men to three single women, there were simply too few girls. As Abe Cahan sagely observed, the *"maidlach es gevehn tsu wenig."*

Emanual H. Saltiel was a South African Sephardic Jew, the owner of a productive silver mine, the manufacturer of concrete building material, the president of the Cotopaxi Town Committee, and, apparently, a first-rate con man. In early 1882 he appeared before the HEAS committee in New York and spoke glibly and persuasively about vast acreage of fertile ranchland in Colorado's West Mountain Valley, highly suitable, he said, for a Russian Jewish farm colony. Impressed, the committee gave him $10,000 to spend on houses, furnishings, farm equipment, and livestock.

But the committee had no inkling of Saltiel's real motivation, in which compassion for the immigrants played no part. Leadville, to the north of Cotopaxi, was in the midst of its heyday. Miners flocked to Silver Dollar Tabor's* Matchless Mine and lesser mines, making it one of the greatest silver camps in the world. Consequently, Saltiel found it impossible to persuade miners to work in his Cotopaxi Placer Mine, for the much lower wages he offered; so he hit on the idea of procuring cheap immigrant labor. Realizing that the HEAS committee would hardly fall in with this plan, he had to get the immigrants out to Colorado for an ostensibly valid purpose. So a group of thirteen Hassidic families, originally slated for Oregon, had their destination shifted. On May 3, 1882, they left New York by rail for Colorado, where they arrived five days later.

Saltiel spoke no Yiddish, and the immigrants no English; but communication was unnecessary for the immigrants to realize immediately that they'd been deceived. Instead of the lush valley ranchland—160 acres for each family—that Saltiel had described so glowingly to the committee, he led them to arid strips of land, about eight miles from Cotopaxi, and a scattering of twelve barely furnished hovels. Other similar sites—most impossible to irrigate—were pointed out as their prospective farms. "It was the poorest place in the world for

---

* Leadville had a large Jewish population for its size, to whom H. A. W. Tabor had given a number of lots for Reform and Orthodox synagogues. In conjectural explanation of Tabor's generosity to Leadville Jews there was the legend that his great love, Baby Doe, had been first brought to Leadville by Jacob Sand, a Jewish miner.

farming," one of the colonists recalled many years later, "poor land, lots of rocks, and no water, and the few crops we were able to raise were mostly eaten by cattle belonging to neighboring settlers." Even the crops they did reap were pitiful—from fourteen bags of seed potatoes planted, they harvested fifteen bags of potatoes inferior to the seed.

Winter would have been intolerable had they any alternative. With no crops to carry them through, their houses hardly able to keep out the bitter cold, with no medical aid at hand, and appeals to Saltiel completely ignored, even their Hassidic singing-dancing joy in God and worship provided feeble solace.

With the approach of Passover, came the problem of how to provide matzo. As yet unaware of the existence of Denver, 192 miles northeast of Cotopaxi, several colonists went to a town nearby—Salida—and in a flour store, chose every tenth sack as specified by Orthodox law. Finally, word of their plight reached the Jews in Denver, and money and supplies were sent from Denver's Jewish community, where Saltiel's reputation was low. Clearly, the Jews in Cotopaxi had to find a more reliable source of livelihood than farming, and the only thing available—by an odd coincidence—was to descend into Saltiel's silver mine with pick and shovel. So every morning at dawn, *yarmulkes* perched on their heads, they set off for ten hours in the silver mines, for which their benefactor paid them in vouchers to be redeemed at the general store—$1.50 on the day shift; $2.50 on the night. But even these wages failed to satisfy Saltiel's ambition for cheap labor. Therefore, before long, he ceased paying the immigrants altogether, and they found work digging trenches and sawing logs for the Denver & Rio Grande Southern Railroad, which gave them the Sabbath off, an indulgence possibly granted them by the president of the Denver & Rio Grande Southern Railroad: Otto Mears, Civil War veteran, Indian *aficionado*, road and railroad builder, Republican politician, and a Russian Jew who spoke the Ute language with a Yiddish accent (*Landsleit* crop up in the unlikeliest places).

Meanwhile, HEAS had received a report of the harrowing conditions at Cotopaxi—"We do not exaggerate when we say that a beast could not subsist on these lands"—and arranged for the colonists to leave for any destination they desired. So, like the colonists of New Odessa, they moved on. Some went to Salt Lake City, some to California, some to South Dakota.

Many settled in Denver, on the Platte River's west bank, to form the nucleus of the Colfax community, which by 1904 had grown to 400 families.

Atwood, a Russian Jewish farm colony in the northeastern part of Colorado, endured a similar fate. Atwood's brief existence—barely five years—was notable only for having been the birthplace of theatrical producer Herman Shumlin, whose parents met and married there.

When there's so much wickedness abroad to wreck an undertaking, it seems totally unnecessary—even inappropriate—for the same job to be done by charity. But there it is, or, at least, there it was, in the Beersheba colony in Kansas.

With rare exceptions, American Jews felt themselves superior to Russian Jewish immigrants in social class, worldliness, refinement, experience, and means. Therefore, though Russian Jews might ask in vexation—and in Yiddish—"where is it written?" *("Vu shteyt es geshribn?")* that *Yahudim* should lead and *Yiden* obey, it often happened that way. On occasion, too, immigrants found paternalism a snug secure arrangement. But generally, the relationship between the colonists and the American Jewish organizations that sponsored them exemplified the blighting effects of overprotection.

Not all the Russian Jewish farm colonies were financially supported by HEAS or, following its demise, by the Montefiore Agricultural Aid Society. The Jewish communities of many cities in the West and Midwest acted as big brother to individual colonies: St. Paul supported the Painted Woods colony; Minneapolis, Devils Lake. Both these colonies were in North Dakota. In Cincinnati, Dr. Isaac Mayer Wise thumped the drum constantly and vigorously *("Ho, for Kansas!")* in the *American Israelite,* urging the establishment and support of agricultural colonies—"It will solve the problem what to do with the Russian Jewish immigrants and be an honor to them and to us." And he set up an organization, the Hebrew Union Agricultural Society, which, together with Cincinnati's Russian Emigrant Aid Society, assumed support of the first "colony of Russian Jews on government land," claimed according to the Homestead Act of 1862. "Reader," Dr. Wise implored in the *Israelite,* "do not stand aloof from the great movement of promoting agricultural pursuits among the Israelites, which will help to suppress prejudice and persecutions among the Hebrews."

In mid-1882, while the Hassidim in Cotopaxi were beginning the struggle with their environment, two young Cincinnati Jews, Charles K. Davis and Leo Wise—eldest son of the doctor and his eventual successor as editor of the *American Israelite*—set out from Cincinnati in charge of "sixty souls in all of men, women and children," on the Big Four & Vandalia Line for St. Louis. They changed to the Chicago & Alton for Kansas City, from which point they expected to lead their group to a site to be called the Beersheba colony, located in southwestern Kansas, on the Pawnee River, twenty-two miles from the Atchison, Topeka & Santa Fe Railroad.

In the two weeks of the journey, a pattern of leader and followers, guardian and wards was established. Under the most auspicious circumstances this relationship would have been difficult to sustain in total harmony. As it happened, the circumstances included those familiar elements of western fiction: the machinations of railroads and the feud between farmers and cattlemen.

Davis and Wise, twenty-nine and thirty-three respectively, were earnest and upright, with a very strong feeling of responsibility for their charges. They also possessed an immense sensitivity to the impression the immigrants might make on anyone—even on the Atchison, Topeka & Santa Fe Railroad, which had acquired the notion "that these Russian refugees are a lot of beggars and paupers whom the Relief Committee of Cincinnati are trying to get rid of . . . and don't want the people located on their road. . . ." (How infinitely fastidious, the Atchison, Topeka & Santa Fe Railroad! Not many railroads fretted about the social position of those living along its tracks.)

It seemed that everywhere they went in Kansas City, they heard "very unfavorable opinions of the land selected for agricultural purposes." Cowboys who hung around the stockyards and the depot expressed serious misgivings concerning Beersheba's location, even declaring "the people would starve there." In desperation, Davis and Wise counteracted such gloomy predictions with statistical data that revealed an increase of rainfall for the Cimarron area—twenty-six miles from Beersheba. Nevertheless they decided it might be prudent for them to go ahead and investigate before they proceeded further.

Left in Kansas City and in charge, young Davis kept a vigilant eye on the immigrants. "This morning," he noted in his journal, "as I usually do every morning and evening, [I] went to the rooms of the different people and made them clean up.

This is a regular thing twice a day, as I don't want the land-lords to make any remarks about their habits."

No one was more conscious of the anomaly of the paternal-istic situation than Davis. He reported: "Today, Chole Ge-danski's wife complained of her breasts aching and I sent Lie-berson's wife to attend her, and she reported to me that it was nothing serious. They come to me each one with his or her troubles and in this act like a lot of children, and at such times I feel as though the responsibility was too great for a young man." Even more awkward than appeals for diagnosis of women's disorders were difficulties with six troublemakers, Skwerski, Roseman, Braselawski, Sasewitz, Boxer, and Suss-man—"the two latter are developing into first-class rascals"—for they stole wine, liquor, and cans of sardines from supplies. A gravely worried Davis wrote, "I want to hide their conduct from the people of Kansas City, especially the Gentiles, who have never seen Russians before, because I don't want them to form a poor opinion of our people. . . ."

Keeping the immigrants in line occupied Davis for about a week in Kansas City. Then he received a report from Leo Wise in Cimarron, refuting all the bad reports they'd heard concerning the land; immediately Davis saw to it that his charges were packed and at the depot to make the 400-mile trip. Arrangements had been made with the Atchison, Topeka & Santa Fe to have a special car on the express train for the immigrants' use. Inexplicably, however, the Kansas City agent for the railroad line declared he had been ordered to put the immigrants on an emigrant train "which is nothing more or less than a freight traveling from 9 to 12 miles per hour," even though they held express tickets.

When Davis was met by Leo Wise, he learned the reasons behind the railroad's attitude—why it "discouraged emigra-tion to this section and also spread bad reports broadcast to the effect that it is only a sandy desert." Davis noted:

In the first place these western counties are new, have no settlers and also are not organized, and as long as a county is not organized the R.R. pays no taxes on its lands, and they own, for twenty miles on either side of the road, every alternate section. It is to their interest then, to keep the emigration East where the counties are organized and they are paying taxes. . . . Secondly, it is to protect the interests of stock men. Cattle are run up in droves of from one to ten thousand (or even more) head from Texas and elsewhere and are run up what is called the trail. . . . These cattle graze on all lands they travel over and spread out for great distances, and wherever a farmer settles in this county, it, of course, takes away so much free grazing ground, and furthermore, the owners of herds are responsible for all damages that they may do any farmer, and as people don't have fences out here, it is no easy job to keep the cattle from running over and destroying crops. . . .

There was also the additional danger of domestic cattle being infected with Texas fever by the Texas herds, whose owners would be liable. For this reason, "both the stock men in this section and elsewhere, and also the cowboys who drive the wild cattle over this trail, oppose and discourage emigration.* Every settler narrows the trail, and finally they dare drive no cattle through the country, and consequently they have to ship their cattle from a point farther west, which causes greater expense."

Of course, these external conditions applied to any new settlers. What young Charles Davis also had to deal with were difficulties "which I had never thought of" (though he probably should have). On Saturday morning when he took ten of the immigrants (a minyan) up to the United States Land Office to be sworn in and have their entries listed for government land, the Orthodox immigrants refused to sign because it was *Shabbas*. Indeed, Edelhertz, the shochet, declared he "would rather not have the land than compromise his conscience." At eight that evening with *Shabbas* over and Edelhertz's conscience intact, the Land Register swore in Edelhertz.

Although the railroads and cattlemen were hostile—the Atchison, Topeka & Santa Fe had unaccountably mislaid a carload of household goods, and $200 had been offered by a cattleman to anyone able to "exert enough influence" to discourage the immigrants from settling—the farmers around the colony eagerly showered help on their new neighbors. "They would show us everything and lend us all the aid in their power, because they said our coming would drive the stock men off this trail and make them go to the state line. . . ."

All kinds of problems beset Davis, the twenty-nine-year-old

* Some years later, the casually bred cattle of the colonists of Kiowa, a Colorado Jewish settlement, were killed off by neighboring owners of purebred cattle, who feared their herds would find the grass greener in Kiowa and breed out of their class.

patriarch, from the missing household goods about which he sent wire after wire to Cincinnati, receiving only unsatisfactory answers, to the colonists' childlike delight with a newly purchased Buckeye mower. ("They acted like a lot of children [and] had to be cautioned many times to be careful or they might lose their fingers or get cut in some way.") Despite the aggravation and weight of responsibility, it's comforting to know that Davis too could indulge in "childlike delight." Emulating the style of the cowboys he admired—"men of nerve and daring and will be crossed by no one"—young Davis sallied forth in the pants of an old blue suit, blue flannel shirt, a broad-brimmed straw hat, and a five-day-old beard, but sans his "shoot iron." ("I'm afraid they might criticize it, as it is only a 38 calibre, while a 44 is regulation out here.") And before he returned to Cincinnati, Davis had seen the fleshpots of Dodge City, "sights . . . that would shock the nerves of many timid persons from the East. . . ." In that city's numerous saloons, he recorded disapprovingly, cowboys were sometimes "regaled with a vile song by an abandoned woman."

Intensely as the immigrants wished Beersheba to succeed, their zeal was exceeded by that of their sponsors, the Hebrew Union Agricultural Society and particularly Dr. Wise, who made constant appeals for money in the *Israelite*. "Go at once," he instructed his readers, ". . . collect as much as you can of either Jew or Gentile . . . no words, no advices, no ifs and no whens are wanted."

Thus benefactors provided the Beersheba colonists with everything they needed—"wagons, horses, steers, harnesses, cows, sheep, poultry, agricultural and mechanical implements, dairy vessels, provisions, tents, cots, lanterns, lamps"—everything but a clear explanation that these supplies had not been given to them, but merely lent. However, the colonists received one permanent addition, a superintendent, Joseph Baum, "said to be an excellent practical farmer." Baum had been given the somewhat ominous authority to withhold "provisions and the benefits of the implements and cattle" from any transgressing colonist. Nevertheless, Rabbi Wise reported approvingly at the beginning of 1883 that the colonists obeyed Baum "as soldiers, they were at first unruly, but now are tractable and docile. . . ."

One year after the establishment of the Beersheba colony, two citizens of Cincinnati—M. H. Marks, the secretary of

HUAS, and Max Isaacs—journeyed to Kansas for the society, to investigate the progress of "our poor Jewish brethren." The buoyant optimism displayed in Marks' report boded well. Eleven families, he wrote, fifty-nine people—twenty-three adults and thirty-six children—lived in excellent health in an area of six miles. Each family dwelled on their own 160 acres, in a whitewashed dugout, to which kitchens and other improvements were being added, "some even making attempts to decorate the interior with bric-a-brac and such fixings as only ladies know the names of—I don't." Overall 350 acres had been plowed, 200 planted in sorghum. They had five yoke of oxen, a team of mules, a team of horses, twenty-three cows, twenty-two calves "and no end of chickens," and on the Sabbath "no labor was performed by man or beast." They owned six plows, five wagons, a set of blacksmith's tools, and harvesting machinery. Though wood was scarce and coal prohibitively expensive, winter fuel was provided by a plethora of what Mr. Marks delicately referred to as "piles of cattle refuse obtained from the great Texas cattle trail close by."

And the Marks report concluded with a fanfare of trumpets:

> but the great question in which we all take such a lively interest—"Can Jews become successful farmers?"—is virtually solved by Beersheba Colony, and that Jews, as well as our Gentile friends, can become successful tillers of the soil, and that the Jewish race can become again that which, according to tradition they have been before, an agricultural people, is established beyond any reasonable doubt.

This compulsion for issuing determinedly bright reports, of declaring victory in the face of defeat ("I pronounce the agricultural colony in the Rocky Mountains a full and complete success," declared the superintendent of the Cotopaxi colony in October, 1882, "and the question whether Jews are fit to become farmers solved and answered in the affirmative"), of proclaiming the campaign to develop Jewish farmers an unmitigated success, stemmed from vital wishful thinking. Otherwise, the dream of the Jewish Man with the Hoe would grow dimmer and more remote and even might fade away entirely.

But in early 1884, shocking news rudely aroused the sponsors of Beersheba from the lulling spell cast by enthusiastic reports. The Beersheba colonists had, independently and without informing HUAS, leased part of their farm property to a cattle syndicate that planned to widen cattle trails. What had happened to Dr. Wise's "tractable and docile" immigrants? Retribution from Cincinnati came swiftly: "Received of Moses Edelhertz property belonging to the Hebrew Union Agricultural Society, J. Baum Agent . . . one pair of oxen, two cows, one calf, one wagon, one yoke, one chain, one well bucket and rope, one shovel, churn, twelve milk pails, two milk buckets, hatchet, wheel barrow, one pr. boots, one straw hat, one bale of wire. . . ."

Rabbi Wise had declared that the colonists obeyed Baum "like soldiers." Now, in their insubordination, seven other colonists who, like Edelhertz, the shochet, had leased their property not only were stripped of their tools, but—instead of having stripes ripped from their sleeves—had that eternal symbol of farm life, the straw hat, snatched off their heads.

However, one Jew in Cincinnati protested. "The matter was entirely misrepresented," Charles K. Davis, the Beersheba colonists' erstwhile shepherd, wrote angrily:

> The transaction was legitimate and had the full sanction of the neighbors. Before the contract was entered into, a meeting of the neighbors was held and a resolution passed consenting to the transaction. This arrangement leaves them as much land as they can possibly cultivate and gives them the means to fence it around and replace stock and implements taken from them and sold by order of the Cincinnati Committee.
>
> Under the contract, made for one year with the privilege for five, eight families received $200 per year, a living in itself. There was no feeling against the Beersheba colony, nor is there any now. If there is any indignation, it is against Baum who induced the Committee to take back the stock, implements, etc., etc., that had been advanced to the colonists, and for his over-zealousness in carrying out instructions.

Despite Davis' arguments, the paternalistic gentlemen of HUAS viewed the colonists' action not as an independent venture or even a mutinous one; but as disobedience. And like disobedient children, they had to be punished. "The colonists reduced thereby to abject poverty scattered to surrounding towns and engaged in odd jobs to eke out a living. . . ." Beersheba lasted barely one more year. By 1885 it had been deserted, many of its inhabitants eventually settling in Kansas and Missouri.

Another factor entered into the collapse of many of the colonies, including Beersheba, one that had nothing to do with barren land, unremitting, backbreaking work, natural disasters, punitive blows from benefactors, or even, as in New Odessa, sex. They simply could not bear the impossibility of visiting relatives—an uncle, a cousin, *machetayneste*—and conversing over a *glezele* tea. To be isolated in small groups out on the Kansas plains, in a forest in Arkansas, or a swamp in Louisiana, away from the rich, soul-nourishing centers of Jewish life, lowered their spirits, sapped their vitality. This, in part, explains why so many Russian Jewish farm colonies "dragged out a short unhappy existence and finally failed utterly." All, that is, except the colonies in New Jersey.

17

Triumph in New Jersey

Perhaps success, like beauty, is in the eye of the beholder, or perhaps defining success, like defining one's faith, is a matter of semantics—after all, according to Mormons, Jews are gentiles. Simply, the Alliance colony was a success because it survived! And because it survived, Alliance and its sister colonies in New Jersey held aloft at least a tattered fragment of the agricultural mystique.

In 1882, a Vineland, New Jersey, lumber firm, known locally as Leach Brothers (though its letterhead read Leach & Brother, marking a small, but no doubt significant distinction between Geo. W. and W. W. Leach), owned well over 1,000 acres a few miles southwest of town, overgrown with scrub pine and third-growth black and white oak. This property was a wedge-shaped piece of Salem County that cut into Cumberland County, in which Vineland was located. And when two bearded visitors arrived in Vineland, on a mission to select a site for a Russian Jewish farm colony to be established under the combined auspices of the Hebrew Emigrant Aid Society and the Alliance Israelite Universelle, they were shown this land.

Vineland had been founded some twenty years earlier by Charles K. Landis, a Philadelphia lawyer and real estate promoter. He designed it as an industrial town, to be run by a Yankee oligarchy and fed by European peasant immigrants who would farm the land in its environs. Since grapes grew abundantly, Landis envisioned a vineyard center complete with a good-humored, dancing, purple-footed peasantry. To give substance to this picture, Landis dispatched alluring descriptions of Vineland to Italy to lure Italian vineyard workers. With the help of an Italian political refugee, Secchi de Casale, publisher of the first Italian-language newspaper in New York City, many Italians were induced to come, settling in an enclave in East Vineland. There the first Italian agricultural colony in the United States was founded in 1878. Though the Italians were hard workers and produced wine from the vineyards by 1881, and though Charles E. Welch, a Philadelphia dentist, opened a grape juice cannery, providing a ready market for the Ives Seedling variety of grape, supposedly best suited to withstand rot and phylloxera, Vineland's vineyards never approached Landis' ambitions for them. Soon the Italian farmers were turning their pertinacity and green thumbs to sweet potatoes.

But South Jersey needed immigrant laborers and farmers, so the New Jersey Bureau of Statistics, revealing an unusual flair, sent off flyers to Southern and Eastern Europe, where peasants of the kind required were presumed to dwell. These flyers extolled the climate of South Jersey as being "like the south of France or the shores of the Mediterranean."

When Moses Bayuk and Eli Stavitsky came to look at the Leach property, Vineland was a small, not particularly prosperous community, whose claim to distinction lay in its carefully planned layout. It appeared a monument to regularity—a mile square, with streets that crossed at right angles off its magnificently wide main thoroughfare, Landis Avenue, and that were lined by trees planted at regular intervals. To Bayuk and Stavitsky, who had come to Vineland from densely packed Castle Garden, the uncluttered prospect of Landis Avenue must have seemed refreshing. Nevertheless, if the climate of South Jersey resembled the Riviera's, its open flat terrain, with its sandy soil and scrub pines, looked dismayingly like the dismal vista of the Russian Pale.

Meanwhile, in Castle Garden forty-three families awaited the return of Bayuk and Stavitsky. They all were members of an Am Olam group from southern Russia, mostly from Odessa, Kiev, and Elizabetgrad, who had a fixed determination to "go to America to become tillers of the soil and thus shake off the accusation that we are merely petty mercenaries, living upon the toil of others." None had been farmers. They did not even know, as one of them later remarked, "if potatoes grew above or underground." They were artisans, peddlers, and *luftmenshn*—with a sprinkling of professional men. And Moses Bayuk, who would choose the site for the enactment of their dream, had impressive credentials. Directly descended from that extraordinary scholar of Lithuania Elijah ben Salomon, the renowned Vilna gaon, Bayuk excelled in Talmudic scholarship and mathematics. He had also been a successful lawyer in his native city of Bialystok.

But neither his lofty forebear nor his own intellectual and professional achievements prepared him to judge the light sandy soil of the Leach Brothers' property; he did not even try. Instead, he and Eli Stavitsky based their decision to buy the 1,050 acres on the fact that the Jersey Central Railroad ran through them. This was not, as it turned out, an unwise criterion. The availability of transportation would be necessary not only for marketing produce, but also in bringing relatives from Philadelphia and New York for visits; in bringing a few *pleasurenikis* to board for the summer; and in taking the colonists themselves to the cities, for occasional visits, perhaps even to see a performance of the Yiddish theater. The sight of that florid Prince Charming Boris Thomashevsky and his *zaftig* wife, Bessie (a farmer's daughter from a colony in Maryland that failed), declaiming in romantic melodrama would send them back to the sweet potato field and hen houses refreshed and invigorated.

Shortly after the Bayuk-Stavitsky decision, in early May, a Jersey Central immigrant train carrying the Am Olamite families stopped at Bradways, a flag station, and "dumped off" its passengers. Until houses were built, House Resolution No. 230 authorized the Secretary of War to lend 1,000 army tents "for the use of Russian Jewish refugees now without shelter at Vineland, New Jersey." (On the same day, Senate Resolution No. 80 was offered "for relief of certain sufferers by the overflow of the Mississippi River," including the Jewish colony at Sicily Island, Louisiana, but it was tabled.) By summer three barracks had been erected; their comforts can be gauged by their having been called Castle Garden by their occupants— or, as recalled by one of the children, "kessel godden."

The first night spent in the Vineland Castle Garden, everyone slept fully clothed, in a huge circle around the room, "so there would be no mix-ups between husbands and wives." These initial precautions must have established the virtuous tone of the colony, for no matter how suggestive its name, Alliance would have no illicit affairs, no brief encounters, no strange interludes. "It was a very moral neighborhood, without adultery or scandal," recalled journalist George Seldes, whose mother was the colony's postmistress; his Aunt Bertha, its midwife; and his grandmother, a keeper of "unfailing records" of the time elapsing between marriage ceremony and birth of first child. Carmel, on the other hand, one of the six other small Jewish farm communities that sprang up in the vicinity of Alliance, proved to be a hotbed of intellectuals. With masochistic zeal, they held concerts, lectures, debates, and Alliance *veiber* (wives) eyed certain Carmel "couples" with the dark suspicion that free love was being practiced—perhaps even perfected.

Life in the barracks, which had interior thin walls bounding an 8-by-14 cubicle for each family, lacked serenity; not even nostalgia could transform it into an experience for which one would yearn.

While the colonists endured these conditions, the *American Hebrew* concerned itself with the selection of a name for the colony. Upon reading Philip Cowen's choice—Washington—Emma Lazarus sent off a letter to him:

> Please *don't* publish this as coming from me, but I hope in the name of common-sense & in compassion for the United States postmasters, that not one more addition to the American villages or settlements of any kind, by the name of Washington will be made—Every state has already an indefinite number of them causing much confusion and unnecessary bewilderment. Why not, if a name must be found, elect that of some friend to the Jewish Cause or some distinguished Jew—such as Eliot, after George Eliot who had such a noble & Eloquent sympathy with us—Montefiore—a beautiful name in itself—or Mendelssohn, or Beaconsfield or Abarbanel. Anything rather than Washington, Lincoln, Jefferson or Garfield.

Cowen published her suggestions anonymously and added one of his own: Schiff, in honor of the foremost member of the HEAS committee. But the colony took its name from another sponsor, the Alliance Israelite Universelle, which had donated $3,000. Thus, Schiff and the other HEAS committee members had to be content with having Alliance streets named after them, while George Eliot and the Earl of Beaconsfield lost out altogether.

By the fall of that year, 1,150 acres were allocated: 150 acres as common property of the colony—for schools, shuls, cemetery, factories—the remainder for sixty-six farms of approximately 51 acres each. The farms were numbered, and each family drew a number, their farm, out of a hat. By grouping the farms in units of four, each set of four families could work cooperatively and share horses and farm implements. In one case, at least, this arrangement led to even more far-reaching teamwork. The Zagers, who had nine sons, lived across the road from the Opachinskys, who had nine daughters; this proximity accounted for three marriages.

The houses were built from the trees on the land, which the Leach Brothers cut down and milled into lumber. Each "shanty" was 12 by 14 feet and 14 feet high—one room and a garret—and "lined with one thin pine board and plastered inside, so that, along with other privations, the settlers suffered from cold in the winter and heat in the summer." Each family was supplied with a stove, necessary furniture, and utensils.

The financial details set up by HEAS—and, after its demise, by a special organization, the Alliance Land Trust—specified: According to each family's mortgage contract, $350 was to be paid in ten years—$150 for the house and well and $15 per acre for the land. Only the interest—3 percent a year—had to be taken care of during the first four years, but after that, the full amount was due in six equal annual payments. Throughout fall and winter, each family received a monthly allowance of $8 to $12, according to the family's size, and, in the spring of 1883, they were given $100 for tools, seed, plants, and implements.

Four small frame synagogues—all Orthodox—arose, and though the colonists weren't equally pious, most were observant. One Hassid among them who acted as the *shammes* would walk down the street with a kerosene lantern in his hand on the night of Selihot when penitential prayers were to be said before dawn, and exclaim loudly, *"Menshn, shtay uff tsu Selihot!"*

The Maurice River, which ran along the colony's shores, served as a *mikveh* for Alliance women, an activity that no doubt sent packing the legendary demon of South Jersey, the

Leeds Devil, reported to frighten horses, but to flee from women, leaving cloven hoof tracks in his wake.*

Though South Jersey's soil, which varied considerably from mile to mile, was superior to that of Cotopaxi, Sicily Island, and Beersheba, the Alliance colonists, nevertheless, had a protracted struggle to wrest a living from it. Alliance had a type of soil, known as Sassafras gravelly loam, which lent itself to sweet potatoes, grapes, and berries; Six Points, another Jewish outpost, had a sandy loam mixed with clay—New Jersey marl—which was best at producing white potatoes, corn, and clover. But before any planting could be done, a process known as stumping had to be undertaken.

After the Leach Brothers felled trees, stumps remained which cost from $18 to $30 to remove. It was a long process, and though HEAS sent a young German Jew to instruct the colonists, he was almost "as ignorant of New Jersey conditions as the colonists themselves." The field had to be burned over, plowed, and set out to blackberries and strawberries. If stump sprouts were kept cut, the stumps decayed and could be removed in about four years by a stump machine. In six years they could be plowed out. But in the interim, farmers planted amid the stumps, where, "to our dismay, the shoots sprouting from the stumps often outgrew the plants."

The original forty-three families had grown to sixty-seven and then to seventy-two. In order to survive those first unproductive years, they had to try other means of earning a livelihood. This accounted for the conversion of two Castle Garden barracks into a cigar factory, employing twenty-six, and a shirt factory that gave work to forty. Sidney Bailey and two fellow colonists, Israel Opachinsky and Sholem Luberoff, contracted with garment factories in New York and Philadelphia for piecework to be done in their homes on sewing machines

---

* According to state historians, the Leeds Devil originated in Estellville in the eighties—perhaps about the time that the 120 Russian Jews sent there by HEAS rioted, refused to remain, and were returned to Alliance—from a perverse wish of an apparently reluctantly pregnant Mrs. Leeds that the stork would bring her not a baby, but a devil. The stork obliged, almost assuredly causing Mrs. Leeds second thoughts. The Leeds Devil has been appealingly described as "cloven-hoofed, long-tailed, and white; with the head of a collie dog, the face of a horse, the body of a kangaroo, the wings of a bat, and the disposition of a lamb." And from all accounts, he spent his time in relatively harmless pastimes: frightening the fainthearted, avoiding women, and discussing Republican politics with a South Jersey judge over breakfast.

provided by Leonard Lewisohn, a New York philanthropist. "All the family would 'sweat' long hours and earned but little money. . . ." Many of the Jewish colonists also hired out to neighboring Gentile farmers, where they learned the hard practical rudiments of farming. But, eventually, they were down at the station—no longer a flag stop, but a full-fledged railroad station—shipping their berries to New York. Grapes were sold in Vineland to Welch's and, after Welch's left, to Allivine, a modern cannery, established by Maurice Fels of the Fels Naphtha soap fortune.

But as the years passed, the poetic quest for spiritual regeneration dissipated—"there wasn't a trace of utopian or any other kind of idealism in the community," wrote Gilbert Seldes—and left only the reality of unremitting hard work by both men and women. "I can well recall," wrote one of the colony's daughters (who became a doctor), "those prematurely old women, plodding along, day after day, through the hot summer, doing the work of man and beast. Clearly can I picture women like Mrs. Rothman, Mrs. Bakerman, Mrs. Helig and my mother wearing, in Old World fashion, a three cornered scarf over their heads, bending low to the ground, slowly following their husbands along the long rows of corn or sweet potatoes. . . ." At night they did accounts, drank tea, and read Yiddish newspapers and books which were among the first things Jewish farmers bought. In 1908, the first Yiddish farm journal, the *Jewish Farmer,* published by the Jewish Agricultural Society, quickly achieved authority among its subscribers. At one home, several farmers sat around a table where an old man read—*davened*—from the *Jewish Farmer,* "interpreting the text in true Talmudic fashion amidst running comment from his interested disciples."

But while colonists at Cotopaxi and Cremieux had worked hard, too, during the brief existence of their settlements, they did not have the spiritual sustenance made possible by easy communication with large Jewish communities. For the Alliance farm family, there were visits from city cousins in the summer and on Rosh Hashonah. They were able, too, to make trips to Rivington and Division streets in New York, or to South Street in Philadelphia, where they could sit and *schmooz.*

The survival of Alliance, its success, was also due in great part to the longevity of its colonists—many lived well into their eighties, still tending their truck farms, or at least gardens. Indeed, the life of the Alliance colony, precisely eighty-seven years, coincided with *their* life. It died in March, 1969, when ninety-four-year-old William Levin died, followed two weeks later by his eighty-four-year-old wife, Lena Bayuk Levin, daughter of Moses Bayuk, and one of the first children born in Alliance.

Alliance ended then, because no succeeding generation continued farming. Having never experienced the Am Olam dream, the sons and daughters of Alliance colonists saw agriculture as unrewarding labor. They turned to a variety of professions. There was one New Jersey Supreme Court justice, a few lower court judges, many eminent lawyers, a brace of doctors, some artists, and a Congressman. The Lubin brothers pioneered in the development of motion pictures—and, incidentally, at the peak of their fortunes, built their parents a house (architecturally Early *Balabatish*) in Alliance and provided them with a chauffeur-driven car. George and Gilbert Seldes became noted journalists and critics, and two of Moses Bayuk's sons went to Philadelphia and started the Bayuk Phillies Cigar Company. Even those who remained with farming worked in related areas. Dr. Arthur Goldhaft, a veterinarian, established the Vineland Poultry Laboratories and led in the research and curing of poultry diseases. (A veterinarian—his mother finally decided, after initial disappointment—"was the same as a doctor.")

For although relatively few children in South Jersey went to high school, Alliance parents saw to it that their children attended Vineland High School even if it meant extra tuition fees and transportation costs. Though the children worked hard on the farm, they were rarely kept home from school to work in the fields. And most went to college.

Thus, in Alliance, the "most successful" of Jewish agricultural colonies, the genuine Jewish tradition of education defeated a contrived Jewish tradition of agriculture.

18

Last Resort in the Catskills

Education didn't deliver the only blow to pure agriculture.

"Sullivan and Ulster Counties lie in the southeastern portion of the state of New York," a 1911 Immigration Commission report pointed out. "Along the line of the New York, Ontario and Western Railroad, traversing the two counties, numerous Russian Hebrews have settled in recent years and have engaged in farming and other pursuits." What were these unspecified, shady-sounding, "other pursuits"? Obliquely, the report was alluding to an occupation not held in high esteem by either Jewish philanthropists or most farmers—summer boarder agriculture. After all, to take in boarders reflected on the ability of Jews to engage in strenuous manual labor, to conquer the soil without the degrading necessity of taking up "nonproductive" trade again. This method of adding to his meager income was characterized as almost "a crime committed by the farmer . . ." and in Europe and America "there is not enough sarcasm to stigmatize these 'make-believe farmers' these farmers 'in name only.'" Undeniably, summer boarder agriculture defiled the mystique.

Jewish farmers, as individuals, had settled in Parksville, Summitville, Mountaindale, Hurleyville, Monticello, Ellenville, Ferndale, Fallsburgh, Greenfield, and Centerville. Several families came in 1899. (One—the Fleischers—arrived in

Fallsburgh and began taking in a few boarders; out of this beginning, the Flagler Hotel grew.) But 1904 saw the greatest influx. Many had arrived first as peddlers and, impressed with the beauty of the area and the *frisha luft* (fresh air), had transported their families from the Lower East Side. Others had come either in ill health or with an ailing wife or sickly children. Still others arrived who had used the country simply as a way out of the ghetto.

In 1909 the Jewish Agricultural and Industrial Aid Society reported 700 Jewish farmers in Sullivan and Ulster counties, but this number was felt to be misleading, for some were "boarding-house keepers who own a few acres of land, but who make no pretense of farming. . . ." Actually all 700, at one time or another, took in at least a few summer boarders. In defending summer boarder agriculture, A. L. Schalit of the Jewish Colonization Association told the directors of his organization:

The city Jew buys a farm. What is this farm? Poor soil fertility or run to grass owing to years without cultivation. What is this Jew who buys it? A man without experience or any sort of agricultural knowledge. This farmer buys his farm for, let us say, $3,000. He pays $800 down; the remaining $2,200 he will have to pay in six annual instalments with 5 or 6% interest. He has just $400–$500 to buy some wreck of a horse, a few second-hand farm implements and a cow or two. He takes possession in April; he must try to get his neglected property into shape. . . . He must prepare, or at least try to prepare something like a harvest, feed his cattle at any rate. The family does the best it can on as little as possible. But November is coming; the first "instalment" with the interest has to be paid, in all $500–$600. Where is he to get them? Even supposing the Jewish Agricultural and Industrial Aid Society has bought up half the mortgage; the farmer, especially the good farmer, will try to improve his property, and the Lord only knows how much he needs it! He will try to get more cows so as to ensure the support of the family through their dairy products; he will try to develop his poultry raising, but in order to do this he must have some buildings, however primitive, and several incubators; he will need a separator for the milk and feed for the cattle. Where can he get the money for all these things? The boarders whom he will take into the house very much against the grain usually, during the summer months, will provide the necessary funds . . . It must not be forgotten that the boarder also means a market right at home, and so much more profitable than the city market for milk, butter, eggs, poultry, vegetables, etc. that the farms produce.

"The Swiss peasants do the same thing," Mr. Schalit added, "and no one thinks of criticizing them."

Though some Catskill farmers eagerly accepted *boarder-kehs,* the circumstances that drove others to take them in had a last-resort aspect. With an employment background of factory or store work in the Lower East Side, few were physically capable of field labor under a hot sun. The immigration Commission reported:

> In many instances, crops failed, live stock died owing to ignorance and lack of proper attention, dairy and poultry products fell off greatly for the same reason, and very often the settler expended more money in producing a crop than it was worth in the market after being harvested. If it had not been for the revenue derived from summer boarders, it is scarcely probable that the Hebrews could have retained their farms, for the crops they raised were entirely inadequate to support their families.

In 1914, for example, Selig Grossinger, a former pants presser, in poor health, had with the aid of Harry Grossinger —who was both his nephew and his daughter Jenny's husband—bought a dilapidated farm in Ferndale for $450. They had come too late in the season for a harvest, and a cow they bought went dry, so the Grossingers decided to take in a few boarders to tide them over. "With cooking like yours," Grossinger told his wife, Malka, "we couldn't fail." And they didn't. However, only a few of those farmers who started out with ill health and a few dollars developed those pathetic assets into vast enterprises that encompassed swimming pools, golf links, an airport, and weekends for singles.

The implications in the criticism aimed at summer boarder agriculture were that it turned man from the poetry of the benign earth, that giving a garment worker and his family room and board for $9 a week was a premeditated evasion of hard work. But did the summer boarder ingredient make everything so easy . . . so *gliklich*?

To keep a dozen or two Russian Jewish boarders happy meant working to near hysteria. For one thing the observance of dietary laws entailed an enormous amount of care to see that not one dish infringed on another, that a *fleyshik leffl* (meat spoon) never touched a *milchik guppl* (dairy fork), or vice versa. It wasn't that they feared God would see—*He* would have compassion—but if a boarder saw, they'd never hear the end of it. While on vacation, a reasonable human being became a boarder, and a boarder demanded services and foods which far exceeded anything to which he was accustomed at home. Before long, privies were no longer good enough, and one farm after another began installing an indoor water supply and bathrooms. As for weather, the owners of the farm dreaded those raw chill mountain mornings when the first greeting from a boarder was a barbed meteorological observation: "Nu, Kaplowitz, I see it's raining—*again*." In addition, the boarders had myriad other ways of "making life a real hell." Invariably from the Lower East Side, they knew nothing whatever about farms or farming. And so they frequently, innocently, ruined fruit trees and trampled gardens. One old lady from Hester Street was horrified to learn that manure was put in the ground right next to the vegetables that were to be eaten. *"Fe!"* she exclaimed in disgust.

Then, still another problem arose. It's a truth universally acknowledged that a single man on vacation is *not* in want of a mate, but a single girl is. And therein lay a headache, an expensive headache. Before he even had the privies paid for, a farmer had to add blandishments to romance: croquet, a little music, a good-looking waiter or so. . . .

"It is hard to imagine the martyrdom of the wife and family of the farmer who has boarders for the season," Schalit told the directors of the JCA:

> I wanted to observe it at close range. Getting up at 3 o'clock in the morning, going to bed at 11 o'clock at night, the whole family worked like convicts to take care of the 10, 15, or 20 boarders, 30 sometimes, that are crowded 2 and three in one room (these boarders are generally of small means). The family sleep where they can, in the kitchen, the stable and out-of-doors. The boarders . . . grumble and criticize all the more they pay less, and it all has to be borne in silence.

Perhaps it was in the area of summer boarder agriculture that Jewish farmers actually came closest to approximating the Man with the Hoe. At the end of the season, had they and their families been asked Markham's rhetorical questions

"Who made him dead to rapture and despair?/A thing that grieves not and that never hopes,/ Stolid and stunned, a brother to the ox?" it's not too far-fetched that they would've snapped back, "Who else—summer boarders!"

19

"Jewish Boys Are Not Willing to Do
What We Want Them to Do"

Since education is an integral, vital part of Jewish tradition, it
was inevitable that when all other attempts at producing a le-
gion of Jewish farmers were failing, a school would be established to do the job. A number of men, some highly placed
Yahudim like Judge Meyer S. Isaacs, favored the idea; or
were less enthusiastic, even irascible about the belief that potential farmers had a need for technical training. Wasn't there
anything Jews could do without going to school for it?

Organizing the first agricultural high school in the United
States—and a Jewish one at that—required drive, determination, *and* money. Hirsch Leib Sabsovich, that "flaming spirit,"
possessed the first two qualities in great degree. As for the
third, he was closely associated with a body that was regarded
as a veritable philanthropic cornucopia. Sabsovich—a tall,
thin, intellectual thirty-three-year-old former law student
from Odessa—had in the midst of the pogroms dropped his
plan for a legal career in order to study agricultural science in
Switzerland and lead Russian Jews back to the soil. In pursuit
of that goal, he arrived in the United States in 1888. His zeal,
his dedication to his task, never flagged. He and his colleague
Dr. Paul Kaplan, former New Odessa colonist, "a warm-
hearted kindly fanatic," spent hours on the East Side, sitting

around cafés, lecturing anarchists, socialists, poets, and scholars "on the beauty of the outdoors and on the good promise of the soil where," they said, "the manifest destiny of the immigrant Jew lay." They were neglecting their bodies, they told their radical listeners, and exhorted them to get away from the city and engage in physical activity. . . .

Though the inspired pair failed to convey their point on East Broadway, Sabsovich had considerably more influence as superintendent of the Woodbine colony in Cape May County in New Jersey. Originally, Woodbine had been 5,300 acres covered with those familiar South Jersey landscape props—scrub oak and stunted pine—and intended as an agricultural settlement that would be strengthened by some industry. But after a few futile years of trying to make "the stingy soil" produce, many settlers left, and the burden of the town's economy rested on a garment factory, a knitting mill, a basket factory, and a machine shop. Of course the celebrated Baron de Hirsch Fund heavily subsidized Woodbine. Of all charitable organizations established for the East European Jewish immigrants, it was the richest, the most all-encompassing, the one with more adaptable stipulations in its bylaws. Consequently, it produced the greatest misunderstanding and inspired myth.

In January, 1891, a deed of trust was issued reading:

> Whereas, I, the Baron Maurice de Hirsch, now residing in Paris, France, have observed with painful interest the suffering and destitution of the Hebrews dwelling in Russia and Roumania, where they are oppressed by severe laws and unfriendly neighbors; and have determined to contribute to the relief of such of my brethren in race, who have emigrated or shall emigrate from these inhospitable countries to the Republic of the United States of America. . . .

As trustees of his fund, the baron named nine of the most eminent American *Yahudim*—Judge Meyer S. Isaacs, Jesse Seligman, Jacob H. Schiff, Oscar Straus, Henry Rice, James Hoffman, Julius Goldman, Mayer Sulzberger, and William B. Hackenberg—who would preside over the expenditure of *"two million four hundred thousand dollars,* lawful money of the United States of America."

Thus to the desperately poor East European Jews, the somber-eyed, sweeping-mustachioed baron became a Jewish Santa Claus. In many homes his portrait hung alongside three other equally admired men; Washington, Lincoln, and Mikhail Bakunin, the Russian anarchist. Stories of De Hirsch largesse swept the East Side. He was going to give every Russian Jew $100, $150 . . . set them up in business . . . send their children to college . . . buy them a farm. . . .

A provision in the deed of trust did call for "instruction in agricultural work and improved methods of farming . . ." so in 1894 the Baron de Hirsch School of Agriculture was opened by Professor Sabsovich on Farms 59 and 60, Woodbine, New Jersey.

"The feet of Jewish youth were to be turned toward a new destiny, leaving behind the peddler's packs and the sweatshops and the slums of their fathers." But to precisely *what* "new destiny" were they to be directed? Two opposing views of the school's goal kept conflict over curriculum at a constant boil. Jacob Schiff, some of his fellow trustees, and Professor Tisserand, the agricultural expert for the Jewish Colonization Association—an international De Hirsch-funded agency that was reluctantly contributing the school's major operating expenses—believed the aim of the school was to simply "produce good rural workmen, able in the course of time to become small landowners or farmers." On the other hand, Professor Sabsovich and Dr. Boris Bogen, a young Russian Jewish immigrant who became principal of the school in 1900, favored theoretical subjects that would also prepare qualified students for professional agricultural positions.

But to Jacob Schiff and other like-minded trustees, the school's function rose above education; it must be a showcase, displaying the Jewish Man with the Hoe in the making. Similarly, when Woodbine in 1903 was incorporated as a municipality with an all-Jewish city administration, "a rather pretentious city hall," paved streets, a fire department, and—of course—the first kindergarten in Cape May County, it was intended as a showcase of Jewish civic virtue, which had to surpass non-Jewish civic virtue.

In this guise, Woodbine *did* attract attention. New York reporters and magazine writers would board a train on the West Jersey & Seashore Line and ride the 130 miles to Woodbine to draw some significant conclusions for their readers on "The First Self-Governing Jewish Community Since the Fall of Jerusalem." Even native Americans from surrounding villages observed curiously the singular behavior of these newcomers to a pluralistic society. Did those heart-rending departures at the railroad stations—the weeping, emotion-racked farewells —mean the traveler was returning to Russia for good? Not at all. He was just going to Philadelphia and would be coming back the same evening.

"Its streets are clean," one writer rhapsodized in *Arena*, "the houses are detached, and built with reference to plenty of air and sunshine. There are no saloons, no disorderly characters and no sweat shops." Reporters also observed that the town had neither a jail nor a house of prostitution.

When Jacob Riis, not only a serious-minded reporter, but an immigrant and slum *mavin*, visited Woodbine, it was to be expected that he would have more sedate observations to make than his colleagues.* And he did. Riis contrasted his first glimpse of Russian Jews in 1882, "herded like cattle in the poorest tenements," with his view of them in the rural environs of Woodbine: "The cattle [not figurative Russian Jews this time, but real cattle] were lowing in the fields. The evening breathed peace. Down the sandy road came a creaking farm wagon. Beside it walked a sunburned bearded man with an axe on his shoulder, in earnest conversation with his boy, a strapping young fellow in overalls."

What Riis saw—that "sunburned bearded man" and that "strapping young fellow in overalls"—exactly fulfilled the trustees' objective. For as one of them expressed it, their aim was "securing a select number who give promise and show a desire of being trained into competent farm hands." There it was! The school's goal did not include turning out students like the Lipman brothers: Jacob G. Lipman, one of the school's first students, was to organize the United States' first department of soil chemistry at Rutgers and later become one of the world's greatest authorities on soil analysis and dean of the Rutgers School of agriculture, profoundly influencing Selman Waksman (another Russian Jewish immigrant), the discoverer of streptomycin. His brother Dr. Charles B. Lipman became a noted plant pathologist. And their nephew Gregory

---

* It might be well to point out that Riis, though he did speak a little Yiddish—that is, he had picked up "scraps of their harsh jargon"—was not as tuned in on certain immigrant attitudes as might be supposed. While visiting one Woodbine home, he recalled to his hosts—Russian Jews—"something we had in common," his "affection for the Princess Dagmar whom I knew in Copenhagen in my youth." Rewarded by the look of a young man, sitting across the room, "a look I have not yet got over," Riis belatedly realized that while Princess Dagmar was now Empress of Russia, neither she nor her husband, Alexander III, could possibly be affectionately recalled by his hosts. "Well for me I did not tell him my opinion of the Czar himself. It was gleaned from Copenhagen itself where they thought him the prince of good fellows."

Pincus, born in Woodbine in 1903, was to be one of the three developers of the first practical oral contraceptive, the Pill. Who needed it? After all, the question wasn't whether Jews could become scientists, but whether they could become farmhands.

"It is our object," reiterated a 1905 school report to the De Hirsch Fund, "to make farmers pure and simple, of the pupils. We should eliminate from our plans the idea of a scientific education as such." It was, therefore, noted as a sinister tendency on the part of Professor Sabsovich to point "with special pride" to the "records of one former pupil who entered Rutgers College and one who entered the junior year at Storrs Agricultural College . . ." and that the curriculum included such esoterica as mechanical drawing, *Thanatopsis,* and algebra.

Before he resigned in disgust, Dr. Bogen spent four years fighting this attitude:

> After working a due period as laborers in the fields, our graduates began to look beyond the horizon and reached for the less laborious stations of the agricultural industry. They went to agricultural laboratories, they entered higher institutions of agricultural learning. . . .
>
> Our directors were distressed. This had not been their plan. They had thought of a contented Jewry working in the fields, tilling the acres of others and eventually their own. They suggested perhaps our method of education was all wrong. We had put visions in the eyes of these boys and, as soon as they could, they lifted their eyes from the ground to follow these visions . . .
>
> They said we must simplify the course to avoid the false ideas which had entered the heads of the boys and were leading them to pursue ambitions far from the soil. Our course was three years long; we must no longer expose the students to higher educational and social influences. Thereafter the work of education must be altogether in the field where they would become inured to the lot of the humble toiler and be content, not knowing any better. Thus we would bring up a toiling class.

The founder of a rival institution agreed. In 1897 Rabbi Joseph Krauskopf of Philadelphia opened the National Farm School a mile from Doylestown, Pennsylvania. *His* goal was to remove Jewish boys from ghetto streets, place them in a more wholesome, rural environment where they would gener-

ate respect by becoming "bread producers," as Count Tolstoy
had advised. (Tolstoy wasn't familiar with the compulsions of
Pennsylvania Railroad conductors, however. At the NFS stop,
they always called out what sounded to the students like "National
Reform School.") And though Dr. Krauskopf and
Jacob Schiff engaged in an acrimonious correspondence over
whether or not the latter had endorsed the establishment of
NFS, both shared a yearning for a "toiling class." When a
young immigrant visited Dr. Krauskopf and asked for his
help in continuing his medical studies at the Jefferson Medical
College of Philadelphia, Krauskopf brusquely told him, "I
can do nothing for you. We have too many doctors as it is."

But alas, after eleven years—during which time the Baron
de Hirsch School of Agriculture had one turnover after another
in administration, had innumerable changes in curriculum,
and even experienced difficulty in retaining matrons
(they tended to grow hysterical after a while)—a report revealed
that an expenditure of $500,000 had realized only 120
young men working at farming. This meant it cost $4,166 per
farmer! To Jacob Schiff, this was a "manifestation of failure."
At a meeting of the De Hirsch Fund trustees at the end of
1905, Schiff made a melancholy admission: He had come to
the conclusion, he said, "that Jewish boys are not willing to do
what we want them to do." Consequently, he favored discontinuing
the school. However, the other trustees opposed this,
for in Judge Sulzberger's words, it "would reflect upon the
Jewish community to acknowledge the failure of our endeavors
to advance farming by Jews."

In the remaining dozen years of its existence, the De Hirsch
Agricultural School continued manfully in the attempt to turn
out "farmers pure and simple," but by 1918 when it finally
closed its doors, a discouraging number of boys had followed
in Dr. Lipman's footsteps and become bacteriologists, plant
pathologists, horticulturists, entomologists, farm economists
and statisticians, teachers, veterinarians—even an editor of an
agricultural journal. Naturally the De Hirsch Fund trustees
weren't ashamed of such alumni—not really ashamed. It was
more a feeling of irritation, annoyance, at the way those maddening
Russian Jews had changed the Man with the Hoe into
the Man with the Microscope and even into the Man with the
Blue Pencil.

PART V

"ALL THE PEOPLE IN DAYTON ARE
NICE AND KIND AND FRIENDLY"

In regard to workmen here . . . I am going to increase the force
as fast as I can work up to it and was thinking I would like to
try out a couple good Jewish fellows. I would like to get about
two that are hustlers. . . . Our cabinet work is all piece work,
a good man can make $2.50 a day or over. . . . We work ten
hours a day. There are only about three Jewish families in Mt.
Carmel. . . . I could not say whether Kosher food is available or
not. . . .
    —From W. E. FLANDERS, foreman, Barlow Furniture Com-
      pany, Mount Carmel, Illinois, to the Industrial Removal
      Office, New York City, 1906

. . . I beg to state that I am afraid in a community like Mt.
Carmel, where there is practically no Jewish life, it will be a
difficult matter to keep Jewish mechanics. We prefer to send
such men to communities where our people can find a little
society which is as important to them as their daily bread. . . .
    —From DAVID BRESSLER, Industrial Removal Office, New
      York City, to W. E. FLANDERS, Mount Carmel, Illinois

When so many Americans are coming East, it is just as well for
the Jews to go West to avoid the embarrassment of the meeting.
    —BERNARD G. RICHARDS, Keidansky's Discourses on Dis-
      persion

20

Selling Jews

In the last decade of the nineteenth century, attempting to pry immigrants from the Lower East Side and send them off into the distant West was the goal of all right-thinking New York *Yahudim.* However, since these good works centered on Russian Jews, they set off fiery opposition. What question had merely two sides? Arguments revealed five, ten, twenty, thirty —an infinite number.

"If a man has the courage to appear on a platform before a crowd of Jewish immigrants," wrote I. M. Rubinow in 1903, "and recommend to them that they should move into the interior, even if he were to promise them material aid, the people of the East Side could rightfully ask him: 'What group could I join upon my arrival?'"

Indeed, problems loomed before a people whose life-style demanded a strong religious community. It was very difficult, for example, to engage a rabbi for small isolated towns, even if there were enough Jews to make up a congregation. As a consequence, once the congregation acquired a rabbi, it was loath to give him up. One such congregation, in a small town in the Canadian north woods, hired a smooth-talking young man who had arrived by train in answer to an ad for a rabbi in a Toronto paper. After he and his wife were settled in a house and after he had satisfactorily performed in the pulpit, a member of the congregation informed Abe Weisman, one of its leaders, that the new rabbi was bootlegging on the side. "I was so mad," Weisman said, "that I could have broken him in half." Instead, he lectured the rabbi, who swore solemnly he would drop bootlegging. All went well for a while; then once again a congregation member came to Weisman with yet another sideline of the rabbi's. Their spiritual leader had established a French-Canadian girl, recently run out of town by the police, in a rented room. "He must be," Weisman was advised, "setting up to be a pimp." Here was a situation that called for stern measures. "Either you get rid of that girl," Weisman told him unequivocally, "or we get a new rabbi." The rabbi got rid of the girl.

Many years later, in retelling this experience, certain aspects of it still troubled Weisman. "I guess you're wondering," he said, defensively, "why we kept him after all this. What could we do? If we fired him, the story would run all over the province—how the Jewish rabbi was a pimp and a bootlegger." It was also true that rabbis content to stay in the Canadian north woods were hard to come by.

Not long after this incident, a prominent religious leader from Toronto—Rabbi Gordon—came to town. After meeting the young rabbi ("that bum"), Rabbi Gordon "seemed to smell something about him even though I didn't mention his bootlegging and his French girl." Following a cross-examination, Rabbi Gordon took Weisman aside and told him that their rabbi was not a rabbi at all, but a fake. It proved a happy release for all, including the phony rabbi, who departed for the less puritanical life of a Texas cowboy.

Despite such problems, there was a great deal to be said for settling in small American communities—out in the great "hinterland" west of Hester Street—and the *Yahudim* said it all. But their rosy pictures, lectures, exhortations, and free train tickets weren't enough, nor was editorial pressure. Though being on the same side of an issue as the *Yahudim* made the Yiddish press uneasy, over a period of five years, it continuously urged its readers to leave the congested ghetto and "go West." Still, so few had been induced to follow this advice that it was necessary in 1900 to organize a dispersion of Jews.

An opportunity to reenact a Biblical episode doesn't come to many men. In the early twentieth century, however, a Diaspora—whose original version had engaged the energies of a remorseless Roman army and, according to exegesis, the punitive powers of the Almighty—was undertaken by a formidable coalition: American Jewish philanthropists, a celebrated Anglo-Jewish writer, and young dynamic members of a new profession—social work.

On a fall day in 1906, twenty-seven-year-old Morris Waldman sat in the compartment of a train as it rolled through the vast expanses of Oklahoma and East Texas. Born in Hungary, Waldman had been brought to New York as a child. He'd spent several years at the Jewish Theological Seminary, worked for a brief period as a reporter, played football with Abraham Brill—then a medical student at Columbia—taught a class at Dr. Stephen S. Wise's Sunday school on Madison Avenue, and made a study of desertion on the Lower East Side for the United Hebrew Charities. Despite Waldman's varied background, he found the sight of Western plains and sombreroed cowboys at the depots beguiling. A crockery and chinaware salesman sharing his compartment complained of the huge expense involved in carrying his sample trunks. "Brother," the salesman then said, "what's your line?"

"Young as I was," Waldman recalled, "and in high good humor at my thrilling excursion into adventurous new fields, I was mischievous enough to want to have a little fun with him. My face assumed an embarrassed mysterious look. I rose and drew the curtain close, returned to my seat and in a low whisper said, 'I sell Jews.' "

Stated baldly, "selling Jews" described more or less what Waldman's job was to be for the next few years. Moreover, he had no need to carry samples of *his* product. "If I had," he said, "I would surely experience some difficulty in disposing of my merchandise."

Waldman was on his way to Galveston, Texas, to establish the headquarters of the Jewish Immigrants Information Bureau, whose working fund of a half million dollars had been donated entirely by Jacob Schiff. Israel Zangwill in Europe supplied the "merchandise"—Russian Jewish immigrants—and North German Lloyd Line steamers were chartered to transport them to the Gulf port. The purpose of this circuitous route was to divert Jewish immigrants from New York or Philadelphia, where they settled comfortably into the ghettos and were so difficult to dislodge. As for the "selling," it was to be directed at the small Jewish communities throughout the South and West, to persuade them to accept the entire responsibility of not only finding jobs for the immigrants but of settling them respectably within their community.

This was the Galveston Movement, an offshoot of the Industrial Removal Office, an offshoot of the Jewish Agricultural Society, an offshoot of the Baron de Hirsch Fund, which frequently appeared to be an offshoot of Jacob H. Schiff.

The IRO had been established five years prior to the Galveston Movement, at the end of January, 1901, under the management of twenty-one-year-old David Bressler. It had the expressed goal of removing "as many of our co-religionists as possible" from large cities "in order to clear the way for the continual stream of immigrants arriving here, but also relieve the prevailing conditions in our Ghettoes." It also had another, less frequently mentioned purpose—to counteract the work of the seven-year-old, Boston-based, Immigration Restriction League. Prescott Hall, one of the league's founders, was a particularly zealous advocate of pure Anglo-Saxon blood. The presence of so many Jewish immigrants in whose veins flowed pure non-Anglo-Saxon blood, of which they were perversely proud, was presumed by the league to be dangerous to the country. So Keidansky, "the oracle of Division Street," proclaimed, "To the South or the West then, or Prescott Hall will catch us."

To achieve these objectives, the Industrial Removal Office dispatched agents across the country to confront American Jews with pep talks, stern lectures on Judaic tradition, and selective bullying. "Upon first broaching the subject I would usually encounter a feeling of distrust," wrote agent Elias Margolis to Bressler. "As they expressed it, they had enough of itinerant 'schnorrers' already, the communal purse was small, etc., etc. . . . Sometimes I would be forced to advance to some of the stubborn or indifferent ones, the argument that they were not fulfilling their obligations to the Jewish People by merely attending to their parochial duties . . . that the problem of New York Jewry was and ought to be the concern of the Jews of the entire country. A good talk invariably had the desired effect. . . ."

Margolis, like Morris Waldman, recognized that IRO work and salesmanship had much in common. "The method of the traveling salesman," he wrote Bressler, "who goes after a man again and again until he lands an account will be one we might adopt with advantage."

The *modus operandi* of the IRO was fairly simple. With whatever persuasive means they had developed, agents obtained the cooperation of local Jewish organizations—particularly the B'nai B'rith—which would find specific job openings and would fill out requisition forms giving the name of the employing firm, a job description, and a person in the community who would look after the welfare of the "removalite." These forms were sent back to the IRO in New York City; from there an immigrant with the necessary qualifications would set out. Agencies appeared in eight large cities, from which agents covered the surrounding area, hunting for employment opportunities. ("Everywhere," Margolis wrote Bressler, "my statement that we could furnish a sober and industrious class of mechanics who could be relied upon at all times, met at first with a smile of incredulity, and upon repetition and emphasis attracted instant attention and interest.") These agents also gave advice to local communities on how to treat the immigrant who was "strongly individualistic, but paradoxical, as it may seem . . . just as strongly gregarious. . . . Above all," they cautioned the committees, "he must not be regarded with a patronizing air."

As for "removalites," Agent Margolis reported:

Max Zin of Huntington, Indiana, sent there in 1906, is in the junk business and is prosperous. He has since married. A. Covnat of Streator, Illinois, sent there in 1903, is working as a tinsmith, and has been employed for the past four years in the same shop. He is making a fair living and is satisfied except that his children cannot get any religious instruction, for there are few Jews in Streator and these few are members of the "Christian Liberal Church." Morris Lapper of Evansville, Indiana, sent there in 1903, worked two and a half years as a presser on overalls, suffered trials and tribulations during that time, opened up a little shop as a presser and cleaner and today is the proprietor of an "Emporium" and as he himself boasted with pride he can buy $300 worth of goods on credit. He is willing to help anyone you may send to Evansville in the future. Alex Bogusin of Quincy, Illinois, sent there twelve months ago by the Galveston Bureau is working in a plumber shop. Despite his residence of but one year in this country he answered my questions in a faultless English (had attended Evening High School during the winter) and as evidence of his rapid Americanization he informed me that he was now a full fledged member of the Illinois Naval Reserve, and more important still he is a good workingman and gives complete satisfaction to his employer. . . .

The arrival of immigrants in cities and towns gave Jewish women a chance to exercise their peerless executive abilities for the first time in the Western Hemisphere. In Milwaukee, Wisconsin, Mrs. Lizzie Kander, a native-born American, descended from German Jews, took one look at the filthy slums and opened the Keep Klean Mission bathhouse for East European immigrants. She persuaded the owner of the brewery next door to let her have their excess steam for hot water. Following this successful enterprise, she organized the Abraham Lincoln Settlement House and taught cooking there.

Mrs. Kander began collecting recipes for use in her classes. When she had gathered a savory number, she approached the gentlemen of the settlement house board for $18 to defray the expense of printing the recipes, for distribution to her students. With kindly condescension, they explained to her that it was too costly, so Mrs. Kander sent her colleagues around to sell advertising to cover the expense. To everyone's astonishment, Milwaukee women willingly paid 50 cents for a copy of her recipe book. Under the influence of this heady triumph, Mrs. Kander offered the board members the profits of her book for the purchase of a building lot. They benevolently consented to "accept any returns from your little venture." By the 1920's $75,000 of its royalties had gone into building the Milwaukee Jewish Center, and at Mrs. Kander's death in 1940, her *Settlement House Cook Book* had reached its twenty-third edition.

Nor was Mrs. Kander the only woman to develop her executive abilities in Milwaukee. One of the Russian immigrant families for whose benefit Mrs. Kander labored was the Mabowehzes from Kiev. The Hebrew Immigrant Aid Society had sent Moishe Mabowehz, a carpenter, to the city in 1903. Three years later his wife and three daughters left Russia to join him. Golda Mabowehz, the middle daughter, cared little for Mrs. Kander's cooking class at the Settlement House and to her parents' displeasure—they wanted her to take a business course—preferred to make Zionist speeches on Milwaukee street corners. Once, after her father threatened to drag her off the stand by the hair if she spoke publicly, Golda warned her friends: "I want you to know that we're going to have a scandal here." But her father returned home after listening to her speak and in some awe reported to his wife, "I didn't know she had it in her." Golda Meir's gift for leadership, however, was to express itself more strikingly in Israel than in Milwaukee.

21

Ship via Galveston

In spite of all the IRO's efforts and those of other agencies, such as the Hebrew Immigrant Aid Society, the fact remained that while approximately 300 Jewish immigrants were dispersed from New York each month, steamer steerages were unloading 6,000 at Ellis Island. This situation gave rise to the Galveston Plan.

In 1906, Jacob Schiff, on a visit to London, met with Israel Zangwill—a head-on encounter of incompatible personalities. Zangwill firmly believed that men of ideas—famous novelists and playwrights, for example—rather than rich bankers, were born leaders. Schiff, on the other hand, agreed with Cyrus Adler, who had written Zangwill in 1905: "Critic, poet, novelist and dramatist you are, and as such I admired you . . . but at no time in all our contact have I ever taken you seriously as a leader in Israel, or even suspected that you took yourself seriously."

In the struggling years of his youth, Zangwill, the son of Polish Jews who had settled in England, had struck Morris Waldman as "a young restless ungainly product of the East End ghetto of London." At forty-two, Zangwill was "nearly handsome in comparison," impressively well dressed, with bushy gray hair, a ruddy complexion, and his "still sharp hawklike features" more mellowed. He had become a genuine literary success, whose books and plays of Jewish ghetto life in London raised him to that lofty peak occupied by Galsworthy, H. G. Wells, and Arnold Bennett. But although he was enormously popular with Russian Jews in the United States—virtually every home had a copy of *Children of the Ghetto*—Yahudim weren't at all keen on him, principally because of his fervent support of Zionism. Zangwill's dedication to Zionism equaled his profound reverence for the British crown—a set of devotions not easily harmonized. In attempting to harmonize them, Zangwill had recently suffered a severe disappointment.

In 1904, England offered Uganda to the Zionists as a homeland, but the World Zionist Organization wouldn't consider a substitute for Palestine. This infuriated Zangwill. "Really," he exclaimed indignantly, "if the British Empire chooses to be magnanimous to the Jews, it is scarcely the place of the Jew to rebuke her." Resigning from the World Zionists, he formed an organization of his own: the Jewish Territorial Organization, usually called ITO*—an abbreviation Louis Marshall once suggested meant "Interminable Talking Organization." The ITO's goal was the acquisition of "a territory upon an autonomous basis for those Jews who cannot or will not remain in the lands in which they live at present."

So when Zangwill met Schiff, he urged him to buy up "some large territory in the Southwest of the United States which eventually could be developed into the Jewish National Home the Zionists were striving for in Palestine with such discouraging prospects."

To suggest to the anti-Zionist Jacob H. Schiff that he buy up portions of Texas and Oklahoma, and turn them into a Jewish state required *chutzpah* of a high order. After disposing of Zangwill's plan—quickly, indignantly—Schiff made a counterproposal, to which Zangwill agreed: The ITO should "direct the flow of emigration from Russia to the Gulf ports . . . from where the immigrants can readily be distributed over the interior of the country."

The choice of a distribution point narrowed down to San Francisco, New Orleans, and Galveston. The first two were dismissed as "too large and attractive" and thus a "temptation to the immigrant to remain there instead of braving the uncertainties of some smaller place in the hinterland." Galves-

* When "Yiddish" in Yiddish is transliterated into English, it is spelled "Iddish."

ton, "a small town on a sandbar in the Gulf," had few things to recommend it as a permanent home. However, it did have one invaluable asset: It had the notable presence of "the Rabbi."

Rabbi Henry Cohen was one of those individuals of whom it may be said—and indeed it was, over and over and over again—that he was a legend in his own time, one who would even achieve apotheosis in a *Reader's Digest* "most unforgettable character" article. A short dynamic young man of twenty-five, afflicted with a stammer ("We'll get used to it," the president of the congregation declared), he had come to the Reform pulpit of Galveston's Temple B'nai Israel in 1888, having served for three years in Woodville, Mississippi; before that, he had ministered to the Amalgamated Congregation of Israelites in Kingston, Jamaica. Born in London, Cohen had gone to school with Israel Zangwill, and in his youth he had spent several years in South Africa, where he had been cracked over the head by Zulus and where he had mastered the click language of the Kaffir tribe so well that he became an interpreter for the British government.

In addition to being a circuit-riding rabbi to some of the 12,000 Jews in Texas, scattered in towns from Nacogdoches to Brownsville, he was teacher, adviser, social worker to virtually all Texas. "When people were in trouble, white or black, Jew or Gentile, aristocrat or plebeian, it was 'the Rabbi' who was first consulted." One need only call, and he would be off on his bicycle to help. He gave "a decent Christian burial" to a prostitute—a service refused by the other clergy. "Where did you study Christology?" a young man studying for the Episcopal ministry was asked. "Under Rabbi Henry Cohen," he answered. And the ubiquitous Rabbi Cohen performed herculean relief work during the disastrous 1900 Galveston flood.

Predictably, when word of the proposed Galveston Plan came to him from Jacob Schiff and his old friend Zangwill, an enthusiastic Rabbi Cohen set off on his bicycle to make arrangements for welcoming the first immigrants. When Morris Waldman arrived in town, he went directly to the gray frame Texas farmhouse at 1920 Broadway to see the rabbi. And when the North German Lloyd steamer *Cassel* docked in early July, 1907, after an eighteen-day, 5,200-mile trip from Hamburg, with its first group of sixty Russian Jewish families, the mayor of Galveston was on hand to greet them with Rabbi Cohen translating his drawled welcome into "fluent, staccato" Yiddish. The rabbi then helped carry the immigrants' luggage to Jewish Immigrant Information Bureau headquarters and saw to it that the newcomers received hot meals and baths.

The Galveston, Harrisburg & San Antonio Railway carried the immigrants to "all points west of the Mississippi River, including New Orleans, St. Louis and West of Chicago." Those who held a JIIB certificate stating that they were "an object of charity" and whose tickets were stamped CHARITY received reduced rates, which were paid for by the JIIB.

Immigrants continued to arrive and depart: one butcher to Kansas City, and another to Fort Worth, a tanner to Omaha, a cabinetmaker to Cedar Rapids. Meanwhile, Waldman and his colleagues crisscrossed the West and Southwest preaching the gospel of *tzedaka*—being righteously charitable—as a means of "selling Jews." "Here and there," he recalled, "we had to overcome 'sales resistance,' " and the most effective weapon was to invoke the magic words "Jacob H. Schiff." Sending a "long telegram over his name, advising a community of my advent, invariably found a delegation awaiting me at the depot."

So when Mr. and Mrs. Schiff made their entrance into Galveston in the aloof splendor of their private railway car and stayed at the Galves Hotel, the city's entire Jewish community experienced a flurry of excitement. Schiff walked the seawall with Morris Lasker, a wealthy Galvestonian, whose son Albert would one be to advertising what Schiff was to banking, and was quietly affable to lesser Jewish citizens of the city. "You know—it's very funny—I've got a son named Mortimer, too," Ben Isaacs, superintendent of Rabbi Cohen's Sabbath school, said to him. "Very funny," Mr. Schiff replied. For years after, Isaacs would approach people with an outstretched hand, saying, "Shake the hand that shook the hand of Jacob Schiff."

Schiff had come to see the Galveston Plan in operation. He reviewed with pleasure the follow-up files of the JIIB that gave first-hand reports on the progress of immigrants after they left Galveston. He also examined the bureau's financial accounts, which occasionally displeased him. For example, he noted the shocking price of pencils. "I buy them cheaper in New York," he told Rabbi Cohen.

22

Dear IRO

It's unlikely that Jacob Schiff, innocent of the impersonality of a computerized world, could entirely appreciate the singular personal quality of the IRO and Galveston operations. It was during the infancy of social work when "case" was just beginning to be used, apologetically, for individuals. And though the labor market occasionally revealed a tendency to view immigrant labor as unused inventory, there were still no mass consignments, no numbered identities, no symbols subject to injury by folding and spindling.

A cross section of the voluminous exchange of letters between IRO and JIIB staff members, Jewish community leaders, potential employers, and the immigrants themselves reveal apprehensions, misapprehensions, and, indeed, the manner in which 79,000 East European Jewish immigrants were sprinkled cautiously like an exotic seasoning over the United States.

(Translated from Yiddish)

South Bend, Indiana
March 2, 1906

Dear Friend of the Removal Office,
    I hereby notify you that I arrived on Thursday to Mr.

Grossman, who on the next morning provided me with a good job. I come to thank you for all the good you have done for me. I am now with Mr. Grossman who is giving me 8 days board and lodging free of charge. . . . I was in a distressful condition and you have helped me out of it. I will recommend your office to all my fellow countrymen and will tell them not to fear riding through the Liberal Removal Office.

I have nothing more to write to you. From me Itzchuk Risman who was sent off Thursday, 6 o'clock in the evening. I beg you dear friends to answer me on Mr. Grossman's address.

ITZCHUK RISMAN THE BLACKSMITH

June 10, 1906

From J. E. LEVY, Demopolis, Alabama, to IRO, New York City

. . . I would like to get two foreign girls to do housework, would like one fifteen year old or a little older and the other grown. Will give them a good home and treat them well. My family is small. Kindly answer as soon as possible and oblige.

From DAVID BRESSLER, IRO, New York City, to J. E. LEVY, Demopolis, Alabama

. . . I beg to inform you that this institution has nothing to do with the question of domestics or servants of any nature. . . .

June 23, 1906

From A. C. FISCHER, secretary, Toledo Metal Trades Association, Toledo, Ohio, to DAVID BRESSLER, IRO, New York City

. . . I will be able to place ten first class lathe hands . . . all the more if they can speak English and are non-union men. There is positively no strike on here, nor do we anticipate one, but we have a great many radical fellows in our shops whose services we wish to dispense with. . . .

From DAVID BRESSLER, IRO, New York City, to A. C. FISCHER, Toledo, Ohio

. . . it isn't likely that we will be able to fill your requisition. . . .

January 28, 1907

Report: MORRIS WALDMAN, general agent, Kansas City, Missouri, to DAVID BRESSLER, IRO, New York City

. . . As I thought the situation in Kansas City is satisfactory. All the people we sent there are at work and are earning comparatively good wages for immigrants.

Yakov Levin is working at his trade and earning $12 per week.

Wolf Baraban is working at the packing house, earning $1.75 per day steady work, has sent 20 roubles to his family— suffers somewhat with rheumatism. Our committee will secure a job for him at a soap factory next week at easier work.

Isaac Waxman is working at his trade (laundry presser) earning $8 per week. If he sticks, will earn more gradually.

Schmedrick did not tell the truth when he said he was a bookbinder. He thought this story would help him. He is working for a factory for $5 per week but next week will secure position with his brother-in-law F. Mishol in furniture place. Mishol is earning $12 a week there at his trade. . . .

The following telegram was sent collect to JACOB SCHIFF in New York City on December 4, 1907, from BENJAMIN KOPERLIK, lawyer and communal worker, Pueblo, Colorado.

Moishe Opotosky arrived Pueblo from Galveston, August 28th. Got him easy work August 30th in bolt shop of Steelworks. He quarreled with other workmen and was discharged, got work September 19th as helper to brick layer. Shortly after he came to me with a black eye and bruised face begging me to get him work in Denver claiming he had fallen off of a brick wall while working and thus injured his face. I investigated and found that he had lied. Have several eye witnesses that injury to his face was due to his getting drunk during the Jewish holidays and falling intoxicated on the street. . . . He was not mistreated while in Pueblo . . . The man is unreliable, inclined to drink and be untruthful . . . he was out of work we fed him . . . He told me that he was coaxed to Galveston and promised big wages . . . I do not believe him.

February 4, 1908

From CLEMENT SALOMON, ITO, London, to MORRIS WALDMAN, JIIB, Galveston

. . . Another serious complaint is contained in the letter I enclose . . . written in Yiddish to his parents by the emigrant Okon who bears an excellent character for truth and honesty and is an energetic hardworking young man . . . A copy of the letter I have sent to Mr. Sulzberger, which even after making all allowances for Oriental exaggeration, has a certain truthful ring about it. . . .

Enc.—Copy and Translated from Yiddish
From LOEB OKON, c/o Hyman Hardware Company, Binghamton, Tennessee, to Parent in Russia

. . . I was sent away from Memphis to a country place, Wedley, and there to a village, where we were told we should have to dig earth and raise a terrace for a railway. There we saw three of our people working very hard knee deep in water and we heard from them that they were earning nothing but their food. To our observation that this was hardly worthwhile, they replied: "We are sold into slavery. We have signed a contract presented to us, and we must not run away after such an agreement." To our question, how they could be such fools, they replied: "We have signed it under threats of being shot down." To our further question as to where they were boarded, they replied, pointing to a man: "With that Christian." On hearing this, I and my two companions who came from Warsaw, wanted to leave immediately, but we were threatened with being shot down to which we intimated by mute signs: "Fire away, then!!" . . . After having wandered about for seven hours, we discovered a house at a distance. We went to it, and found there a couple of Blacks, husband and wife [who] gave us bread which we ate with onions. Then he put his horse to his cart and took us to the town of Wedley, where we found a Jew, who gave us a dollar and a half each, and sent us off to Memphis. Now we are thanking and praising our dear God for having saved us from evil hands.

From MORRIS DUBOIS, Dayton, Ohio, to IRO, New York City

Now I thank you. I with my wife and children what you took us out of trouble. I thought that my whole life time I would have to suffer with my whole family in New York. Now I don't know how to thank you and the committee in Dayton. They treat me like a father with children, they got me a good position and I am making a good living. All the people in Dayton are nice and kind and friendly. It is a nice and healthy country.

23

"Richer Than Jacob H. Schiff!"

"There was a man—a greenhorn—believe me he couldn't talk a word English. He goes to a brother-in-law, a tailor in Indiana—or maybe it was Idaho. Well, so this brother-in-law, he gets him a job. What kind of a job? Scrubbing out a dairy floor in big gum boots. This is a job? Wait. Wait! He puts by a dollar or two. Then it comes a chance to rent a little store—a hole in the wall. So what does he sell in that store? Clothes? Shoes? Groceries? Maybe newspapers, cigarettes? Not him. You wanta hear? A few fine combs. *Fine combs! A meshugganer,* everyone said. Who could tell that from fine combs you can make a living. So you know what that man is today? A millionaire. A millionaire? Richer than Jacob H. Schiff!"

The foregoing is a *bobbe-myseh.* And *bobbe-mysehs* of success, rich in lavish exaggeration, worked together with the Jewish magnet theory—one Jew draws relatives—as the East European Jews' very own vehicle of dispersion. For though the IRO and the Galveston Plan merely promised respectable jobs and a wholesome atmosphere in which to live, *bobbe-mysehs* concerning vast wealth, magically accumulated, enticed untold numbers of immigrants to head westward. As a gesture to verisimilitude, *bobbe-mysehs* were occasionally seasoned with a grain of truth. After all, a Jew from New York did go out to Oklahoma and struck oil and built his own shul. Did Jacob Schiff have his own shul? Certainly not—unless one counted Temple Emanu-El. Sometimes a simple remark could, through the accretions of retelling, become a satisfying *bobbe-myseh*. For example, some years after he had settled in a small Midwestern town, a former Jewish immigrant exclaimed grandly, *"Mein veib shlepzich aroum in a Nash!"* How more gratifying in the retelling, to give his wife not merely one Nash in which to *shlep* around, but three and, in addition to them, a White Steamer and a liveried chauffeur.

But material success didn't represent the whole of Jewish aspirations. East European Jews might go out to Des Moines and struggle upward from a penniless state to affluence. But was that enough? Another element—*takhlis*—a solid, worthwhile, high-minded objective for one's life—figured concretely, despite its seemingly intangible nature, in *shtetl* culture. It also lay firmly rooted in the conscious thinking of immigrants.

"I used to arrive at my lodging for the night completely frozen, but with a bank balance growing steadily," recalled a former immigrant who began life by peddling in Maine, ". . . yet from time to time the old question would come to mind. What is the *takhlis*? Am I going to be a peddler all my life? No, I cannot spend my lifetime this way, I thought."

What constituted *takhlis* differed, to an extent, with individuals, but learning always led to *takhlis*, while money only occasionally did. (There were still other Jewish concepts—*yiches*: pride in one's family or ancestry. Jews might have *yiches* and achieve *takhlis* and still be without money. Such Jews were invariably philosophers. There was also *naches*: pride and satisfaction, usually derived from the achievements of one's children. Probably Samuel Ribicoff, formerly of Grodno, Poland, saw little *takhlis* in being a bread salesman and a factory worker in New Britain, Connecticut—when he settled there in 1905. But as the father of Senator Abraham Ribicoff, he was able to *kleyb naches* [gather satisfaction].)

If success, *takhlis*, or a blend of both came from Lower East Side strivings, the process was a slow, backbreaking, obstacle-strewn one. Therefore, for many, the road to success beyond the Hudson seemed a more romantic byway, and eventual *takhlis* appeared enticingly closer in Houston, Texas, than on Houston Street. Thus, if the IRO or another charitable agency didn't send one West, then the adventurous set out by themselves—generally via peddling. Operating out of peddlers' warehouses at key points in the South, Midwest, and Far West, they would traverse their route, week after week, always eyeing their territory for a good business location where one could open a dry goods store and call it The Emporium or The Bon Ton or The New York Store. Soon after one of them settled in a rural community with his family, a brother might join them or a nephew. His wife's cousin might leave New York to settle in an adjoining town. In this way, a sprinkling of Jews became a part of small towns all over the country. By 1910 even Nevada had ninety-eight Jews who listed Yiddish as their mother tongue.

However, not all peddlers established stores in their pursuit of *takhlis*. Simon Fishman peddled through Oklahoma, Texas, and Colorado, grew wheat in Nebraska, and then moved to Kansas to become the Wheat King of West Kansas. Sol Levitan, too, used a nonmercantile formula. Fresh from Lithuania, nineteen-year-old Levitan landed in Baltimore in 1881, peddled over Pennsylvania and Ohio, and finally settled down in Green County, Wisconsin. By 1907 he had founded and was director of the Commercial National Bank of Madison and a close associate of Bob La Follette. Later he became a Progressive Party leader. (There can hardly have been *many* Progressive Party leaders who were bank presidents.) Levitan eventually became treasurer of Wisconsin; he kept a sign on his office door: "Uncle Sol, Your State Treasurer Welcomes You," until a ruffled building superintendent removed it with the comment "that it made the capitol look like a Jewish fire sale."

It hardly came as a surprise to Jews scattered throughout the country that they were not always welcomed. From time to time, irate natives charged Jewish peddlers with using unsportsmanlike means to achieve success. In the South, for example, local businessmen claimed that Russian Jewish peddlers and storekeepers prospered because they did "a great many things the white man of the South would not do. They have no objection at all to calling the negro 'mister' and they are pleasant to him. . . ." Naturally, reactions of this type often set off the *tsitterdik* syndrome among American Jews. "I consider it very unjust and unwise," wrote a man from Defiance, Ohio, to the *American Israelite,* "to send the refugees to very small places as they made a great deal of *richus.*"

In general, most American small towns, composed of English–Scotch-Irish–German mixtures, received Jewish families with a blend of friendly curiosity and condescension. But there were periods of extreme nativism. A small-town Jewish storekeeper was the first to know that the Klan was going to burn a cross, for individuals—who he knew rarely, if ever, changed their bed linen—came in and bought new sheets. A special situation existed in the innumerable little mining towns in western Pennsylvania. An East European Jewish family might find itself surrounded by an entire population of East European Christians, who, in Russia, might have taken part in pogroms. Yet in their new surroundings—without the venomous pressure of the imperial government and united by a common bond of language, Russian, Polish—amicable relationships and enduring friendships flourished between them. Indeed, the spectacle of a Jewish storekeeper—a former yeshiva *bochur*—and the local Russian Orthodox priest indulging in their weekly pinochle game was not a sight likely to have warmed the heart of Konstantin Pobyedonostzev. (Not only former *pogromschiks* emigrated, but Cossacks, too. In 1906, uniformed and booted, 5,000 of them disembarked at Ellis Island—but probably they didn't head for Delancey Street.)

Actually, anti-Semitism was more likely to occur in larger cities and usually during hard times—when success eluded everyone. In the depression winter of 1892, a New York charitable agency sent 600 Jewish immigrants to Fall River, Massachusetts. Work was scarce in the city's cotton mills, and competition from alien laborers was bitterly resented. Ominous anti-Semitic rumblings sounded, and rumors of riots spread. Hurriedly, members of Boston's Jewish community raised funds and distributed the immigrants elsewhere, averting trouble.* An anti-Semitic riot in Fall River may also have

* While anti-Semitic incidents occurred from time to time in different parts of the United States, they represented individual malice or stupidity, never government policy. Still one medieval reminder of imperial anti-Semitism turned up as late as 1928 in Massena, New York, a small community near the Canadian border. A four-year-old girl disappeared *erev* Yom Kippur, a timing which struck Massena's mayor as more than coincidence. He sent a state trooper to bring in Rabbi Berel Brennglass of Massena's Congregation Adath Israel to the police station for questioning. "Can you give any information," the rabbi was asked, "as to whether your people in the old country offer human sacrifices?" Whether the mayor and trooper were convinced by the rabbi's outraged denial of blood ritual, it became academic. The next day the child was found, unharmed. She had wandered off and fallen asleep in the woods. Apologies were adamantly rejected by the rabbi and his congregation. Eventually, the trooper and mayor wrote long fulsome apologies, and the matter was closed. But a rabbi in New York City suggested that Jews "should issue standing invitations . . . to their non-Jewish friends to visit homes and synagogues when they carry on religious rituals," presumably to attest to the paucity of human sacrifice.

been diverted because—by late summer of that year—the citizens had turned their attention to a new and horrifying drama. On August 4, it was charged, one of their native daughters took an ax. . . .

But anti-Semitism notwithstanding, the pursuit of success *cum takhlis* continued. Thousands and thousands of East European Jewish immigrants peddled their way to all points of the compass or were drawn via the Jewish magnet. Why did Ted Lewis' parents settle in Circleville, Ohio, Harry Hershfield's in Cedar Rapids, Iowa, Al Jolson's in Washington, D.C., Jack Benny's in Waukegan, Illinois, Dinah Shore's in Winchester, Tennessee, the Friedman girls'—Abigail Van Buren and Ann Landers—in Sioux City, Iowa? Some immigrants simply settled in towns that struck their fancy, or some established a business at a crossroad. Avrom Hirsch Goldbogen, for example, who later changed his name to Mike Todd, grew up in Bloomington, Minnesota, where his father, a poor part-time rabbi, ran a crossroad general store. Others started a town. Sol Abraham, a sawmill owner, founded one in Oregon which he named Julia for his wife. Ultimately after an argument with Abraham, the Southern Pacific Railroad struck back by changing the town's name to Glendale. And in Vermilion Parish, Louisiana, Abram Kaplan established the city of Kaplan and became a pioneer rice planter. Many immigrants achieved success in the clothing and movie industries, in intellectual fields, in public service. But two of them derived *takhlis* in what at the beginning of the twentieth century were unique areas.

One of the two was Laibel Willcher. As a nine-year-old, he had emigrated with his parents to Philadelphia from a *shtetl* near Kiev. Several years later the family moved to Washington, D.C., where they had relatives. After doing a four-year hitch in the Navy, his name now anglicized to Arthur L., or Al, Welsh, he married and settled down near Washington as a bookkeeper. However, in 1909, when Welsh saw the Wright brothers' experimental flights at Fort Myer, Virginia, he determined to learn to fly. He became one of Orville Wright's five original pupils and ultimately, according to Wilbur Wright, "the PEER of any man in the world as a PILOT." As a flight instructor at the Wrights' Dayton school, one of his pupils was Hap Arnold, later chief of the Air Force during World War II. Welsh won a prize for being the first aviator to fly more than two hours with a passenger and another for a continuous flight of three hours and five minutes. But in 1912,

his career ended tragically. He crashed and was killed while
testing a plane with a minimum speed of 45 miles per hour
and carrying a 450-pound load.

The other, Louis Blaustein, emigrated to the United States
from Lithuania in 1888. He peddled over eastern Pennsylvania for several years, then married, settled in Baltimore and
briefly ran a small wholesale grocery store. He worked for a
small oil jobber in Maryland until Standard Oil of New Jersey
eliminated him from competition. In 1910, Blaustein and his
eighteen-year-old son Jacob started the American Oil
Company, operating out of an old Baltimore stable. Their
staff consisted of one man who drove the tank wagon. On Ca-
thedral Street in Baltimore, the Blausteins set up a gas tank
with a meter that showed gallons and price. They called it the
Lord Baltimore Filling Station—the first drive-in gas station
in the United States. Another Blaustein development was an
antiknock gasoline, which they named Amoco. It fueled the
Spirit of St. Louis from New York to Paris.*

Encompassing *takhlis* and wealth, the career of one former
peddler was really in a class by itself. Indeed, it was a living
bobbe-myseh! In 1892 fourteen-year-old Samuel Zmuri left
his parents, three sisters, and two brothers in a Bessarabian
shtetl and traveled with his aunt in steerage to the United
States. Though they landed in New York, they moved south-
ward, drawn by the Jewish magnet. His aunt had relatives in
Georgia—and he lived in Savannah briefly before moving to
Selma, Alabama, where he worked as an errand boy, as a me-
chanic, and for an old peddler who traded tinware for pigs.
"In those days," he reminisced proudly when he had become
enormously wealthy, "I could outrun any pig in Dixie."

By the time he was eighteen Samuel Zmuri had brought his
whole family to Selma, and, at twenty, his name spelled more
pronounceably Zemurray, he arrived at the great turning
point in his life. He noticed that the price of bananas in Selma
fluctuated from week to week. On making inquiry, he learned
that very ripe bananas could sometimes be bought cheaply
and thus sold for less. So Zemurray went down to the Mobile
wharf, bought several stems of ripe bananas, brought them
back to Selma, and sold them to a grocer at a small profit. Inspired by this triumph, he invested $150 in ripe bananas,

---

* Among Jacob Blaustein's other distinctions, he became the first
president of the American Jewish Committee of Russian Jewish descent
—a momentous event that didn't occur until 1949.

wired grocers along the railroad line to be down at the depot if they were interested in buying bananas. This venture netted him $38. By 1903 he had sold 336,000 bunches of bananas, by 1910, 1,713,212, and he was known as Sam the Banana Man. Such a name—at once endearing and patronizing—immediately evokes that ubiquitous character of folklore—the humble little Jewish peddler. But Zemurray was nothing of the sort. He towered well over six feet. He was thin, with a thick shock of dark hair. He balanced a quiet, reflective aspect with occasional flares of temper, fueled with an extensive profane vocabulary in English and Spanish, to which he could add virtuoso curses in a number of Central American dialects. A rich Russo-Yiddish accent contributed still more flavor to his fierce outbursts.

Sam Zemurray had entered a business dominated by Boston goyim. Before 1870, bananas were exotic curiosities. Jewish immigrants landing in Boston in the eighties and nineties were frequently offered "a queer slippery kind of fruit," called bananas as a precursor of all the wonderful new treats in store for them. Few knew whether they were to be cooked, eaten raw, or exhibited as tropical ornaments. (Indeed, as late as the 1940's Chiquita had explicitly to educate Americans on the care of bananas.) Then, in 1870, Lorenzo Dow Baker, of Wellfleet, Massachusetts, captain of a fishing schooner with a run to Jamaica, brought back 160 bunches of bananas, for which he'd paid a shilling a bunch. He sold them in Jersey City for $2 a bunch, netting a profit which brought a sparkle to his eyes. Disregarding the derision of his neighbors on the Cape, he began to include more and more bananas in his cargo, unloading them in Boston, where a produce firm sold them on commission.

In 1885, Baker, ten members of the produce firm, and one ship formed the Boston Fruit Company. By the turn of the century it had merged with smaller companies along the East Coast to become the United Fruit Company, whose ten ships constituted the Great White Fleet. Captain Baker bought up land extensively in Jamaica and miles of Cape Cod property, including beachfront and cranberry marshes—"enough blame cranberries," he exclaimed, "to give a bowlful of Thanksgiving sauce to the whole dadblamed world."

Meanwhile, 2,000 miles south of Boston, Sam Zemurray was expanding, too. He went down to New Orleans and observed that the United Fruit Company's Great White Fleet threw huge quantities of bananas overboard because they were too ripe for shipment. He contracted with United to buy the "ripes" but refused to tell what he planned to do with them. Innocently, they assumed he hoped to transform them into a salable wine. Instead, to their great annoyance, Zemurray sold the ripe bananas to local markets at lower prices than those charged by the United Fruit Company.

When United offered to help finance Zemurray's purchase of the bankrupt Cuyamel Company, he gave up his contract for "ripes." He bought two old freighters—formerly of the Liverpool-Argentine run—for $60,000 ($5,000 cash) and progressed from banana jobber to banana importer, buying from independent planters in Honduras. His method of operation—tough and direct—contrasted with the behavior of United Fruit executives who stayed in Boston and favored replacing "tropical tramps" with ambitious young college men.

By this time Zemurray, who decided to go one step further and become a banana planter, had married Sara Weinberger, whose father, Jacob Weinberger—"The Parrot King"—was an old-timer in the banana game and the subject of many of the trade's favorite *bobbe-mysehs*. He was certainly not United Fruit's idea of executive material. Early in his career, Weinberger, a native Southerner, sailed along Caribbean shores, trading peddlers' ware—clothes, notions, cottons—for green bananas, coconuts, and parrots that swore in two languages. The latter he sold to pet shops in the United States, and the former went to jobbers in New Orleans. He made and lost fortunes with startling rapidity—once in a period of six hours. He transformed Nicaraguan swamps into productive banana plantations and was a popular figure among the natives. Thus, when Sam Zemurray formed the Cuyamel Fruit Company and bought land in Honduras, he sent his father-in-law there to handle production. However, in the midst of his expansion—irrigation experiments, railroad building—an obstacle arose in the form of Honduran-Wall Street politics.

In 1910 a new commercial treaty between the United States and Honduras was about to be signed. It stipulated that J. P. Morgan & Company would advance money to Honduras and be repaid by a percentage of custom duties. This arrangement displeased not only many Hondurans, including their deposed president, Manuel Bonilla, then hiding out in New Orleans, but also his friend Sam Zemurray. When Secretary of State Philander Knox objected to Zemurray's paying the Washington hotel expenses of two Hondurans lobbying against the treaty, Zemurray explained his position:

I was doing a small business buying fruit from independent planters, but I wanted to expand. I wanted to build railroads and raise my own fruit. The duty on railroad equipment was prohibitive—a cent a pound—and so I had to have concessions that would enable me to import that stuff duty free. If the banks were running Honduras and collecting their loans from custom duties how far would I have gotten when I asked for a concession? . . . I'm not a favorite grandson of Mr. Morgan's. Mr. Morgan never heard of me. I just wanted to protect my little business. Manolo Bonilla and I were working for the same thing. Why shouldn't I help him?

Why not, indeed! So in pursuit of their mutual goal of forestalling the treaty, Zemurray lent Bonilla money to buy the *Hornet*, a yacht built twenty years earlier for Henry Flagler, with an engine room armored by the Navy during the Spanish-American War. Two legendary soldiers of fortune, Lee Christmas and Machine-Gun Maloney, summoned from an evening of frivolity at Madame May Evan's bordello on Basin Street, accompanied Bonilla, a case of rifles, 30,000 pounds of ammunition, and a machine gun aboard the *Hornet*. They set off for Tegucigalpa, the Honduran capital. It was captured without bloodshed, without battle, with only a few cross words. The government was overthrown, and Bonilla became president again. The Morgan interests collapsed; Sam Zemurray got all the concessions he needed. (It may have been—as many of Zemurray's radical *landsleit* on the East Side preached—that the only way to shake off the oppressive bonds of Wall Street was through revolution.)

From then on, the Cuyamel Fruit Company prospered. Under Sam Zemurray's guidance, Cuyamel led in irrigation and soil experiments, drainage systems, railroad and steamship facilities, and company morale. Consequently, it also led in producing bananas for the market and irritation for the executives of the United Fruit Company.

Their irritation wasn't merely caused by the formidable competition or by Cuyamel's success in hiring away some of United's best men at higher salaries. Zemurray himself perplexed and bothered the Boston-based executives of United Fruit. That company's first president had spoken of Zemurray admiringly, as "a risker, a thinker, and a doer," but its second president disdainfully referred to his exceedingly tall competitor as "that little fellow." And Sam Zemurray was, indeed, a curious mixture. He loved a good *haimish* (cozy) chat with

people in the trade—peddler, planter, shipper, researcher—
Yankee or Honduran. He could converse and listen with
equal interest concerning sigatoka—the banana blight, or the
colic of Honduran babies. He had boundless energy and curiosity, often walking over miles and miles of plantation, or riding muleback instead of traveling by private car. And yet for
all his gregariousness, he insisted stubbornly on privacy. He
never made speeches and refused all public honors. Few people north of New Orleans—except in Boston—had ever heard
of him.

Finally, in 1929, United Fruit persuaded Zemurray to sell
Cuyamel for 300,000 shares of United Fruit stock, worth
$31,500,000, making him a director and United's largest
shareholder.

A millionaire many times over, Zemurray retired to his
four-story town house at 2 Audubon Place in New Orleans,
across the way from Tulane University, attended by his son,
and to which he had presented a chair of Middle American
research and a collection of Mayan relics. He bought and
began rehabilitating a 25,000-acre plantation in Tangipahoa
Parish. He played golf, hunted deer, pheasant and wild duck,
spent intervals boating at his summer home in Pass Christian,
Mississippi. (*Takhlis* in Pass Christian? Why not?)

As any empire builder would attest, the monetary rewards
of such endeavors pale before intangible ones: pride of creation, satisfaction in the results of one's life's work—*takhlis*.
So in 1932, when United Fruit's stock plummeted, and the
company was floundering on the verge of disaster, its inept
administration in Boston threatened not only Sam Zemurray's
$31,500,000, but his past achievements. Thus, on a cold day
in January, Zemurray appeared—tanned and determined—in
the rarefied atmosphere of United Fruit's boardroom on Federal Street, threw down his shares on the conference table,
and exclaimed, "You've been ———— up this business long
enough. I'm going to straighten it out."

Takhlis not only had to be achieved, but had to be pre-
served.

PART VI

"IT IS NO JOKE!"

. . . these Jews form the lower class in the Ghetto and they are known as Russian Jews.

—M. J. McKenna, *Our Brethren of the Tenement and Ghetto*

The Jews in America have revolutionized the tailoring trade by practically destroying the market for second-hand clothing. For the same price and even less than had to be paid for second-hand clothing ten years ago, one may procure new clothing. The value of this from the hygienic standpoint cannot be overestimated.

—"The Russian Jew in America," *Review of Reviews*

There are three million Jews in America and we have just as much right to have our own criminals as any other part of the population has to have its criminals.

—Judge Mayer Sulzberger

We might be able to do something for the Russian Jews if it were not for the students who are always stirring up discontent among them by their socialistic teachings.

—*American Hebrew* editor to New York *Times* reporter

It is about time that the Jews of Russia familiarize themselves with the life of the Jews in New York City. It is no joke!

—I. M. Rubinow, *The Jewish Question in New York City*

24

Unwashed Alien Bodies

Though it was debatable just how many American tourists sailed off to Europe for the specific purpose of seeing "a genuine Jewish ghetto," in 1897 the New York *Times* advised its readers that such a trip was quite unnecessary. In New York City, right at their doorstep ("No expensive steamship fares need to be paid"), south of Houston Street and east of the Bowery, there was the real, the bona fide article, "those interesting glimpses of typical Russo-Jewish life. . . . Even the daily drudgery and toil of these immigrants is worth the study of the careful student of humanity."

Despite the *Times* travel-guide tone, the Lower East Side lacked tranquil, picturesque tourist attractions. Rather, the situation in its Seventh, Eleventh, and Thirteenth wards— three-quarters of whose population was Jewish—set off alarms, dire predictions, warnings, and helpless hand wringing. Seventy percent of the East European Jewish immigrants settled in already grossly overpopulated tenements. As sociological statistics presented it, the Eleventh Ward had 1,774 people per acre and the Tenth, 1,526 per acre, while the Bombay ghetto had a mere 759.66 per acre. Those East Side acres —more than 500 of them—"enjoyed the distinction of being the most densely populated in the United States." It was maintained that there was not enough standing room on a street for the people who lived on it. One corner—at Hester and Orchard streets—was so thickly jammed with people and pushcarts that it was declared the most congested on the face of the earth. "The stores cannot hold the goods, the sidewalks cannot accommodate the buyers and the streets cannot contain the mass of carts that are pushed upon, into, and toward its asphalt pavement." They swarmed, they teemed, they infested, they herded, mobbed, packed . . . verbs applied with anguished distaste. Had the same situation prevailed in all New York City, the city would have had 150,000,000 people. (Yet only a decade earlier Abe Cahan had submitted a story about the East Side to the Sunday editor of the New York *Sun,* who read it with great interest and then said to Cahan, "Pardon me, you use a word about which I must ask. What is a ghetto?")

And all uptown observers, Jew and non-Jew, who considered themselves—with sporadic accuracy—"careful students of humanity," found East European Jews more perplexing than the Irish and German immigrants who had previously lived on the same streets. Simpler days long past even evoked a certain nostalgia. "The great thieves that once dominated the street are gone," Frank Moss, a former president of the New York Police, wrote poignantly, "there is nothing to keep them, and no place for them to rest and think and hide and plan. Billy McGlory, the fiend, the king of dive keepers and the ruiner of an army of girls, once kept his Armory Hall at 158 Hester Street, but he is gone."

Not infrequently, a downright unfriendliness could be detected. "Such faces, such names, such voices, such sounds, smells, such intense haggling, bargaining, trading!" Yet occasionally someone spotted a virtue. In contrast with other immigrant neighborhoods, the New York *Herald* reported approvingly, few saloons were to be found among Jews. Instead, they had delicatessens and coffeehouses—whose chief beverage was tea. (On the other hand, at *Yahudim* teas the chief beverage was coffee.) It may have been that in 1893, borsht, gelfilte fish, lox, and Hungarian strudel were as addictive for Jewish laborers as gin was for their Irish counterparts, or perhaps uninhibited *noshing* provided the same wicked thrill as booze, for no less an authority than a government report from Washington solemnly declared that "among Russian Jews, gluttony is considered a sin."

Usually, however, philanthropists, sociologists, clergymen, government officials, police, medical experts, missionaries, and journalists formed a critical audience—prepared to analyze, sermonize, admonish, and reveal their bleak opinions through rhetorical questions. "What is the outlook? Will these people improve? Can they be fused into the mass of American citizenship without debasing it?"

The major obstacle to their reaching any effective conclusions was their total misunderstanding of the nature of East European Jews. Thus, an individual as sensitive and well meaning as Jacob Riis could maintain—in the face of the rich store of culture and tradition the immigrants brought with them—that the reason the Russian Jew was the ripest material for citizenship was that ". . . he comes to us without a past. He has no country to renounce, no ties to forget." One must bear in mind that much of Riis' information came from Max Fischel, "a little old round happy Jewish boy," who gathered the facts from which Riis wrote his articles. However, according to Lincoln Steffens, Riis "trained his boy Max to see and understand as Riis did."

Even the adjectives used to describe Russian Jewish immigrants emphasized the exotic and led to misinterpretation. For example, the experts often applied "Oriental" to East European Jews. They meant the term to indicate the Mongol type common among Russians—smooth dark hair, broad high cheeks, and the Mongolian eye, "placed obliquely or slanting, so that the external angle is higher than the inner angle and the aperture is much narrower than in ordinary eyes." And this alien appearance intensified a hostile conviction that so outlandish a people must surely be up to no good.

Consequently, they presented a sinister spectacle to many: bearded old *zayde*s, still in caftans and streimmels, slowly trudging headdown toward home or shul; women, their *shaitels* clamped tightly on their heads, picking feverishly over food or clothing on pushcarts, with small children clinging to their skirts; older children—after school—their arms heaped high with garments they and their families had sewn at home, on their way to deliver them to one of the neighborhood sweatshops; middle-aged men, hollow-eyed, depressed—some of them would become either suicide* (*"Er hot genumen de gez"*) or desertion (*"Er hot avekgelufn fun heim"*) items in

---

* According to Dr. Maurice Fishberg, an anthropologist, "Jewish immigrants in New York City are much given to self-destruction, although in their native homes suicide is very rare." Indeed, by 1907 a Yiddish newspaperman estimated that "there are six Jewish suicides on the average weekly in New York City." Suicides also abounded on the

the Yiddish press; ambitious young men, clean-shaven, wearing derbies, walking quickly, dreaming of moving their families from Rivington Street to the solid middle-class comfort of the Bronx. All these people were somehow thought to have qualities unlike other nationalities, to harbor some cabalistic, unsporting "Oriental" appurtenance known as a "subtle Hebrew brain."

Yet only when they were seen en masse, all on stage simultaneously and moving rapidly—even if it were only ten-year-olds hurrying to *chedar*—did they appear overpowering to uptown observers, the more nervous of whom might sooner or later begin muttering of a coming "preponderating Semitic influence in the United States." Inside, in the dismal rooms in which they lived, the immigrants impressed observers as vulnerable, pitiable. "At night the floor is covered with the sleepers who are fortunate if they have mattresses to interpose between themselves and the boards." Presumably, affected by the airless, dim surroundings, "the workings of that wonderful machine, the Jewish mind," ground to a halt and turned to *shmaltz*.

It appeared easier to come up with solutions for the wretched conditions of the tenements than to divine the behavior and appearance of the people on the streets. And the simplest way to improve tenement conditions was to acquire a better grade of poor people to occupy them. According to one journalist, the Russian Jews "cannot be lifted up to a higher place because they do not want to be," and according to another, "the most incorrigible slummers, paupers and vagrants are Italians and Jews."*

In cold fact, however, tenements in all their deplorable state existed in New York long before the immigration from unfashionable parts of Europe had commenced. Early slums consisted of old houses divided into one- or two-room flats.

---

stage of the Yiddish theater, but while these histrionic versions were almost always ascribed to "intellectual despondency," the real thing among East Siders was far more likely to be caused by degrading living and working conditions.

* Jewish and Italian immigrants were continually linked by slum watchers for possession of the same negative traits. According to these experts, both groups positively relished squalid living conditions and nourished criminal tendencies. In reality, they did share certain characteristics. Neither had proclivities for heavy drinking, and both had a weakness for gambling. Both Jews and Italians were emotional, warm-hearted, and had a high degree of natural humor. Moreover, together they produced the best mayor in the history of New York.

Backyard privies were surrounded by hastily and shoddily built shanties to hold more lodgers. At one time the city also had 300 underground lodging houses. During a visit to the United States in 1846, Charles Dickens had alluded to New York slums in typical Dickensian prose: "What place is this, to which the squalid street conducts us? A kind of square of leprous houses. . . . What lies beyond this tottering flight of steps that creak beneath our tread?—a miserable room, lighted by one dim candle, and destitute of all comfort, save what may be hidden in a wretched bed." Four years later the New York *Evening Post* proudly reported the erection of a new building:

> built with the design of supplying the laboring people with cheap lodgings and will have many advantages over the cellars and other miserable abodes, which too many are forced to inhabit. The depth of the building is two hundred and forty feet, with a front of thirty-five feet. Each tenement consisting of two rooms and a hall, is nearly eighteen feet in width and about twenty in length; giving twenty-four residents to each floor. This is a praiseworthy enterprise and well worthy of imitation.

This "praiseworthy enterprise" was the first railroad flat. Imitated over and over and over again, it transformed the decaying slums of the old city into the decaying slums of modern New York. Nevertheless, driven by the need to use available rectangular lots in the most financially advantageous way and still to adhere to a law which forbade any construction covering the lot solidly, tenement designers did progress beyond the railroad flat. (The first New York apartment house—as distinguished from the tenement—was the Stuyvesant on Eighteenth Street, built in 1869 and designed by Richard Hunt who had modeled it after fashionable Parisian multiple dwellings and called it a "French Apartment.")

From railroad flats, the only direction tenement architecture could take was up, thus even the dumbbell double-decker was an improvement. Still, had East Side Jews who lived in them been told that their design had once won a prize, they would have quite likely reacted with astonishment and a muttered *"Es is eichet an America,"* an expression—"This, too, is an America"—which they felt explained all the Golden Land's aberrations. The prize was won shortly before the Jewish exodus from Russia. A trade magazine, the *Plumber and Sanitary Engineer,* initiated a competition for "an ideal plan for tenement houses to be constructed on an interior lot 25′ by 100′." Of the 200 plans submitted, the one by James E. Ware of New York City received the award. His original design was of a building with a narrow middle—12½ feet wide —that gave the structure the shape of a dumbbell and a future as a perfect firetrap. The open stairways formed a flue, and the air shaft on each side served as a chimney through which fire could—and did—flame upward, consuming six or seven decks or stories, on each of which were four apartments —two on each end, with the narrow hall between in which stairs and landing were jammed.

In 1885, three years after his experience on Wards Island, George M. Price was appointed sanitary inspector on the East Side, for an area that included 11,000 buildings, in which 10,000 families—nine-tenths of them Russian Jewish immigrants—lived. "The horrible sights" he repeatedly saw depressed and sickened him:

> The buildings in which the Jews lived were crowded, damp, without elementary sanitary facilities, half in ruins. . . . The flats were dark, dank, emitting an unbearable stench, particularly those flats which also served as shops. The inhabitants were in a poor state of health. Children died like flies during the frequent epidemics. . . . Parents were forced to have their children help them in tobacco or tailoring work, or else send them—at the age of six or seven—to work in a shop, which meant physical, psychological and moral deterioration. . . . Not infrequently we came across buildings housing one hundred families with eight hundred persons.

Frequent fires caused new regulations which caused new circumlocutions. For example, the bars of mandatory fire escapes were often made to conform with the legally required thickness by numerous applications of "black wash," a cheap coating. And the paint used in the rooms, which firemen called "three-month paint," was highly inflammable. Tenements occupied by Jews were particularly susceptible to fires on Friday nights, on the eve of Yom Kippur, and during Chanukah, as well as other holidays which required the lighting of candles. But when alarmed rabbis instructed their congregants to place their candlesticks in basins of water, East

Side fires on holidays diminished to the normal, secular twenty-five a day.

In the later models of double-deckers, two toilets were added to the middle section. Frozen in winter and overflowing in summer, these primitive facilities constantly inspired revolted uptown investigators to find just the right sensory-emotive adjective: "unspeakably filthy," "disease-ridden," "foul," "stinking." The meager water supply, usually a tap outside the building, discouraged even those who had an excessive attachment for bathing. Nonetheless, a finger of reproach pointed to the "Russian and Polish Jews" as "the most unclean population which the city has," and "cleanliness is an unknown quantity to these people." When Adolph Ochs' New York *Times* described the Lower East Side as "the filthiest place in the western continent," the *Yahudim* were aggrieved. Indeed, they associated a disinclination to bathing with radical politics—and a neat haircut and clean collar with Republican respectability. Deep down, they felt that socialism and anarchism—even Tammanyism—could be dissolved by soap and water. So in 1893 the immaculate gentlemen of the Baron de Hirsch Fund established free public baths on the corner of Henry and Market streets. In so doing, in sending the immigrants to showers, they changed the bathing habits—though not the politics—of all America. For the essential principle of the German rainbath, which they adopted, was "the abolition of the old-fashioned bathtub." Instead of soaking in a tub, "the bather is standing in a rain of luke-warm water falling upon him with some force while he is soaping himself, and thus gets rid of all accumulations on the skin, the latter being washed away by the force of the douche and flowing at once away in the drains provided for each bath."

However, far more than unwashed alien bodies troubled the *Yahudim*. Of the numerous fears concerning East European Jewish immigrants, one of the most overriding was that they would inevitably produce criminals. Earlier Jewish immigration had been responsible for a number of noteworthy contributions to the underworld. And though no one cared to boast about these crooks, they *had* excelled in their profession. Who could overlook Felonious Fredericka, the ineffable Mother Mandelbaum, Queen of the Fences, 250 pounds of villainous womanhood? Enchanted reporters described her as "not beautiful but massive," with remarkably large sensual features, an excessively florid complexion, and a protruding underlip. A widow with four children, she bravely carried on her "little notions business" in a small dry goods store on the corner of Clinton and Rivington streets. She lived in two elegantly decorated floors above, their eclectic but handsome furnishings harvested from some of the most opulent homes in New York. "There were many unique assemblies about her table, for she gave 'swell' dinners to her thieving associates . . ."

In a 25-foot frame wing, adjacent to her shop, she received the swag of a network of burglars, "house-and-bank sneaks," and pickpockets, both Jewish and non-Jewish. (Mother M. was above religious prejudice; merit alone counted with her.) She kept her associates in expense money and that renowned legal firm of the underworld, Howe and Hummel, on a $5,000 yearly retainer. At the height of her gang's power, it was maintained that they committed 80 percent of the bank robberies in the United States.

But despite certain congenial arrangements with New York police, Pinkerton detectives employed by a district attorney who didn't care for congenial arrangements nabbed her in 1884, at the age of fifty-two. She was arraigned on seven counts of grand larceny in the second degree and with a count for receiving stolen goods.

When Mother Mandelbaum, her son Julius, and her confidential clerk, Herman Stoude, skipped bail and fled to Canada, her attorney, William Howe, genially explained her disappearance to reporters. She was of a philosophic turn of mind, Howe said, and believed "absence of body was better than presence of mind." She spent the rest of her life in Canada, though she made occasional visits to New York which the press duly reported. But the police—despite their familiarity with her distinctive appearance—apparently never noticed her.

Mother Mandelbaum's absence was felt, but there were other *gonovim* to carry on. There was Abe Greenthal, leader of the infamous Sheeny Gang, "acknowledged to be one of the most expert pickpockets in America," who had delusions of grandeur so extraordinary that he not only called himself "General Greenthal," but also, although born in Poland, claimed to be "a German." The East Side was also the habitat of Sheeny Mike Kurtz, burglar and safe blower. Sophie Lyons, née Levy, con woman, pickpocket, and "adventuress"; Emmanuel Marks, "the red-headed Jew" bank sneak and skin gambler. To say nothing of Silver Dollar Smith—Charles

Solomon—who ran the Silver Dollar Saloon* (whose entire
floor had silver dollars cemented—firmly—on it) on Essex
Street. Silver Dollar Charlie's lawyer was Max Hochstim, who
ran a protection racket and who, after harsh treatment at the
hands of the Lexow Investigation Committee, was heard to
mutter sourly, "Them Reformers have given us a bad name."
The Max Hochstim Association held an annual outing at
Long Island pleasure resorts, which it was advisable to attend
at $5 a ticket. "The Association will assemble at Head-
quarters, Number 47 Delancey Street at eight o'clock A.M.,
sharp," the ticket read ominously, "and march in a body to
the boat." (Hochstim, though he had an accommodation pact
with many members of the police, was not above ingratiating
himself with a judge by a flattering word or so. "Your
Honor," he once said winningly, "you sure look swell in the
judicial vermin.")

These were isolated individuals, playing no part in a huge
ethnic criminal band. But after the turn of the century, when
New York's Jewish population had grown to 1,000,000, it was
noted that its crime rate had increased accordingly. On the
face of it, this statistic should have surprised no one. A small
percentage of every ethnic group had resorted to crime in its
rise from poverty. Yet in 1902, officials observed that "within
the last year or two the Hebrews also have shown tendencies
to the grosser vices that have never before characterized
them. It can hardly be doubted that a people of their general
habits with respect to temperance and the family relation
must have fallen under some alien influence to bring about
such conditions as are now found to exist on the East Side."
The "alien influence" equaled the desire to succeed in America which, in the minds of many of the young East Siders, required them to disavow their parents' way of life and traditional Jewish values. "The Russian Jew comes here with his
reverence for the law, with his Old World notions of submission, and lo! within a few years there grows up around
him a set of young people—more American than Americans,
with reverence for nothing and submission to nothing but
their own desires."

Attempts of Jews themselves to deal with this explosive sit-

* In 1890, with the passage of the Raines Law, which permitted the
sale of liquor on Sunday only in hotels, the Silver Dollar became a
"Raines Hotel." Thus, bars were magically transformed into hotels—
and, in fact, many actually became hotels by renting rooms for purposes
of prostitution.

uation started in 1908, when an uptown lady began *hokking a tchynik* about unlicensed pushcart peddlers, and ended in 1917 when the agents of the Bureau of Social Morals, an authentic Jewish vice squad, closed its investigations. Then the warning hissed for more than four years throughout the East Side underworld—"Cheez it! Jewish societies are watching!" —was heard no more.

25

With Friends Like This ...

Few of her colleagues in the higher echelons of New York City public education, or her neighbors at 330 Central Park West, or her family connections—the Altmans and the Proskauers—would have had the temerity, or the command of Yiddish, to call Miss Julia Richman a *tsutcheppenish*. Any such sentiment—pinning Miss Richman down as a pest, an irritating vexation that clings tenaciously—would have had to emanate from the Lower East Side, where Miss Richman's popularity sank like a stone in the spring of 1908.

A highly esteemed pioneer in education, Miss Richman was at that time a formidable maiden lady of fifty-three. She was the first woman in Manhattan to attain the post of district supervisor of public schools, and her list of achievements was truly imposing. She introduced eye examinations into public schools, the dispensation of corrective glasses to those who needed them, and special instruction for retarded children. Her participation in Jewish community life was equally distinguished, particularly in matters dealing with the East European immigrants. In 1894 she recommended in a report to the Hebrew Free School Association that the *chedar* be abandoned, because the teaching of Hebrew loosened ties with the public schools. She was the first president of the YWHA, a charter member of the National Council of Jewish Women—

an organization founded primarily to protect young Jewish immigrant girls from white slavers who lay in wait for them at the docks—and a founding member and director of the Educational Alliance. For some years, she had also directed *Helpful Thoughts,* a magazine for Jewish children.

In all these positions she evidenced, as one admirer asserted, "her sincere desire to obviate evils or irregularities." As one example of her vigilance, Educational Alliance minutes reveal that "Miss Richman called attention to the fact that owing to an error, Mr. Stern was re-elected a trustee at the last annual meeting when his term had not expired, whereas Messrs. Seligman and Blumenthal, whose term had expired, had not been re-elected." Yet despite all her good works on behalf of Russian Jews, the pushcart controversy brought the wrath of the East Side down on her pompadoured head.

Pushcarts "gently gliding by" exist only in the world of song lyrics. In the reality of 1908, uptown critics regarded them as a noisy nuisance, a fire hazard, an odorous embarrassment that also clogged street space where, it was declared indignantly, children might otherwise play. To downtowners, pushcarts were a livelihood and a source of good cheap food and clothing. To a politician like Senator Jacob Javits, having a mother who was a pushcart peddler was the "New York equivalent of being born in a log cabin."

A city ordinance required pushcart peddlers to have a $15 license, but the city issued only 4,000 licenses, forcing about 10,000 or more unlicensed vehicles to ply the streets illegally. Investigation of police records on the Lower East Side revealed the huge increase in the Jewish crime rate was due primarily to arrests for Sunday violations and of unlicensed pushcart peddlers. The police, however, did not trouble a large number of unlicensed peddlers who had either paid the requisite $5 bribe or whose association had promised to deliver their votes solidly for Tammany. (If these votes weren't forthcoming, they were told bluntly, there would be trouble—*"vet sein tsuris."*)

Pushcarts were one of those vexing issues with which all New York City administrations, sooner or later, had to grapple. Any decision was bound to offend a huge bloc of voters. All politicians, therefore, from corrupt Tammany Democrats to upright reform Republicans approached this political hot potato with a mien of outward civic rectitude masking inward trepidation. They next employed that timeless trinity of political convenience: (1) Appoint an investigative committee; (2)

disregard its findings; (3) fuzz the issues until a new administration comes in. The gavotte was then repeated, step by step.* Consequently, lower Manhattan became a jungle of rickety pushcarts—before Jewish holidays every kind of vehicle was used, even old baby carriages—laden with cheap merchandise and fragrant and not so fragrant food. The sound backdrop to this scene, an incessant hubbub of clamorous Yiddish.

This inelegant display outraged Miss Richman's sensibilities; she therefore demanded that Police Commissioner General Theodore Bingham rigidly enforce the law. General Bingham, a West Point man, had retired from the Army after an accident in which he had lost a leg. And though Mayor George McClellan, under whom he served, regarded him as "utterly tactless and arrogant," apparently Bingham's personality also encompassed unexpected depths of *rachmones*—and compassion is commendable even when inspired by political expediency.

"You don't want to be too hard on the poor devils," he told Miss Richman. "They have to make a living."

"I say, if the poor devils cannot make a living without violating our laws," Miss Richman answered with characteristic authority, "the immigration department should send them back to the country from which they came."

The angry outcries evoked by Miss Richman's widely circulated declaration daunted her not at all. In speeches, she continued to recommend that violators of pushcart ordinances be deported. Before long, downtowners circulated a petition, addressed to the Board of Education, demanding that Miss Julia Richman be transferred to another district. Upon receiving a copy of this petition for his signature, Louis Marshall replied with a stirring panegyric to good intentions:

Is a lifetime spent in good works to go for naught, because of an occasional over-emphasis of expression? Are years of acknowledged usefulness to end in shipwreck because of the use of superlatives or misconstrued metaphors? . . . Nobody can make me believe that your characterizations of Miss Richman are justified, or that your adjectives are applicable to anything she has said or done. Her methods may not have

* The resolution of the pushcart problem did not occur until the late thirties, when Mayor LaGuardia put all pushcarts under a roof; then, like a king conferring knighthood, he told the peddlers, attired in white coats for the occasion, "Now you're merchants."

been the best, her words, on occasion, have been unwise, her discretion may sometimes have lapsed, but her motives have been unimpeachable.

Miss Richman survived as district supervisor, perhaps because by the fall, the erstwhile protector of the pushcart peddlers, Police Commissioner Bingham, became the target for even greater downtown hostility.

In an article for the *North American Review,* "Foreign Criminals in New York," Commissioner Bingham stated that 50 percent of the criminals in the city were Russian Jews, who numbered only 25 percent of the population.* "They are burglars, pickpockets, firebugs and highway robbers," he wrote, adding somewhat gratuitously, "when they have the courage." (Bingham was later to say that in writing his article, he had felt not "the slightest malice, prejudice or unfriendliness." This raises the speculation that it may very well have been Commissioner Bingham—or Julia Richman—who inspired that well-worn Jewish axiom "With friends like this, who needs enemies?")

The East Side erupted over the article, and the downtown press demanded Bingham's resignation. The *Warheit* informed its readers that the article in the *North American Review* wasn't Bingham's first venture into anti-Semitism. In the November, 1907, issue of *Harper's Weekly,* he had declared that 1,200 out of 2,000 pictures in the rogues' gallery were of Russian Jews.

The violence of the reactions came not just from wounded pride or resentment at being unjustly maligned. Bingham's statistics provided a ready weapon for those, in and out of Congress, who were urging immigration restrictions. If Jews produced so many criminals, why allow such a great number of them to enter the country? Thus the editorial storm provoked by Bingham's article contained an urgent plea for de-

* New York City was not alone in making the charge that East European Jews had a strong disposition for criminal pursuits. In London the police regarded the East European Jews who had settled in the Whitechapel district with great suspicion. Indeed, the head of the CID maintained that Jack the Ripper was "a low-class Polish Jew," though in 1888, Scotland Yard received a communication denying that identity among others: "I'm not a butcher, I'm not a Yid,/ Nor yet a foreign skipper,/ But I'm your own lighthearted friend,/ Yours truly, Jack the Ripper." And, of course, a more recent theory identifies the Ripper as a high-class heir to the British throne: Victoria's grandson, Prince Albert Edward—a non-Jew.

fense. The *Tageblatt* thundered: "We have a million Jews in New York. Where is their power? Where is their organization? Where are their representatives?"

Uptown, where the power, organizations, and representatives usually were, a relative calm reigned. In the beginning, anger had been expressed at Bingham's "venom and prejudice," but soon circumspection moderated emotion, for American Jews were struck by the horrendous possibility that Bingham's statistics might be accurate. Who knew what those wild Russians were up to?

Jacob Schiff remained silent for more than a week; then he conveyed his "shock and astonishment at the reckless statement of the Commissioner." Comment from the 30 Broad Street office of Louis Marshall turned out to be even more succinct.

But some blocks northeast of Untermeyer, Guggenheimer & Marshall, on East Broadway, the *Tageblatt* thundered once again. This time it asked a rhetorical question, reviving the Seligman-Grand Hotel controversy: "When someone refused to allow a Jewish aristocrat into a Gentile hotel, the Jewish four hundred did not rest until the guilty party had been dismissed; and now . . . they are quiet! Is it because the ones insulted are Russian Jews?"

In rebuttal, on Friday, September 11, the *American Hebrew,* "organ of the Jewish four hundred," lectured downtowners on "Jewish Sensitiveness." The Bingham incident, they editorialized, "illustrates the excessive sensitiveness of Jews with regard to any statements derogatory to their highest claim. So many of them have passed their lives under the withering face of repression, that in this land of liberty they tend to go to the other extreme and insist upon the right of freedom with undue emphasis. . . ."

"Is this the Torah of Americanism which you teach us?" The *Tageblatt* demanded. Instead of guiding them in becoming proud citizens of a free country, "you preach the old Torah of fawning to bend the back quietly and be still."

Much of the downtown press eyed with distrust not only the *American Hebrew* and the Conservative movement it represented, but also the non-Yiddish-speaking uptown reform "reverends," especially the American Jewish Committee, organized by Louis Marshall and Jacob Schiff two years earlier. The announced purpose of the AJC was to protect the civil and religious rights of Jews all over the world. So where,

asked the Yiddish press, was the committee now? Only reti-
cence emanated from the committee's officers.

Meanwhile, as the editorial war between uptown and downtown went on, Louis Marshall, who opposed countering
Bingham's statement "by any sensational methods," covertly
closeted himself, in *shtadlan* tradition, with Mayor George
McClellan, Jr., and Deputy Police Commissioner Arthur
Woods. A carefully worded retraction written by Woods and
Marshall emerged—though one suspects the major contribution was Marshall's*—which they "had every reason to believe Commissioner Bingham will give to the press tomorrow," on his return from vacation, provided the East Side
would drop demands for his resignation and consider the matter closed. To this, downtown leaders agreed.

According to the retraction statement, which Bingham
promptly issued, "the figures used in the article were not compiled by myself, but were furnished me by others, and were
unfortunately assumed to be correct. It now appears, however, that these figures were unreliable.† Hence it becomes my
duty frankly to say so and repudiate them. . . . I withdraw the
statements challenged frankly and without reserve."

Triumphantly, Marshall wrote Judge Mayer Sulzberger on
the day the retraction appeared that although to the East Side,
"we are still not entirely kosher, we are not so *trefa* as we
would have been had the fight not been made. . . ."

Nevertheless, in a letter to the *Tageblatt*, which it published
the next day, Marshall scolded the immigrants: "What has the
great east side, with all of its protests, done to obviate and
cure the existing evils, and to eradicate the causes which have
led to juvenile delinquency. . . . It is possible that some of the
so-called Jewish magnates, whose coolness you deprecate,
may have influenced this dignified solution of an unpleasant
episode. . . ."

The *Tageblatt* responded fiercely, defensively. "Had we on
the East Side remained silent and awaited salvation from on
high, Bingham would not have taken his words back. If our
prominent Jews from the upper circles used their influence it

---

* In a statement to the New York *Times*, Marshall guilelessly approved "the manly and courageous manner" of Bingham's retraction.

† An accurate investigation of crime statistics in New York City
revealed that out of 2,848 felony convictions in 1907, 460 were of Jews
—16.14 percent, not 50 percent. And 6.1 percent of every 10,000
criminals were Jewish.

was due to the storm we raised on the East Side. . . ." But in closing, the *Tageblatt* struck a note that was central to the entire conflict between the *Yahudim* and the Russian immigrants. Everyone on the East Side, it said, was aware of the importance to American Jewry "of a Jacob Schiff and a Louis Marshall." However they also wanted "self-recognition": "we wish to give our famous Jews their honored place in an American Jewish organization in the measure that they have earned it. But we wish them to work with us and not over us."

After all the rhetoric and rejoinder, the claims and counterclaims, the Bingham incident forced the whole downtown Jewish community to realize that New York's 1,000,000 Jews needed an organization to represent them. But in 1909, the consolidation of 1,000,000 Jews in one cohesive, more or less congenial group smacked of the unachievable; it meant uniting uptown and downtown, *Deitchen* and Russian, Zionist and Anti-Zionist, Litvaks and Galitzianer, Republican and Socialist, Citizens Union and Tammany Hall, the American Jewish Committee and the Workmen's Circle, Reform and Orthodox, religious and atheist, philanthropist and *shnorrer*.

For so redoubtable an undertaking, it seemed only suitable that its leader should be not only a visionary, but a blend of the constituency; that he be of East European descent, but just married to the sister-in-law of one of the most influential *Yahudim* in the United States; that he should be a graduate of the Hebrew Union College, where Zionism was anathema, and also a founder of the Order of the Sons of Zion; that he should be a Reform rabbi at Temple Emanu-El, but also have had a grandfather who was a Hassid.

26

Shoenfeld to Magnes to Gaynor

Judah L. Magnes, a remarkably handsome, thirty-one-year-old frustrated baseball player from California, met every demanding requirement.

Born in Oakland, where his father had emigrated from Poland in 1863, Magnes' boyhood was often lyrically described as "typically American." He had yearned to be a professional baseball player or a great orator and was devoted to the works of Horatio Alger and Oliver Optic. Still, "Oriental"—used to characterize the exotic qualities of East European Jews—might certainly have been applied to the Magnes home, in which kashrut was strictly observed by the Chinese cook.

In 1900, when Judah Magnes graduated from Hebrew Union College at the top of his class, he became the first native California Jew to be ordained and had already won a reputation as a highly gifted speaker. A decade or so later, when HUC began acquiring many students of East European descent, some from orphanages, officials corrected noticeable esthetic defects—by capping teeth, treating acne conditions, and providing the ministrations of an elocution teacher to eradicate unrefined accents and implant in their stead that rolling Reform baritone so pleasing to God and Reform congregants. Had Judah Magnes been among them, it would not have been necessary to lift a finger, for he possessed—as the admiring *American Hebrew* itemized—"a straight limbed carriage, well-poised head and pleasantly modulated voice." Although he had a tooth missing in his upper jaw, he was rather proud of this one defect. "I have always been considered too pretty-pretty," he explained. "This gives me a fierce bizarre effect."

Magnes spent the new few years in Germany studying the Talmud, religion, philosophy, becoming more and more obsessed with the Zionist idea. "I wish to live now more like a Jew," he wrote alarmed parents, "that is, an Orthodox Jew. . . ." And Louis Lipsky, a leader in the Zionist movement, noted that "when he returned, he seemed like a man who had put on the shining armor of knight errantry and was eager to conquer the world. He wore a beard and observed the dietary laws."

Aware of the constantly increasing number of East European Jews in the United States, Magnes began studying Yiddish. He wandered over to the East Side, reveling in the atmosphere, joined the Zionist organization, and spoke at Zionist meetings.

Nevertheless, Magnes spent the next year as librarian at HUC, whose president, Kaufmann Kohler, was the leader of classic Reform doctrine and, as such, intransigently opposed to Zionism. Magnes organized a Zionist club in Cincinnati and made frequent and pointed analogies between Reform and Zionist ideologies. Warned by Dr. Kohler to stop these Zionist appeals, he resigned from HUC and accepted a Reform pulpit at Temple Israel in Brooklyn.

The continued pogroms in Russia—the massacre in Kishinev and other cities—led Magnes, shortly after his installation in the Brooklyn pulpit, to organize the first protest parade in American Jewish history, in which 100,000 East European Jews marched solemnly up Broadway and Fifth Avenue following Judah Magnes, who had become the only idol American Jews had provided for young Russian Jews.

By 1906 Judah Magnes had been scouted by Louis Marshall for the pulpit of *the* Reform temple, Emanu-El, where it was hoped he would appeal to the congregation's young people. The *Yahudim*, too, were having trouble with rebellious children, but the predicament of the Temple Emanu-El parents was just the reverse of that suffered by immigrant parents. As Magnes described the conflict, it "was between parents who are estranged from Judaism and children who have yearnings towards it." The new rabbi succeeded in attracting young people, so well, in fact, that he married one of them, Beatrice Lowenstein, the young sister of Mrs. Louis Marshall.

Had anyone but Judah Magnes advanced the idea of a kehillah, he would not only have been driven from the temple, but from the shul, too. The kehillah was a communal organization in *shtetl* life. Magnes, with his customary keen enthusiasm, was certain that such an organization would "wipe out invidious distinctions between East Europeans and West Europeans." Its officers would be democratically elected, but it would be allied with the American Jewish Committee, whose officers "never wanted any elections."

At the conclusion of the Bingham incident, in the fall of 1908, the need to "lift the feeling of the [Jewish] community from the subconscious state into full consciousness" became obvious. With Magnes, who possessed a single-minded determination, employing the full force of his charm and personality alternately to cajole, suggest, persuade, urge, pacify, and conciliate, uptown and downtown delegates met and argued at several conventions. By the end of February, 1909, the delegates had adopted a constitution for the Jewish Community of New York City. The kehillah had become a reality.

If two Jews were alone on a desert island, according to the old—and not too far-fetched—cliché, they'd form three organizations. Magnes' achievement in coalescing the majority of New York's 1,000,000 Jews into one organization was therefore something of an administrative phenomenon. Moreover, the whole concept of the kehillah—organizing on a sectarian basis—ran counter to the goal of assimilation in which most American Jews believed. The *American Israelite* regarded the kehillah as evidence of "that crazy nationalism which is the latest form of Jewish hysteria." To the *Israelite* such an action indicated that Jews regarded themselves as different, that they wanted to isolate themselves from other Americans and their way of life. This complete denial of the Americanizing process, as the directors of the Educational Alliance were quick to point out, perpetuated a *shtetl* tradition on the free soil of the United States. (One uptown gentleman, who believed that the quicker Jews "get rid of their Judaism the better," refused to give a contribution to the kehillah when he found out its Bureau of Education would teach Hebrew. He had been under the impression that the kehillah was organized chiefly to inculcate "better American manners.")

As downtown journalist Bernard Richards observed, the

objectives of the *Yahudim* were different. "They were simply interested in philanthropy, charitable work as such. And they didn't plan to organize Jewish life on any kind of religious or national conceptions, which are more involved and more in line with ancient, old time feeling and traditions." However, despite all their apprehensions, *Yahudim* allowed themselves to "be persuaded against their will" to support the kehillah, because of their admiration for Judah Magnes and by a concession they exacted from him: The American Jewish Committee, composed solely of *Yahudim,* would work in conjunction with the kehillah, operating on a national level in matters of Jewish interest, while the kehillah would deal with local situations in New York City.

This was a fortunate division of territory, for a new "local situation" erupted at the end of 1909, which the gentlemen of the AJC were ill equipped to handle. Blood ritual accusations, yes; prostitution accusations, no. In its pursuit of evil, the November issue of *McClure's* contained "Daughters of the Poor," written by George Kibbe Turner, a quiet, unassuming muckraker, who charged that among Jewish immigrants there "were a large number of criminals who soon found that they could develop an extremely profitable business in the sale of women in New York."

Turner's exposé presented the poor Jewish girl, fresh from Galicia, unable to speak English, doomed to an abysmal existence from meager sweatshop earnings, and lured by the "weird Oriental hieroglyphics of Yiddish posters" into cheap dance halls—"Castle Gardens"—in reality the chief recruiting grounds for the white slave traffic. Here the girl sat forlornly on a bench along the wall and waited for Prince Charming. Prince Charming, according to Turner, was generally a "cadet"—the somewhat inappropriate name then used for a procurer—whom Turner graphically described as "a delightful young Jewish American man with plastered hair, a pasty face and most finished and ingratiating manners."

Portions of the *McClure's* article were translated into Yiddish for the edification of East Side readers. But even the affronted cries that again issued from downtown couldn't drown out the shrill truth in the Turner article. Immigrant girls *were* being drawn into prostitution and often by Jewish cadets, but Turner erred in thinking these criminals were the immigrants. Almost invariably, the cadets were an American product, individuals alienated from Orthodox Judaism by the drive to Americanize, who had absorbed the ethic of getting ahead. And prostitution—called by the more delicate-minded "The Social Evil"—was a major industry, one that had raised the living standards of countless Tammany politicians, their rival Republican bosses, and many members of the New York police to remarkable heights. Occasionally even the madams and their girls profited. In 1909, Mother Rosie Hertz, who in 1882 had been a mere streetwalker, operated the most successful houses of prostitution. "From the smallest beginnings" —a one-room apartment—her business continued to prosper until she owned the buildings in which three of her "resorts" were located. Together with two associates, she operated eight houses on the Lower East Side. Just like any self-made man, Mrs. Hertz took great pride in her achievements; frequently, after she had gathered her girls together for their daily accounting, gave inspirational lectures "on how to succeed in business and by what trials of strength and endurance she had built up her business."

Though the inevitable brouhaha over the *McClure's* article took place, nothing substantial was done about the problem. Organization plans for the kehillah were under way, but Dr. Magnes was having his own trouble at Temple Emanu-El, where his sermons were sharply critical of the congregation and of the direction Reform Judaism was taking. Louis Stern —one of the trustees of the temple, whose daughter married a titled Catholic Hungarian in a ceremony in his home conducted by a priest—was so bitterly offended by Magnes' censorious sermon on the marriage that he resigned.

In the spring of 1910, Rabbi Magnes came up for reelection by the trustees, and in a sermon on Passover, he made his views explicitly clear:

> Insofar as it is Reformed, your Judaism and mine has something of a parasitic nature, and just as the parasites may at times have more outward beauty than the parent tree, so have the richer Reformed congregations an outward appeal in the beauty of their buildings, their glorious music and their perfect decorum. . . . Unless it is your desire to become less Jewish rather than more Jewish, the one direction this congregation can take is that leading towards the Living Jewish people where living Judaism is to be found.

Although in the beginning, the Temple Emanu-El congregation had been indulgent toward Magnes' "extreme Jewishness," perhaps, as one observer speculated, as a "vicarious

atonement for their assimilation," there was considerable relief when Magnes left Emanu-El and a year later was induct-
ed into B'nai Jeshurun, a Conservative congregation.

Finally, in the late summer of 1912, after a series of unre-
lated incidents, substantial action was taken in the matter of
crime on the Lower East Side. From Police Commissioner
Bingham's maladroit remarks on the high incidence of Jewish
criminals sprang Rabbi Magnes' miracle—the kehillah. However, Bingham hadn't written the article as an exercise in anti-
Semitism. He was simply indulging in that perennial ploy of
public officials, pointing up a threat to get an increased budget
from one's department. Commissioner Bingham had revealed
a grim and frightening picture of foreign criminals on the
streets of New York "solely to make a plea for a secret service fund." He wanted this extra appropriation for a special
police arm who not only were trained in Jewish folkways and
customs—East Side policemen who didn't call seltzer *sulzar
warter* or offer *marseltoffs* to a newly married couple—but
would know the immigrants and have their trust.*

It was undoubtedly cold comfort to General Bingham that
the kehillah, which partially owed its existence to him, should
finally carry out his original purpose: sending a special investigative body to fight crime directly among the Jewish immigrants. It was certainly an unconventional idea. In 1912 the
New York Jewish community had countless regular relief
agencies, agencies for the relief of the sick, child care agencies, free loan societies, old age homes, educational agencies,
and free burial associations. But it had no vice squad.

The mere idea of the gentlemen of the American Jewish
Committee and other powers of uptown Judaism acquiescing
to so parochial an action as an independent Jewish police
agency for the kehillah seemed patently absurd. It had been
uphill work to persuade them to support the kehillah itself—
"a movement," Judge Samuel Greenbaum stated disapprovingly, "which seems as uncalled for as it is un-American."

* According to Tammany leader and State Senator George Washington Plunkitt, suiting a man to the people in his district was a vital
element in Tammany Hall's success. As an illustration of what can happen when a man wasn't also suited for the work he had to do, he told of
a repeater in Albany who had been hired to go to the polls early in a
half dozen election districts and vote on other men's names before those
men reached the polls. At one place, when he was asked his name by the
poll clerk, he rashly answered, "William Croswell Doane." "Come off it,"
the poll clerk said, "you ain't Bishop Doane." "The hell I ain't," yelled
the repeater.

For Jews to organize along any other lines than religious seemed to them a reflection on their status as American citizens. But two incidents in 1912 forced them to reverse their attitude. One—concerning the efforts of a convicted thief to get out of Dannemora Prison—affected Jacob Schiff personally, and led him to give his financial support to the kehillah crime agency; the other—the murder of gambler Herman Rosenthal—brought to worldwide attention such notorious East Side figures as Big Jake Zelig, Sam Schepps, Gyp the Blood (Harry Horowitz), Lefty Louie (Louis Rosenberg), Dopey Benny, Bald Jack Rose, and Little Kishky, names that fell with unsavory emphasis on the ears of the *Yahudim*.

In January, 1912, Foulke Brandt, a prisoner at Dannemora, addressed an appeal for the commutation of a thirty-year sentence to Governor John Dix in Albany. The circumstances of Brandt's conviction were these: In 1907, Brandt—a tall, handsome, twenty-one-year-old Swedish immigrant—had been a servant in the home of Mortimer Schiff, only son of Jacob Schiff, and had been dismissed for "writing an impudent letter" which he had handed to young Mrs. Schiff with her tea. Mortimer Schiff released the "impudent" contents of the letter to the press after Brandt's commutation appeal, when the case began to grow into a *cause célèbre*. It read:

Dearest Lady,
    . . . I am a poor fellow but I have a heart I should part with to a Lady which I love dearest on Earth (It is you, dearest Lady.) . . . I do not know if you are interested or like my person but I do know that I am awfully fond of you. . . . Inside my heart is the eternal feelings which cannot be expressed in words. (only actions can speak.) . . .

Lovingly . . .

Alarmed by these expressions of passion, Mrs. Schiff had run to the nursery and locked herself in with her two children until her husband came home and fired Brandt. On a Friday evening about a month later, Brandt entered the Schiff home through an open window and lay in wait in the study, dressed, for some inexplicable reason, in his former employer's dressing gown. When young Schiff came in, Brandt assaulted him and stole some stickpins. After his arrest, Brandt pleaded guilty and was sentenced. His commutation appeal, five years later, declared he was innocent and had pleaded guilty because he had been promised a short sentence. Schiff hired a number of expensive lawyers to fight the appeal, which Governor Dix subsequently refused.

Then, in late January, the New York *American* and other papers picked up the Brandt case and began publishing "scandalous and infamous stories" that implied Brandt's "theft of stickpins was a chivalrous blind to cover by the appearance of a crime, the real purpose of his presence" in the Schiff home. The obvious implication: Young Mrs. Schiff and Brandt had been carrying on an illicit affair. A titillating story indeed! Yet it lost some of its credibility when it was learned that the man responsible for it, Carl Fisher-Hansen, a disbarred lawyer and Brandt's adviser, had circulated the same story about a burglar and another woman two years earlier and that Brandt had a record of robbing four former employers and forging $15,000 worth of checks. Nevertheless, the Schiff name and the hints of dalliance on Fifth Avenue ensured wide coverage in the papers and required New York politicians to declare themselves for or against Brandt—and, thus, for or against the Schiffs. State Attorney General Thomas Carmody and New York City District Attorney Charles S. Whitman believed that Brandt had been "a victim of a conspiracy," while Mayor William Jay Gaynor of New York held that the Schiffs were being victimized. Whitman was a Republican whose untiring ambition and facile handling of the Rosenthal murder case would make him governor of New York, also led him to make sensational statements over trivial items in order to keep the scandal running. His sly methods particularly angered Schiff. On the other hand, Mayor Gaynor, who had run on a Tammany ticket and whom Schiff had opposed in 1909, acted with discretion and his usual independence. Finally, the Schiffs withdrew their opposition to the commutation when Brandt recanted the allegations he had made and also swore that he wouldn't "appear in public upon the stage or otherwise in connection with the case, to gain notoriety in the writing the history thereof, or discussing it in public." Brandt was last seen leaving by train for Minnesota.

The Brandt-Schiff story had barely subsided as a public spectacle when the horrid disclosures emanating from the Rosenthal murder—with its unlovely cast of Jewish thugs—replaced it. Thus for a whole year the front pages of New York papers prominently featured stories involving Jews. That the Schiffs in the former case had been the victims mattered not at all. The thin line of distinction between victim and victim-

izer is often blurred in the public eye. But the rapport that had
arisen between Mayor Gaynor and Jacob Schiff during the
Brandt case would now have definite consequences. Schiff,
who had held the strongest views against secular Jewish organizations, offered the sum of $5,000 a year for an anticrime
agency in the kehillah, with which Mayor Gaynor agreed to
cooperate.

The name of the agency changed several times, going—
with progressive euphemism—from Vigilance Committee to
Vice Committee, to Bureau of Information, to Welfare Committee, and, finally, to Bureau of Social Morals. Its operation,
based on the understanding arrived at with Mayor Gaynor in
the fall of 1912, was a unique arrangement. William Jay Gaynor was a notable eccentric. Spade-bearded, cold-eyed, acerbic,
opinionated, irascibly independent (so independent that in 1909
he sued the New York *World,* which was supporting him),
he was also a compulsive letter writer. People wrote him from
all over the country on every conceivable subject, and he shot
off crotchety answers. To a man from Kansas looking for a
wife: "How is this? Why do you send up here to New York
for a wife: . . . You may not be as attractive as you think you
are. . . ." Professing to dislike reformers, he carried on fierce
feuds with two crusading clergymen, the Reverend Charles
Parkhurst and Rabbi Stephen S. Wise, although he himself
was certainly a reform-minded mayor. His frequent scolding
of "that little pinhead in authority" (any city official who
wanted to arrest socialist speakers), his denunciation of police
who clubbed strikers, and his reply to a missionary requesting
a license to preach conversion to the Jews on the East Side
("Do you not think the Jews have a good religion? . . . Did
not we Christians get much or the most of what we have from
the Jews? . . . Why should anyone work so hard to prosely-
tize the Jews?") had won him a loyal following among Russian Jewish immigrants.

Without Gaynor's cooperation, without his constant prodding of Bureau of License officials, his persistent *nudzhing* of
police inspectors, the Bureau of Social Morals would have
been ineffective. Instead, it achieved almost immediate results.
Four investigators were appointed, headed by Abe Shoenfeld,
the son of Meyer Shoenfeld—a former East Side union leader. Shoenfeld, acclaimed by Magnes as "an excellent young
Jewish man with considerable experience," and the other investigators focused their attention on the First Inspection District, which encompassed the six precincts of the Lower East

Side. They collected information on such operations as stuss-houses,* bordellos, horse-poisoning rings, fences, and pick-pockets, which was sent along a chain of command: Shoen-feld to Magnes. Magnes to a police inspector. If no action was taken by the police—a not uncommon situation—Magnes went directly to Mayor Gaynor, who immediately began prodding and *nudzhing*.

If there was one thing that embarrassed the police officers of the First Inspection District, it was having "Jewish socie-ties" interfering in their territory. When the order came down from Mayor Gaynor to put four stusshouses "out of busi-ness," the First's Inspector Cornelius F. Cahalene marched over to see Rabbi Magnes and deny the accuracy of Shoen-feld's findings. With Inspector Cahalene listening, Magnes phoned Shoenfeld and reported what the Inspector had told him.

"You tell Inspector Cahalene," Shoenfeld said, "that his graft collector. Bob Clifford, can be found right now at the Sagamore Hotel . . . that he gets $125 a month from each stusshouse and I say he [Cahalene] is a grafter and I say he also has a graft collector . . . who sells the bottled beer to all the stusshouses."

The four stusshouses were closed the next day. And broth-els, poolrooms, gambling halls, gang hangouts went the same way. No place was safe from "Jewish societies." They closed down Mother Rosie Hertz—after she had been at the same address for thirty years. They had Yoski Nigger, King of the Horse Poisoners. put away for a long stretch. For six years—while Yoski (Joseph Toblinsky) was on the loose—horse poi-soning was the bane of East Side stable owners who refused to pay extortion money. Yoski's "Yiddish Blackhand Associa-tion" was responsible for poisoning 300 horses. But by April 1913, Mayor Gaynor. answering an invitation to a reception of the Horse Owners Protective Association, wrote approving-ly that "whereas 14 horses a week were poisoned in 1912, such poisoning of horses has ceased altogether."

After a year of investigations, Shoenfeld wrote a sixty-page report for Magnes to present to Jacob Schiff and the other ke-hillah sponsors. He itemized 103 illicit establishments shut down by the kehillah, with detailed accounts concerning each one, and 200 thieves, drug peddlers and practitioners of im-

---

* Stuss was a simplified form of faro. Because it originated around 1885 on the East Side, it was called Jewish faro. And because hood-lums like Kid Twist ran stusshouses, they were invariably crooked.

moral behavior put out of circulation. Proudly, he concluded: "It can easily be seen how closely our investigators are in touch with the condition—we creep right into their home affairs—into their lawyers' offices, and we know what goes on. There is not a time we cannot lay our hands on them, and there is not a man on our lists who is not known to one or more of our investigators."

But in September, 1913, Mayor Gaynor died suddenly, and the Bureau of Social Morals never received the same cooperation again. Without Gaynor, Schiff's interest in the bureau faded, and his annual contribution dropped to $1,000. The new city administration considered the unconventional arrangement embarrassing, and by 1917 Rabbi Magnes' energies had shifted to opposing America's entry into World War I. Thus, quietly, without fanfare, East Side crime once again became the responsibility of professionals.

27

Up from the Poolroom

The kehillah crime agency's theory that sordid surroundings were not only evil in themselves, but a dangerous source of corruption for impressionable minds, was one with which not everyone agreed. One Jewish immigrant from Rumania, Marcus Ravage, who later became a journalist for the *New Republic* and the *Nation,* maintained the lessons he learned at age sixteen, while standing behind the bar or while pouring out miscellaneous drinks to the people at the card tables in a Division Street saloon, taught him more of the "rich wisdom of life" than the three universities he later attended. There was little character to save, he declared, in someone who would "go to perdition at the mere sight of evil." Of course, Ravage had been well treated by the owners of the bar, a couple named Weiss. Mrs. Weiss fed him chicken soup, lectured him on the importance of courtesy, thrift, and the most effective hair dressing, while Mr. Weiss paid for his haircuts and even offered to teach him English. "But of this I did not avail myself," Ravage said, "because I noticed he always referred to Mrs. Weiss as 'he.'" However, most East Side saloons and poolrooms—traditionally the lair of small-time hoods, thugs, and *mumzorim* of all kinds—were usually run by less kindly types than Mr. Weiss: burly, hard-eyed gents on the order of Silver Dollar Smith.

There were also other exceptions. About fifteen years before Dr. Magnes and his kehillah agency began their assault on East Side crime, two young men, eager to quit working in sweatshops, opened a poolroom on the Bowery—"The Othello Poolroom. Props. S. Cohen and J. Rubenfeld"—an establishment with fifteen tables. Their proprietorship lasted about a year.

Successful from the beginning, the Othello was diagonally opposite a saloon run by Steve Brody, whose leap off Brooklyn Bridge had made him a celebrity, and it was patronized by Himself—Big Tim Sullivan, the East Side Tammany boss. Big Tim would amble genially through the poolroom, speaking to everyone, pointing out "the glories of Tammany," and dispensing largesse in the form of bags of coal, with Tammany's compliments.

In one corner of the poolroom, Sam Cohen's father opened a cigar and soda-water stand. "He had never been in such a place before," his son recalled, "and he was at first quite bewildered by the looks and ways of our clientele. They did not much resemble the people he met in the clothing trade or in the synagogue and there was seldom a Jewish face in the place. . . . He couldn't stop commenting on the habit the really big shots had of waving away their change. This was the closest he had ever come to finding gold on the streets in America."

The habitués of the Othello resembled those who hung around other poolrooms: thieves, pimps, grafters, dope fiends, policy and number racketeers, drunks, prizefighters, and pickpockets. One, a character known as the Yiddish Napoleon, was a short dark boy who did look like the Little Corporal and who claimed illegitimate descent from him. (It hardly seemed possible, but Napoleon *did* march through Lithuania in 1812. . . .) The Othello even received a visit from Theodore Roosevelt, then police commissioner, who strode in alone. "After that," wrote Cohen, "I never doubted stories of his bravery."

TR demanded to see the owner and was momentarily taken aback when young Sam Cohen approached him. "Your place is infested with nothing but thieves and panhandlers and robbers!" he bellowed at the young man. "I know about the betting that goes on, too! Someday I'm going to back in here with a wagon and pull you all in!"

Cohen shrugged. "There isn't anything I can do about it if

you feel like it. I hire a bouncer, I call in police, and nothing
helps."

Never one to dwell on hopeless situations, TR left and
never returned. Had his visit occurred on a weekend and had
he looked behind the soda-water stand, he would have seen
Sam Cohen's younger brother, Morris, then a City College
student and later one of the most eminent twentieth-century
philosophers, bent over a book—possibly *The Decline and
Fall of the Roman Empire* which he read at the Othello—jot-
ting down "a few of my sentiments justifying Gibbon against
the assault of Guizot and Millman. . . ."

Few dens of iniquity on the Lower East side harbored a
Morris Raphael Cohen tucked away in a corner, but even one
was not at all a bad average. Moreover, Marcus Ravage and
Morris R. Cohen represented a far stronger—more flourishing—element in the character of the East Side than crime:
intellectualism—the turbulent, troublesome kind of intellectualism that bred unionism, radical politics, vegetarianism,
free love, and the utopian concept and whose proponents not
only felt a compulsion to remodel society but were certain
they could.

"Moishe," pleaded a former immigrant to his nineteen-
year-old brother who had landed a few hours earlier and was
already expounding on the way to improve the United States,
"do you want to do an older brother a favor? *Fix mir nicht
dos land.*"—"Don't fix up the country for me."

28

Worse Was Better

Following Appomattox, a frenzied burst of industrial growth —stimulated by laissez-faire and protective tariffs—transformed the United States. Pausing briefly for a financial panic in 1873, the country proceeded onward to affluence, comfort, and a stockpile of ignored social problems. A network of railroads diminished distance, and so did the newly invented telephone (with which, the Bell Telephone Company assured its subscribers, one could carry on a conversation easily "after slight practice and with the occasional repetition of a word or sentence"). One after another, new inventions appeared before an awed public: the incandescent lamp, the talking machine, the kinetoscope—primitive forerunner of the motion picture which would make possible the rise to wealth and power of Adolph Zukor, Samuel Goldwyn, Lewis Selznick (who once wrote a letter to Nicholas II offering him a movie career), and other East European Jewish immigrants. An inexpensive fountain pen was available, and so were typewriters. Central heating, indoor sinks, and flush toilets heralded a future of unbounded elegant living for the middle class. The expanded ready-made clothing industry made it possible for men of small means to be less provincially dressed. Until the eighties, women's clothes were custom-made for the rich, homemade for the poor.

Poor Cousins

The year 1889 marked the beginning of the children's ready-made clothing industry, when Louis Borgnicht, a poor young Galitzianer immigrant peddler, set out to find a product that no one was producing. He tramped all over the Lower East Side, surveying the marketplace and taking notes. He discovered that no one made children's aprons—then an essential part of a child's wardrobe. Borgnicht and his wife made a few sample aprons, which sold immediately. Then they began turning out children's dresses, meeting with even greater success. Observing his triumph, others undertook the manufacture of children's clothes—dresses, knee pants, and reefers. But Borgnicht held the title "King of the Children's Dress Trade," and since he and his wife had twelve children, it was appropriate on all counts.

However, to produce all these miracles of American ingenuity, to man the machines in the factory, to mine the coal that powered the factories, to lay the rails for transcontinental lines—the United States needed a far larger laboring class than it possessed.

To meet this need, child labor thrived; children of the poor were in the factories, in the mines. The potential child labor market was unlimited, for if the poor had anything at all, it was children. Still, with all its advantages, child labor provoked criticism. ("The golf course lies so near the mill that nearly every day the little children can look out and see the men at play.") The ideal would consist of adults who would work long hours at tedious tasks in unpleasant surroundings for inadequate pay and without complaint. Immigration, therefore, had been encouraged. Nevertheless, it soon became infuriatingly apparent that welcome, docile European peasants turned rapidly into independent American laboring men —who joined unions.

The garment industry, in particular, affected Jewish immigrants. At one time, it had been dominated by German Jews, but now, little by little, it was being taken over by those who had been tailors in East Europe (11 percent of the immigration) and by "Columbus tailors"—the unskilled and inexperienced who took up tailoring when they landed in America. They made a unique contribution to the fifty-year-old English-imported sweating system—a division of labor called the task system. "The Hebrew tailors of New York," declared an Industrial Commission report, "have devised what is perhaps the most ingenious and effective engine of overexertion known in modern industry."

Slum experts among *Yahudim* and Christians, however, invariably attributed the appalling conditions of East Side Jews to the immigrants' refusal to deviate from the letter of Orthodox Judaism and their children's refusal to cling to it. Rarely was the matter of exploitation mentioned as a significant factor. But the immigrants, unsophisticated through they may have been, quickly perceived that if they and their children didn't have to work twelve to sixteen hours a day for $12 a week in a highly seasonal trade and live in a decaying, fetid, rat-infested, and crowded tenement, there might be a marked improvement in their spiritual well-being. Consequently, while Reform Judaism and the Jewish Theological Seminary failed to moderate the Orthodoxy of the pious and the irreligion of the young, the development of the Jewish labor movement managed to do a little of both.

Many approaches were tried for improving East Side labor conditions. But for approximately a half dozen years, the most popular approach among young immigrants disdained not only labor organization but all organization.

Anarchism, despite its advocacy of free love, was not a frolicsome doctrine, encouraging as it did such forthright individual enterprise as lighting the fuse to a pipeful of dynamite and placing it "in the immediate vicinity of a lot of rich loafers who live by the sweat of other people's brows." Furthermore, anarchism fiercely opposed participation in "palliatives" and "opiates"—*i.e.*, unions, political action, and religion.

Anarchist leadership in the United States was chiefly in the hands of non-Jews—German immigrants, an occasional Englishman or Russian nobleman—whose fiery speeches were delivered in their native language. But among Russian Jewish immigrants in the eighties there was a small group of students —the intelligentsia—who understood Russian and German. Most of them were members of Am Olam who had originally planned to go to Oregon but, once in New York, had decided to stay and live in commune style on the Lower East Side. It was a kind of New Odessa East, with a Vilna commune on Essex Street, a Kiev commune on Catherine Street, and an Odessa commune on Bayard Street. After the abandonment of the New Odessa colony, veterans of the Oregon Am Olam group drifted back and joined their comrades on the East Side. These young men and women, products of a secular education in Russia, had forsworn Judaism as an outmoded garment is discarded and had dipped into an assortment of radical underground activities with zealous idealism. They worshiped the memory of the executed nihilist conspirators who had assassinated the czar, and when they settled on the Lower East Side, they chose a radical ideology from the wide range available: from the violent Bakunin variety to the philosophical anarchism of Prince Kropotkin. When these young radicals began gathering in Justus Schwab's saloon at 50 First Street and in the East Sixth Street Anarchist Hall to express their impatience with the capitalistic system, the ominous tone of their intemperate rhetoric reverberated uptown in the homes of *Yahudim*. Moreover, the Americanization plans so dear to the heart of those *Yahudim* evoked only derision from young radicals. Indeed, nothing could surpass the contempt with which European intellectuals regarded America. For them, it was a well-established fact that one need only be a first-class bluffer to succeed in the United States, an opinion *Yahudim* understandably found offensive. "America," Abe Cahan was to write some years later, "is looked upon in Europe in the same way anti-Semites look upon Jews."

One German anarchist leader—Johann Most—gained formidable influence over Jewish radical students. He was a thirty-six-year-old short, volatile, bitterly frustrated actor with a carefully cultivated arrogant manner. As editor of the German-language paper *Freiheit,* he had arrived in the United States in 1882—fresh from a prison term in England for having written an editorial on the czar's assassination entitled "At Last!" Though his appearance at first repelled—for a graying dark beard didn't entirely conceal the badly disfigured left side of his face, the result of incompetent surgery in his wretched childhood—he had a fine resonant voice and a flamboyantly dramatic style that made him a great crowd pleaser, even though not everyone in his audience understood him. Most's prison terms in Germany, Austria, and England had fanned his hatred of society and increased the stridency with which he goaded his listeners to commit terrorist acts. To help them in this endeavor, he had worked in a New Jersey explosives factory, taken notes, and written the *Science of Revolutionary Warfare,* "A handbook of instruction in use and preparation of Nitroglycerine, Dynamite, Gun-Cotton, Fulminating Mercury, Bombs, Fuses, Poisons, etc. etc."

Not long after his arrival in the United States, Most's militant and reckless oratory had crystallized anarchist dogma in this country. And Jewish students under the spell of his "primitive power," his radiation of "hatred and love, strength and inspiration," flocked to the cause. Some later declared they hadn't been so much anarchists as "Mostoists."

In their fervent efforts to promote anarchism among their own proletarians—East Side Jews—the *anarchistlach* organized the Pioneers of Liberty. And since the first step in spreading anarchism was to loosen the grip of religion, the Pioneers for a number of years held a gala to lure the Jewish working class away from shul. At their notorious Yom Kippur Balls, tea (with milk) was served with ham sandwiches on which hot sharp mustard was spread lavishly, in order, one observer recalled, "to kill the taste." However, they were disillusioned to discover that Jewish workers—even those who aspired to the intelligentsia—would obligingly cheer radical sentiment, which invariably included ridicule of Judaism, yet turn up at the synagogue every Friday night. There's no recorded case of a Jewish anarchist refusing to strike a match to light a bomb fuse because it was *erev Shabbas,* but at a radical meeting, held with proper defiance on the Sabbath, an anarchist lit a cigarette and was attacked by his comrades for his sacrilege. "And what would you say," he exclaimed in exasperation, "if I told you I didn't believe in God altogether?"

Nevertheless, inspired by the magnetic rhetoric of Johann Most, young Jewish anarchists argued over tactics to advance the cause and to lead the Jewish masses to world revolution. "Is better worse," they asked one another, "or is worse better? Which will bring the people closer to the Social Revolution, improved or worsened conditions?" The truly committed claimed worse was definitely better.

Of course, anarchists and *Yahudim* would have been outraged at the suggestion that there were any similarities at all between them. Yet they both suffered the same frustrating experiences in their separate attempts to shape up the mass of Jewish immigrants. They also shared a strong distaste for Yiddish and an open opposition to labor unions. But anarchists wished to eliminate Orthodox Judaism (all Judaism, for that matter) and transform the immigrants into world revolutionaries, while *Yahudim* merely desired to Americanize Orthodox Judaism and lead the immigrants into the GOP. Consequently, both were suspected by some extremely Orthodox Jews of being Christian missionaries in disguise. As things turned out, both anarchists and *Yahudim* could claim some degree of victory. To the latter's relief, East European Jews did become Americanized, but they brought it about in their own individual way—through Yiddish, labor unions, *and* radical politics.

29

Emma and Sasha . . . and Johann

Among those young East Side Jewish anarchists, the two *cha-verim* most devoted to the cause were Emma Goldman and her Sasha—Alexander Berkman. Emma, a warmhearted, idealistic, romantically turbulent girl, occasionally felt a twinge of doubt concerning anarchism's wilder tenets. Sasha, however, was rigidly exacting in his judgments. "A good anarchist," he declared, "is one who lives only for the Cause and gives everything to it." Characteristically, when Johann Most made the gallant gesture of presenting Emma with a large bouquet of violets, Sasha exclaimed, "Violets at the height of the winter with thousands out of work and hungry!" But Emma, who was not adverse to the use of "Dynamite, Bombs, Poisons, etc., etc." for social justice, became irritated at the predisposition of the cause—*and* Sasha—to be a killjoy. An example of this occurred when Emma returned from a strenuous two-week speaking tour. It had been her first experience in facing the public, and she had urged workers, as Most had coached her, to drop the struggle for an eight-hour workday* and strive rather for the "ultimate overthrow of the

* Opposition to the eight-hour workday came from both left and right and took the form of scare tactics. Anarchists warned workers that reducing the workday from its normal fourteen, twelve, or ten hours would just perpetuate their conditions as wage slaves, while capitalists alerted them to the danger that so short a workday as eight hours would leave leisure time in which they would overindulge in drinking and fornication.

capitalist system." That evening she attended a dance and was "one of the most untiring and gayest" of dancers. Before long, Sasha sent his cousin over to Emma to whisper gravely that "it did not behoove an agitator to dance," at least not with such "reckless abandon." Her frivolity, she was told, would hurt the cause. Indignantly, Emma turned on her assembled comrades, including a darkly disapproving Sasha, and exclaimed that she was tired of "having the Cause being constantly thrown in my face." Furthermore, she added, the cause "could not expect me to become a nun. . . ." (The cause, of course, had no such expectation. Wisely, it restricted itself to what it considered the attainable—the "ultimate overthrow of the capitalist system.")

Emma and Sasha met for the first time in 1889, at Sachs' Café on Suffolk Street, where the elite radical Jewish intellectuals congregated to consume Mrs. Sachs' cheesecake and debate great issues. On any night at Sachs', one might see editors of anarchist and socialist papers; members of various radical factions (usually holding cigarettes, between thumb and forefinger tips, whose esoteric brands—Marx, Engels, Bakunin, Kropotkin—revealed their ideological persuasion): poets of the sweatshop; actors and playwrights of the Yiddish theater; a reporter or two from the New York *Times, Herald,* or *Post,* collecting material for yet another article on the East Side; and every once in a while, several members of the Bomb Squad "in very evident disguise."

Earlier on that eventful day, twenty-year-old Emma had journeyed down from Rochester, New York, where she had spent her first three years in the United States. In that city, she had experienced the grim reality of exploitation as a clothing factory worker, had twice married and twice divorced a husband who was impotent, a compulsive gambler, and a terrible bore. (She had also quarreled with her parents, who had wanted her to remain married, apparently believing her to be entirely too fussy.)

Sasha had come straight to New York City from Russia, arriving during the Blizzard of '88. A year younger than Emma, he was a dark, intense youth with "a high studious forehead," the inevitable wire-rimmed spectacles of the radical intellectual, and paradoxically, the torso and appetite of a longshoreman. (The first time Emma saw him, she heard him call out in "his powerful voice" to the waiter at Sachs', "Extra-large steak! Extra cup of coffee!") His firm jaw indicated an uncompromising nature, and he spoke incessantly and eloquently, in an accent even more heavily Russian-Jewish than Emma's, on the need of revolutionists to sacrifice all on the altar of "the beloved People." Both had been deeply affected by the 1887 execution of the four Chicago anarchists convicted of throwing the bomb at the Haymarket riot. Emma, in fact, traced her radicalization to that event.

Their association with Johann Most was a stormy one; indeed, by 1892 the intricately interwoven love life of Emma, Sasha, and Most—to say nothing of Fedya, a fun-loving anarchist painter for whom Emma posed in the nude—had become an authentic East Side *scandale*. Although Sasha never expressed so bourgeois an emotion as jealousy, he did from time to time drop remarks to the effect that Most "cared only for women physically,"* that "Germans were that way," and that Most was a spendthrift and a drain on the cause. As for Fedya, Sasha regarded him as incorrigibly addicted to beauty, which was, indeed, true. While Emma and Sasha deplored the conspicuous opulence of the millionaires' mansions along Fifth Avenue, "while the masses live in poverty," Fedya objected to their ugliness. "Such bad taste," he complained. Most, for his part, expressed his jealousy directly, accusing Emma—his *Blondkopf* and his "blue eyes"—of preferring that "arrogant Russian Jew," who had the effrontery to call him to account on "revolutionary ethics."

During her many years of notoriety, newspaper cartoonists invariably depicted Emma as "Red Emma," a wild-eyed, demoniac fanatic. But at twenty-three, she was, as Most called her, a *Blondkopf*—though, not of course, exclusively his—with curly hair, blue eyes, "a saucy turned-up nose," and fine complexion. Barely five feet tall, she weighed 120 pounds, so that she was ... plump. Her own objective appraisal concluded that she was "too large in the hips for my age," which she unkindly attributed to having come "from Jewish stock."

In July, 1892, Emma, Sasha, and Fedya were running an ice-cream parlor in Worcester, Massachusetts, to earn the fare back to Russia to "engage in conspiratorial work." This wasn't their only foray into capitalist enterprise—they had also had a photography studio in Worcester—but the ice-cream parlor proved more successful, owing to Emma's superlative coffee and "dainty dishes."

During that same July, Henry Clay Frick, partner and gen-

---

* Some time later, when Most exclaimed to Emma, "Love, love—it's all sentimental nonsense. There is only sex!" Emma thought, "So Sasha was right after all."

eral manager of the Carnegie Steel Company, fortified the
Carnegie Homestead works with a 15-foot-high, 3-mile-long
fence laced with barbed wire. He also imported 300 armed
Pinkerton men from New York, evicted strikers' families
from company houses, and prepared "to teach our employees
a lesson."

Upon reading newspaper headlines of the violence at
Homestead over the shoulder of her only customer, Emma
went into action. She shooed the customer out and closed the
shop. With the day's receipts—$75—she and her two partners
left for New York City, to plan an *attentat*—"propaganda by
deed"—against Henry Clay Frick.

"Sasha had never made bombs before," but with Most's
book of instructions in front of him and $40 worth of dyna-
mite, he worked every night for a week in constructing two
bombs—one to test and one to use on Frick—while Emma
kept a nervous watch:

> I lived in dread every moment for Sasha, for our friends
> in the flat, the children and the rest of the tenants. What if
> anything should go wrong—but, then did not the end justify
> the means? Our end was the sacred cause of the oppressed
> and exploited people. It was for them that we were going to
> give our lives. What if a few should have to perish?—the
> many would be made free and could live in beauty and
> comfort.*

But when Sasha returned from Staten Island, where he had
tested the bomb, Emma saw "by his expression that something terrible had happened . . . the bomb had not gone off."
Forty dollars shot and no bomb!

Unable to raise much money from their friends, Emma and
Sasha decided only he could go to Pittsburgh. When he arrived, he would have to wait until Emma sent him at least $20
more for a new suit and a gun—the former so that he would
look presentable enough to get in to see Frick and the latter to
shoot him.

After seeing Sasha off at the Baltimore & Ohio Station,
Emma cast around frantically for a way to raise the necessary

---

* Forty years later when Emma was writing her autobiography, she
had come to a different conclusion. "It was my religiously devout belief
that the end justifies all means. The end, then, was my ideal of human
brotherhood. If I have undergone any change it is not in my ideal. It is
more in the realization that a great end does not justify *all* means.

money. The next morning she awoke with the answer—"I would go on the street." Sonya in *Crime and Punishment* had become a prostitute to support her little brothers and sisters and consumptive stepmother. If "Sensitive Sonya could sell her body," Emma asked herself, "why not I?" Furthermore, her cause was greater than Sonya's. "It was Sasha—his great deed—the people. But should I be able to do it, to go with strange men—for money?" She endured the lectures of her conscience—"Sasha is giving his life, and you shrink from giving your body, miserable coward!" (Nazimova once remarked that she would like to play the title role in a play about Emma Goldman.) Finally, outfitted in a white linen dress ornamented with "Caucasian embroidery," under which she wore homemade flesh-colored underwear—the material bought with borrowed money—Emma tottered off on unaccustomed high heels to join the procession of streetwalkers on Fourteenth Street.

Despite her lofty—or low—resolve, every time a man approached her Emma hurried away, repelled by his "vulgar glances." And "vulgar glances" were, of course, the least of it. By eleven o'clock she was exhausted; "my feet hurt from the high heels, my head throbbed. I was close to tears from fatigue and disgust with my inability to carry out what I had come to do." Finally, a tall white-haired old gentleman invited her into a Union Square saloon for a drink. "You're a novice in the business," he stated categorically, after they were seated. When Emma admitted she was, he pointed out that prostitution had little to offer, "unless one had the knack for it. You haven't got it," he said with finality, "that's all there is to it." Thereupon, he thrust $10 on her and sent her home.

In Pittsburgh, Sasha converted the money Emma sent him into the deed's prerequisites: suit and gun. Then, ignoring a porter's declaration that "Mr. Frick was engaged," he walked into the industrialist's office, shot him twice, and stabbed him twice. As Frick's staff pounced on Sasha, he popped a capsule of fulminate of mercury into his mouth, "enough to blow us all to bits." In addition to being mean and ruthless, Frick had acute powers of observation in times of crisis. "What's he chewing?" he called out—in time for the capsule to be forcibly removed from Sasha's mouth.

Though Sasha maintained "the vital thing was the motive not its physical success or failure," it was depressing that as he began serving his twenty-two-year prison sentence—later reduced to fourteen—Frick bounced back to splendid health, more intransigently anitlabor than ever. "My poor tortured boy!" Emma recorded. "I could read between the lines how crushed he was at the realization that Frick remained alive."

They had expected—and were pleased with—the screaming denunciation by the "capitalistic bourgeois press." But that the Homestead workers should condemn his act, as they did, was a brutal blow. (Emma had always had some reservations about the "beloved People." "I had worked with proletarians in factories and I did not always find them helpful and generous.") Equally depressing was the public sympathy Frick received from the same people who rallied against Frick's cruelty to his steel workers. Though Johann Most didn't go so far as to commiserate with Frick, he did turn on Sasha. After years of writing fiery editorials and exhorting anarchists to go out and shoot, bomb, or poison for the cause, shortly after Sasha had shot and stabbed, Most repudiated the whole "propaganda by deed" concept and implied Sasha had "shot off a toy pistol," that he had been hired to attack Frick in an attempt to draw public sympathy. Many thought Most's motivations were a mixture of simple bourgeois jealousy of Sasha's relationship with Emma, irritation at Sasha's self-righteousness, and fear that any association with the Frick shooting would send him to jail once again. Whatever the reason, Emma was furious. She sat in the first row of a Most lecture, several months later, dressed in a long gray cloak under which she clutched a whip. When Most rose to speak, Emma sprang up and, in a loud strong voice, exclaimed, "I came here to demand proof of your insinuations against Alexander Berkman." According to the New York *Times* account, Emma, identified as "the woman who drinks beer in Peukert's Anarchist saloon," uttered "select anarchist billingsgate" and leaped to the podium. As Most muttered, "Hysterical woman," Emma lashed him several times across the face and neck, broke the whip dramatically over her knee, and threw the pieces at him.

Anarchism, always on shaky ground on the Lower East Side—for one reason or another—never fully recovered from this episode.* And many of the young Jewish radicals drawn

---

* Emma continued the work of spreading anarchist propaganda. In 1901 she was arrested on suspicion of having inspired Leon Czolgosz to kill President McKinley but was later cleared. Released from prison, Sasha rejoined Emma, but in 1917 they both were imprisoned for two years on a charge of opposing America's participation in the World War. At the end of their sentences, in the midst of the 1919 Red Scare, the

to anarchism by Johann Most gradually drifted into one of socialism's myriad forms.

One such young man, about ten years older than Emma and Sasha, had shared their genuine romantic idealism and, for a time, their belief in anarchism. But his disillusionment had come earlier when "instructing servant girls, for example, on how to poison the soup of their capitalist masters or teaching workers how to make bombs with which to kill individual manufacturers" ceased to make sense to him. As editor of the *Jewish Daily Forward,* he was to become the most influential man on the Lower East side, where his unique blend of socialism, pragmatism, and *Yiddishkayt* led Jewish immigrants into twentieth-century America.

---

authorities deported them to Russia. Disillusioned with the Soviet experiment, she and Sasha left after a few years. Emma lectured not only on radical subjects—in many countries, including the United States—but on drama and modern literature. Sasha died in 1936, and Emma four years later.

30

*For the Little Old Lady
on East Broadway*

On September 1, 1951, the New York *Times'* obituary page
carried a column-wide picture of a very old man—thick white
hair brushed back, sharp eyes staring defiantly, a full white
mustache, a strong, stubborn chin. Alongside appeared his
obituary:

> Abraham Cahan, retired editor of the *Jewish Daily Forward,*
> died yesterday in Beth Israel Hospital. His age was 91. He had
> been living recently at the Hotel Algonquin. . . . A Russian
> revolutionist at 20, a successful American novelist and journal-
> ist at 30, editor of a moribund little Socialist Yiddish daily
> at 40, he became the dominant force of the greatest Jewish
> daily in the world at 50, a position which he occupied to the
> end of his life. . . .

Anna, Cahan's wife of sixty-two years, had died in 1947.
They had no children; the Jewish immigrants, it was often remarked, were his children.

"Tall and well built," with a high-bridged nose and slightly
crossed eyes, Cahan had had unquenchable enthusiasm, a
soaring ego, an infectious humor, and an absolute passion for
"the thrill of truth," for portraying *"real life* with its comedy

and its tragedy mingled"—a penchant he carried out superbly in his novel of immigrant life *The Rise of David Levinsky*. Opinionated, he held grudges tenaciously and could lash out at his enemies with venom. He was also capable of great kindness and compassion. The complete urban man, he had been a devoted bird watcher. Of all his paradoxical characteristics, Jewish immigrants had been most affected by his philosophy of pragmatic radicalism.

At the nonreligious service held for Cahan, 500 people jammed the second-floor auditorium of the Forward Building, 175 East Broadway. Ten thousand more filled Straus Square and Seward Park, and still others, stationed in the windows of surrounding tenements, listened to the service, piped through loud speakers, for "the Lower East Side's first citizen." Mayor Vincent Impelliteri spoke, as did Secretary of Labor Maurice Tobin, David Dubinsky, Cahan's associates on the *Forward*, functionaries of the Workmen's Circle, United Hebrew Trades, and the International Socialist Movement. The Israeli ambassador to the United States, Abba Eban, alluded to Mr. Cahan's role in preserving "Jewish consciousness and culture against the tide of assimilation" and diplomatically ignored Cahan's having been—for much of his long life, as even a right-wing socialist had to be—anti-Zionist.

Abe Cahan liked to dilate on his early ideological confusion. In his native Vilna, following the usual period as a yeshiva *bochur*, he had been a student at the Vilna Teacher Training Institute and an active member of underground radical groups. After the czar's assassination, he was subjected to a series of police searches for forbidden materials. The police didn't always know precisely what they were looking for. "What does this mean?" a police chief asked, pointing to *A Critique of Political Economy*, the subtitle of Karl Marx's *Capital*. "Oh," Cahan said quickly, "this is a book about business." One couldn't, of course, count on such innocence forever, so Cahan decided he'd better leave the country. He reached Castle Garden in the spring of 1882, twenty-one years old, a revolutionary anarchist to whom the word "leaflet" had a "sacred sound," but before long he began questioning the cause's dogma: "On the one hand, how can we possibly yield to everyone when each individual's will is different from that of every other individual? On the other hand how can we abolish voting without at the same time leaving all the decision-making to a despot or group of despots?"

When he spoke to a veteran anarchist concerning this dilemma, the suggested solution was "the inherent goodness of human nature." Following this discussion, Cahan concluded "anarchism was a most confusing amalgam of contradictions and nonsense," and he joined the Socialist Labor Party and eventually the more moderate Social Democrats.

But from his early days in the United States, American politics had held such fascination for him that he had scarcely been able to restrain himself from asking President Chester A. Arthur for his autograph. ("How would it look for a socialist to ask for a souvenir from a capitalist President?") While Emma Goldman and Alexander Berkman remained revolutionaries to the end of their days, Cahan epitomized the larger group of young, more flexible East Side radicals who adjusted their ideologies to American conditions. Thus, when the New Deal came on the scene, Cahan gave his support to the Democrats.

But though at first Cahan and his fellow radicals loftily scorned any interest in the parochialism of American life and opposed "befuddling the workers with a little ballot box," they wished, nevertheless, to lead sweatshop workers in the class struggle. Consequently, their Propaganda Association for the Dissemination of Socialist Ideas Among Immigrant Jews persisted in attempts to win a following. But their fiery speeches in German and Russian, exhorting the workers to throw off the chains of economic slavery, were understood by only a small number. Little wonder then that among exhausted sweatshop workers the complex theories of Marxism and radical dialectic terminology evoked only puzzled looks, philosophical shrugs, and an occasional *"vos hokkt er a tchynik?"*

Cahan differed from his radical colleagues in a number of respects. He could identify and empathize with the uneducated Jewish immigrant. He loved Yiddish ("Even though some of my friends showed contempt for Yiddish, I defended it"). He possessed an eminently practical nature and an extraordinary curiosity about every aspect of urban American life. Once, after a Propaganda Association meeting, he asked Mirovich, the group's leader, a simple question—but one with portentous results:

"If it is for Jewish immigrants," I asked him, "why are the speeches in Russian and German?"

"What language do you suggest?" he asked derisively. "What Jew doesn't know Russian?"

"My father," I replied. . . .

When I said that one should make speeches for Jews in Yiddish, all who were standing around us laughed . . . the idea that one could make a serious political speech in this homey language seemed comical to them.

"Well, why don't you deliver a speech in Yiddish?" Mirovich taunted me.

"Why not?" I replied daringly.

The kind of Yiddish Cahan used in addressing an audience of 400 Jewish immigrants in mid-August, 1882, was a "simple Yiddish—like Mother used to talk," very different from the kind of Yiddish, heavily larded with German, tolerated by the intelligentsia. His use of it as a vehicle of socialist propaganda was revolutionary.

Yiddish in the United States had no status at all. Called Judeo-German, "a veritable linguistic ugly duckling," Yiddish was not even acceptable to early Yiddish theater companies which fastidiously chose a broken-German, broken-Yiddish "refined" blend known as *"deitchmerish,"* a dialect spoken by the socially ambitious in an attempt to pass as German Jews. Heroes often spoke straight German, and only the low comic spoke Yiddish. When a group of Jewish actors wanted to organize and join the United Hebrew Trades, they specified that the UHT representative couldn't address them in "coarse and common Yiddish, but in German, the language of poets and thinkers." And obviously, whenever uptowners spoke of Yiddish as the common language of the Lower East Side "common" was precisely what they meant. This attitude lasted for years. When Abe Cahan and an associate published (until their $10 ran out) a newspaper in simple Yiddish, their friends were shocked. One told Cahan, "I always knew Litvaks have a lot of *chutzpah.*"

Nevertheless, as the only radical who could speak the Yiddish of the proletariat "fluently, lovingly and artistically," Abe Cahan became an object of envy to other radicals. In his first two Yiddish speeches he covered Marx's theory of surplus value, the class struggle, and an appeal (accompanied by "elaborate Vilna curses") to "march with iron bars and axes on Fifth Avenue and to seize the palaces of the rich." Upon mature reflection, Cahan considered this suggestion had "more fire than practical sense." Still, Yiddish—"a racy and powerful" language—inspired extravagant expression. Indeed, labor organizers and politicians could not hope for a better vehicle. When, for example, union organizers or socialist agitators would cry out in the vernacular as they frequently did, that bosses or Tammany Hall or uptown capitalists were "drinking the blood" of workers or voters, it wasn't taken literally. "My mother," Samuel Chotzinoff recalled, "often accused me of drinking hers."

In 1897 Abe Cahan passed the hat at a socialist meeting, and Jewish workers threw in money and "their watches and rings." This collection totaling $800 was for the purpose of starting a Yiddish socialist paper, the *Jewish Daily Forward*. It would be a cooperative venture, "organized not for profits but for the spread of Socialism." Elected editor, Cahan almost immediately clashed with the rest of the staff over their determination to feature the interminable, acrimonious exchanges of socialist factionalism. Within eight months, he resigned.

Much more aware than the others on the *Forward* of the isolation a ghetto imposed, Abe Cahan spent the next five years as reporter for the *Commercial Advertiser,* a daily edited by Lincoln Steffens. Cahan couldn't have had a more sympathetic or encouraging superior. As an assistant editor on E. L. Godkin's *Evening Post,* Steffens had "become as infatuated with the Ghetto as eastern boys were with the wild west." To the amusement of his Jewish friends, he had a mezuzah nailed to his office door and fasted on Yom Kippur. His vignettes and sketches of old Orthodox Jews and their conflicts with their American children drew complaints from uptown Jews:

> Mr. Godkin himself required me once to call personally upon a socially prominent Jewish lady who had written to the editor asking why so much space was given to the ridiculous performance of the ignorant foreign East Side Jews and none to the Uptown Hebrews. I told her I had the satisfaction of telling her about the comparative beauty, significance and character of the uptown and downtown Jews. I must have talked well, for she threatened to have me fired. . . .

Steffens assigned Cahan to the police beat where Cahan learned not only how to use the telephone, but how to evoke human interest:

> "Here, Cahan," Steffens would call to him, ". . . a man has murdered his wife, a rather bloody, hacked-up crime. We don't care about that. But there's a story in it. That man loved

that woman well enough once to marry her, and now has hated her enough to cut her all to pieces . . . find out what happened between that wedding and this murder. . . ."

Cahan also wrote innumerable articles about East Side Jewish life. He covered stories at training camps during the Spanish-American War, queried returning soldiers on how bullets sounded—calling the article "The Song of the Bullets." He reported on prisons, the Fifth Avenue Easter Parade, and even a cakewalk at Madison Square Garden. He reviewed plays—usually the Yiddish theater—he was too critical of the American stage. ("Not even your star actors seem to have any sense of the reality of a conversation. They don't talk, they declaim.") Both plays and books had to meet his severe criteria of realism. He interviewed diverse American personalities: Admirals Dewey and Schley, Theodore Roosevelt, President McKinley, Tammany boss Richard Croker, Buffalo Bill and Russell Sage, an unredeemed capitalist, for whom "penurious" was too extravagant a word—*Sage was cheap*. When Cahan asked him why he had so much money, Sage replied ingenuously, "Just for the fun of making it," though Cahan suspected he relished holding onto it even more. It was a unique confrontation. How many downtown socialists, after all, had met their sworn enemy, a flesh-and-blood capitalist, face to face? Not any—except for Sasha.

Aside from his work on the *Advertiser,* Cahan had already written a well-received novel, *Yek'l,* and had written articles and short stories for a number of well-known magazines. The Hapgood brothers—Norman and Hutchins—admired his work, as did Steffens and one of the most noteworthy of American novelists, William Dean Howells.

Thus, in 1902, when the *Forward* implored Cahan to return as editor—twenty years after his arrival in the United States as a dogmatically dedicated anarchist—he explained his views to one of the *Forward*'s staff:

> Lief, I am afraid that you are making a mistake. The comrades are the same as ever; I—am not. I spent some time in the outside world. I found out that we Socialists have no patent on honesty and knowledge. The outer world is more tolerant of us than we are of them. They seek to understand us. We don't know the outer world. You and your comrades are steeped in the spirit of sectarianism. Should the *Forward* remain as it is it will go no further. The great public will not come near it, be-

cause it doesn't concern itself with all life—interests which interest the great masses, outside of their daily economic struggle. I say to you, Lief, it's just as important to teach the public how to carry a handkerchief in one's pocket as it is to carry a union card; to have respect for someone else's opinion is just as important as to have an opinion of one's own. . . .

In the early days of the paper, Cahan had written a policy statement that declared support by the *Forward* of *"that* socialist movement," which would best "reflect the free flexible principles" of the *Forward*. But the freedom and flexibility Cahan exercised on the paper outraged dyed-in-the-wool socialists; with revulsion, they watched the transformation of the *Forward* from a six-page socialist forum to eight pages of what they scornfully labeled *"veiberishe* business."

Unquestionably, Cahan did direct much of the *Forward*'s contents to women. Though, up to this time, Jewish women's reading had consisted mostly of Yiddish prayers, many who couldn't read learned how in order to read the *Forward*. "See that woman," Cahan said to one of his staff, while pointing out the *Forward*'s window at an *alte bobbe*, in *shaitel* and shawl, on East Broadway. "That is your reader. She must understand you."

So they dumped abstract essays on the class struggle. In their place, human interest stories about East Siders appeared that portrayed the class struggle in vivid, identifiable terms and were written for that little old lady on East Broadway in simple "Yiddish-Yiddish," clear as chicken soup. He invited contributions from readers on the nature of luck: "What is *Mazel?*" ("*Mazel,*" wrote the winner "is somebody else's *schlimmazel.*") A column dispensed medical advice to mothers, and popularizations of American history went to citizens in the making. (Cahan wrote a multivolume history of the United States in Yiddish.) The paper also offered simplified features on science and literature, a diagram of the Polo Grounds, and "the Fundamentals of Baseball Explained to Non-Sports." (About a dozen years after the publication of the latter, John J. McGraw of the New York Giants—dazzled by a golden vision of thousands of Jewish fans trooping up to the Polo Grounds—initiated a frantic search. He offered $100,000 for a Jewish baseball player.) The *Forward*'s Sunday edition, shipped all over the country, featured a department, "Gallery of Missing Husbands," with pictures and descriptions of East Side men who had deserted their families.

Thus, when Jewish males came into a community for the first time, local ladies subjected them to microscopic scrutiny. The *Forward* received many excited telegrams from such vigilant Jewish women—in Chicago, Terre Haute, Oklahoma City, and all points—turning in someone's errant husband . . . at least they were almost certain he was an errant husband.

Cahan appealed to Jewish pride (his socialist critics called it chauvinism) by highlighting stories of the sacrifices made by parents to send their children to college. There seemed to be no socialist dictum he wouldn't violate. A mother appealed to the *Forward* for advice on her son's refusal to recite the mourner's prayer for his father. "He says he would be a hypocrite if he said Kaddish because he does not believe in God. What can I do? He reads your paper. He is a Socialist. Can you make him? Can you help me?"

> You have refused to say Kaddish because you don't believe it would do your father any good, and so you think it would be hypocritical. But you are wrong. For you *know* it will do your *mother* good, and so, when you go to the synagogue, you will not be a hypocrite, but only a kind son who is comforting a broken old mother. If her religion is sincere, we should all respect it.

Former ham sandwich *fressers* at Yom Kippur balls could only ask one another, what *kind* of socialism was this? However, of all the assaults on radical sensibilities the most severe was caused by the "Bintel Brief"—a Bunch of Letters. They presented Cahan's "real life," domestic tragedies and comedies in the form of two to six letters—depending on length— which appeared daily in the *Forward*. Advice was sought on problems familiar to all Jewish East Siders: socialist children of religious parents; a Litvak mother-in-law beset by a Hungarian daughter-in-law ("Be glad," they told the mother-in-law, "she isn't Roumanian"); how, with a jealous husband, can you take in a boarder?; a Philistine husband with an intellectual wife, and vice versa; a socialist son whose mother exclaimed to the editor, "Socialism is socialism, but getting married, too, is a human affair"; a daughter complaining of a heartless mother—"We hate capitalists, she likes capitalists. What we do not like, she likes to spite us." "I am a socialist, and my boss is a fine man," wrote a garment worker, "I know he is a capitalist, but I cannot hate him. Am I doing the wrong thing?" From all these predicaments came entertainment and conversation and a feeling of identification for Jewish families wherever the *Forward* went.

But the socialist journalists whom Cahan assigned to answer the letters suffered, and the scorn of their comrades, who called them "Bintel Briefniks," compounded their agony. To all of them Cahan was fond of repeating an analogy which he felt conveyed his approach in helping Jewish immigrants adapt themselves to America. "If you want to pick a child up from the ground," he told them, "you first have to bend down to him. If you don't, how will you reach him?"

Another Yiddish paper also tried to reach the immigrant, but it did not bend, it merely looked down.

31

"A High-Class Yiddish Newspaper"

Around the turn of the century, Louis Marshall seated himself each day and, applying his recently acquired skill, read
the downtown Yiddish papers. Of the dailies, the *Tageblatt*
was Orthodox and pro-Tammany Hall; the *Abend-Blatt* was
antireligious and doctrinaire socialist; the *Forward* was semi-
antireligious and union-oriented socialist; the weekly *Freie
Arbeiter Stimme* was antireligious and anarchist. Instead of
attempting to emulate the New York *Times* or even the
American Hebrew, they all shamelessly aimed at the Hearst
and Pulitzer formula: sensationalism and demagoguery.
(One theory maintained that Hearst's *Evening Journal* acquired a new body of readers every six years—immigrants
graduating from the foreign-language press. But when Jewish
immigrants reached the English-paper stage, they continued
to read Yiddish papers "for news about Jews.") Apart from
their deplorable politics, their style offended Marshall. "A
Yiddish newspaper's freedom of expression," remarked a
downtown editor to Hutchins Hapgood "is limited by the
Penal Code alone." Nonetheless, libelous name calling and
bloodcurdling invective filled columns, whether the subject
was factional socialist polemics, union and labor discourse,
city or national politics, the review of a new volume of Yiddish poetry, or merely the usual internecine feuding—and the

fury of feuding Yiddish journalists and writers would have terrified Judas Maccabeus. Moreover, *so* irresponsible were they that in reference to uptown Jewish philanthropists, all Yiddish papers adopted a sarcastic, irreverent, impudent tone.

The only thing to do, Marshall decided, was to publish "a high-class Yiddish newspaper"—not Tabloid Yellow or Radical Red, but *Parve* Ecru. Consequently, in 1902, when Zvi Hersh Masliansky, the East Side Zionist preacher, and several other Yiddish journalists bought the plant of the *Abend-Blatt,* which had just folded, with the idea of starting a new paper— *Di Yiddishe Velt (The Jewish World)*—Marshall agreed to raise the money for it. Obviously, Marshall could be as pragmatic as Abe Cahan. Zionism was an aberration to Marshall and most uptowners. But Masliansky counterbalanced it by embracing the Educational Alliance school of starry-eyed American patriotism. Moreover, he was a spellbinding orator and very popular among Jewish immigrants. Still, Marshall provided himself with a safeguard. He stipulated that those who subscribed money for starting the paper would control its policy, which Marshall said would be "everything that the existing Yiddish newspapers are not, namely clean, wholesome, religious in tone; the advocate of all that makes good citizenship and so far as policies are concerned, absolutely independent. . . ." Furthermore, the control was to be a covert one. A trust fund would shield subscribers' names—Jacob and Mortimer Schiff, Felix Warburg, and an affluence of Seligmans, Strauses, Guggenheims, and Lehmans—from suspicion-prone East Side Jews, who might otherwise believe that *Yahudim* were out to control the policy of a downtown Yiddish paper.

Marshall felt Yiddish papers had one reason for being: to Americanize the immigrants. His idea of effective content therefore included a Yiddish translation of the Declaration of Independence; a serialization of an American history; injunctions to the reader on his duties "towards the noble country which protects his life and property . . ."; a presentation "in a dignified and instructive manner of the Republican side of the political issues"; and more news about the Jewish Theological Seminary than anyone on the East Side wanted to know.

Even subsidized by *Yahudim* to the tune of $100,000, the *World* lasted scarcely two years. The *Forward* did present American history and other educational features, but written simply and garnished with anecdote, analogy and relevancy to immigrant life. The civics lessons offered by the *World,* however, came across as pompous and patronizing and—even worse—remote from life in the sweatshops. Moreover, its Yiddish was of the scholarly variety, and "clean and wholesome" though it may have been, the total effect was dull. The *World*'s journalists—like all Yiddish journalists—were socialists, anarchists, labor agitators, Zionists, or poets of the sweatshop. But under Marshall's tight supervision, his staff curbed their impulses. "Every line was written carefully without teasing exaggeration." (No bosses ever drank the blood of their workers in *World* editorials.) And though he had set out to show the downtown press how to put out a Yiddish paper, in the end, when he finally sold it, Marshall was only too eager to get "this incubus" off his hands.

32

The Koshered Political Animal

Uptown Jews believed stubbornly that there was absolutely no such thing as a Jewish vote. "It is purely a figment of the imagination," the *American Hebrew* editorialized sternly. In truth, a discernible Jewish vote made *Yahudim tsitterdik* simply because it was invariably cast for nonrespectable political parties. The Democratic Party wasn't considered wholly undesirable. The conservative wing led by Grover Cleveland—or, as he was known downtown, *der grober* Cleveland—was highly regarded. But to have a large bloc of Jewish votes go to Tammany Hall, for example, created a gnawing uneasiness, conjuring up visions of bribery, corruption, and other such un-American vices. Actually, their fears weren't completely illusory, as anyone could attest who'd seen Tammany workers lurking in tenement hallways and distributing marked ballots from white cotton bags, while holding seductive dollar bills enticingly between their fingers. As disturbing as the possible Tammany capture of immigrant Jews was to *Yahudim*, the efforts of young radical Jewish intellectuals to spread socialism among the immigrants agitated them even more.

In certain circumstances a Jewish vote was acceptable. It is safe to say, for example, that if every Jewish immigrant citizen had voted for William McKinley, not one uptown Jew would have been embarrassed. On occasion, *Yahudim* solicited Republican votes with poignant desperation. In 1899, following his jubilant descent from San Juan Hill, Theodore Roosevelt ran for governor of New York. A Yiddish circular, distributed over the Lower East Side by Jewish members of the Republican State Committee, appealed to all Jews to vote for TR because owing to him and the Rough Riders, "the long felt Jewish desire to see Spain fall was finally fulfilled. Every vote for Roosevelt's opponent is a vote for Spain!" (Roosevelt turned out to be the most popular of Republican candidates among Jews, who occasionally named their children for him.)

In addition to the Democratic machine, a Republican machine existed on the East Side, whose claim to ethical superiority over Tammany Hall lay principally in its poor following. However, its hierarchy contained a Jewish boss or so and a few Jewish ward heelers. Sam Koenig, a Hungarian Jew, became increasingly powerful in downtown politics. And after years of being a Republican boss, Silver Dollar Smith, né Charles Solomon, "having changed his convictions," became a Democratic boss. (High-minded wings of both parties failed miserably in the ghetto. Reform or Fusion or Citizens Union or County Democracy or Good Government clubs were always offering tenement dwellers dignified stuffed-shirt candidates like Seth Low and pushing such issues as the enforcement of the Sunday closing and peddlers' licensing laws.) Actually, the downtown Republicans and Democrats enjoyed the most amicable of relationships. As State Senator Plunkitt, of "the most perfect political machine on earth," elucidated:

> Me and the Republicans are enemies just one day in the year—election day. Then we fight tooth and nail. The rest of the time it's live and let live. . . . You see we differ on tariffs and currencies and all them things, but we agree on the main proposition that when a man works in politics he should get something out of it.

Into this atmosphere of good fellowship, came the young, Jewish radical immigrants, incapable of perceiving the advantages of political accommodation. Though when they saw Martin Engel, Tammany leader of the Eighth Assembly District (who also ran a kosher chicken racket) driving around "de Ate" in an open barouche, his fingers and flashy cravat gleaming with diamonds, "they dimly realized what benefits accrued from keeping in with the forceful ones."

Since East European Jews had had no past experience with the Democratic processes and the free election system, a socialist machine didn't exist. It was generally believed that when they did venture into an American political campaign, some arcane acculturation process would take place—even among socialists. And it did.

Abe Cahan believed that when he worked "with all his energy" for Henry George in the 1886 mayoralty campaign, it straightened out much of his ideological confusion. Not single taxers by any means, socialists supported George to encourage opposition to the two capitalist parties. For them, this campaign approached the ideal "class struggle." On one side, the Tammany candidate, Abram Hewitt, and the Republican, Theodore Roosevelt, "the rich and their corrupt political lackeys" and, on the other, Henry George, "political purity and labor." Moreover, as the impressed Yiddish papers pointed out, George, an American *geborner*, fought with them against the capitalists and for the workers. The Eighth—the most solidly packed Jewish district—gave George a greater vote than Hewitt, who won the election and received 22,442 votes more than George. (Roosevelt ran well in the Eighth, too, but came in third in the whole city. He never let *that* happen again.)

Shocked by the brazen swindling at the polls, Abe Cahan saw Tammany's resourcefulness at first hand. Often when Henry George supporters arrived at the polls, they were told the records showed they had already voted. "That meant," Cahan wrote, "that a vote had already been cast for Hewitt in that person's name." When it was pointed out by George poll watchers that a man answering to the name of Schloma Rabinowitz had a curiously thick Irish brogue, the alleged Mr. Rabinowitz had a ready explanation: "And where do yez think I learned me English if not from the Irish, God love 'em?"

As it turned out, Tammany itself underwent acculturation of sorts. Impressed by the vote Jewish immigrants had given George, Big Tim Sullivan, replete with *yarmulke*, began attending *brises*, Bar Mitzvahs, weddings and funerals. And John J. Ahearn, whose Fourth district contained equal numbers of Irish and Jews, found it was "all the same to him whether he takes off his hat in church or pulls it down over his ears in the synagogue."

But Tammany Hall had an innate flexibility. Young Jewish socialist intellectuals did not . . . yet. Had they been able to compromise earlier, to absorb one of Tammany's basic tenets to look after your constituency, their influence among East

Side immigrants would have been felt sooner. First, they had to overcome their reluctance to occupy themselves with ethnic or religious problems as such. In their eyes, they weren't Jewish socialist; they were "Yiddish-speaking socialists." Mankind was their constituency. The Dreyfus case, for example, which deeply disturbed practically all Jews, was dismissed cursorily by the Yiddish voice of the Socialist Labor Party, the *Abend-Blatt:* "How can you compare a single instance of the wrong suffered by one man from capitalism and its main support, militarism, with the wrongs that millions of workers suffer day and night?"

But a number of Jewish socialists—among them Abe Cahan, Morris Hillquit, and Meyer London—were moving to the right—their enthusiasm for revolution diminishing while their enthusiasm for the concept of class struggle increased. The Socialist Labor Party to which they belonged had for some years boiled with discord and rebellion. This friction centered on "the quarrelsome and intolerant tactics" of the SLP leader, Daniel De Leon, a dark-bearded, handsome man in his forties who had a grand manner and a malicious tongue. A former lecturer in international law at Columbia, De Leon had in a decade's time gone from the utopian socialism of Edward Bellamy to a fanatical espousal of revolutionary Marxism. He possessed a brilliant mind, a magnetic personality; his aristocratic demeanor, in particular, impressed Jewish socialists. His background was rather mysterious. Jews believed him Jewish, though he occasionally exhibited hostility toward Russian Jews, but then, at one time or another, he exhibited hostility toward everyone. Ambiguous about his antecedents, he did claim direct descent from Ponce de Leon. Sam Gompers, who loathed him, maintained De Leon's ancestry to be a mixed bag of Spanish Venezuelan, Dutch, Jewish, and black, "which makes him," Gompers said with relish, "a first-class son of a bitch."

More to the point, perhaps, De Leon had an unbearably arrogant and dictatorial manner. He was as intransigently fixed in his own opinions as he was contemptuous of those held by others. Not one to countenance someone else's arrogance, Abe Cahan led a group of fifty-two Jewish socialists out of the SLP and eventually into publishing the *Daily Forward,* based on socialism, trade unions, and the class struggle. In 1901 they joined with the Hoosier socialist Eugene Debs, "a real American," to form the Socialist Party of America, where political theorizing would give way to political action.

Then in 1903, on two days in early April—the regular pogrom season—the worst pogrom in Russian history ripped through the city of Kishinev. Forty-five Jews were killed; hundreds maimed and crippled. Not yet conditioned to murder in genocidal numbers, these figures appalled the whole world. Petitions of protest inundated an irritated Czar Nicholas II, who refused to receive them. Even the Kaiser remonstrated. In the United States, where American Jews were preparing to celebrate the two hundred and fiftieth anniversary of their initial arrival, Jews and Christians reacted with mass protest meetings all over the country, at which funds were collected to alleviate the suffering in Kishinev.

Yahudim had always frowned on Jews organizing for secular reasons, but following Kishinev, Jacob Schiff and Louis Marshall formed an organization of *shtadlonim*, the American Jewish Committee, to protect "the civil and religious rights of Jews in any part of the world." Jewish workers on the East Side stepped up the formation of *landsmanshaften* by 80 percent. Each of these mutual benefit societies consisted of *landsleit*—those who came from the same *shtetl*, city, or province. In addition to the nostalgia and *haimish* comfort they provided, these societies—*fereines*—also offered sickness and unemployment benefits, medical care, and funeral plots. (And in later years, they featured theater parties.) Granted that the Upmann-cigar-*balabatish* milieu of the American Jewish Committee conference rooms differed from a meeting of the Zosleh *Fereine*, held in a small shul on East Fourth Street amid Sweet Caporal smoke and steaming glasses of tea, still the same impulse created them—the imperative need for security conjured up by the Kishinev pogrom.

As for the cosmopolitan socialists, Kishinev produced a stunning change in them. "In our enthusiasm for the Socialist dream," one remarked sadly, "we have forgotten the tragic needs of our own brothers." One group formed the Jewish Defense Association, which raised $30,000 to arm Russian Jews in the event of more pogroms. (The association even received a $100 check from Jacob Schiff, who under normal conditions strongly opposed such activity, but then *everyone* was acting out of character.) In the wake of new massacres in 1905, 125,000 Jews dressed in mourning led by Judah L. Magnes (and organized by the Jewish Defense Association) marched to Union Square with the bells of churches along the way tolling sympathetically.

Equal in significance to the effects of Kishinev and the

1905 pogroms on Jews in the United States was the new influx of Jewish immigrants that followed the pogroms—more than a quarter million in four years. Among them were young socialist intellectuals, former Bund members, destined to put new life in the Jewish labor movement, cultural life, and East Side politics. Now they didn't consider themselves "Yiddish-speaking"; they were *Jewish* socialists. They soon "began to evoke an undefined Jewish feeling . . . began proclaiming that Jewish socialists must be 'first and foremost, Jews.' " Suddenly Zionism burst into bloom as a popular movement on the East Side.

Meanwhile, Tammany Hall proceeded along its customary devious paths, winning elections on the Lower East Side without exerting itself unduly. In 1900, as a gesture to its Jewish voters in the Ninth Congressional District, it gave them Henry Goldfogle, a forty-six-year-old municipal court judge, son of German Jews, but a New York *geborner*. A good sound organization man, Goldfogle—in six terms in Congress—offered resolutions of sympathy for Russian pogrom victims to be read into the *Congressional Record* and upheld the passport rights of American Jews traveling in Russia. Louis Marshall, however, accused him of being "more interested in introducing resolutions and making speeches for home consumption than in seriously and efficiently dealing with this situation." And on the subject of working conditions in sweatshops, Judge Goldfogle was generally mum.

At first, Tammany viewed the fiery speakers of Socialist campaigns with detached amusement. ("We got our bookworms, too . . . but we don't make them district leaders, we keep them for ornaments on parade days"); but as each election passed, the Socialist vote grew in size and significance, and the organization had to up the price of votes, had to keep hopping to send repeaters and floaters down to the polls.

In 1914 the Socialist candidate opposing Judge Goldfogle was a labor lawyer, Meyer London, idealistic, uncharismatic, and rumored to be a saint. During the labor turmoil of the preceding years, he had worked unceasingly for the workers and "had to be browbeaten into accepting fees for his services." But as genuinely popular as London was, his victory over Tammany Hall was due in great part to Abe Cahan's *Daily Forward,* whose grass roots tenement-to-tenement electioneering revealed a keen understanding of American politics.

When Meyer London went to Washington in 1914, he was

the first Socialist Congressman from the East. Moreover, he had been elected by what purportedly did not exist—the Jewish vote. Signaling this era, a cartoon in a Yiddish humor magazine showed London standing amid the tenements of the Lower East Side with hand outstretched to shake the hand of Uncle Sam, stationed at the Capitol Building. "Hello," Uncle Sam said, speaking in Yiddish, of course. "You are truly a different sort of Jew. I like you."

33

Downtown Gibson Girls

Still in her teens, Clara Lemlich blended unnoticed into the bleak mass of sweatshop girls—she was, in East Side parlance, "a nothing." But in the fall of 1909 a single impulsive emotional act gave her a moment's individuality. It also galvanized a faltering labor movement, and this, in turn, gave the immigrant Jew a shove away from parochialism. At the time, Clara was thin and intense, spoke a fiery Yiddish, and was a Gibson Girl.

No doubt Charles Dana Gibson would have had difficulty associating Clara with the idealized American girl he drew—poised, exuding wholesomeness, confidence, the American spirit, and a total ignorance of Yiddish. Still, by drawing his girl dressed in a shirtwaist, he created the most popular fashion in America for a generation. Thus, Clara and some 15,000 other girls—Jewish and Italian—were his creation, too; but these real-life Gibson girls worked fifty-six hours a week, plus overtime during the busy season, to produce shirtwaists for as little as $3 a week in approximately 600 shirtwaist shops downtown.

One of the largest manufacturers of shirtwaists, the Triangle Waist Company, was located on the east side of Washington Square Park and occupied the top three floors of the Asch Building. (On a Saturday morning in March, 1911, flames would gut the Asch Building and incinerate 146 Triangle shirtwaist workers.)

The Triangle shirtwaist—a moderate-priced number, $1.50 wholesale—was made under the notorious subcontracting system. This meant the manufacturer dealt only with a contractor who would hire young girls—the greener, the cheaper— and show them how to make the component parts of a shirtwaist: sleeves, bodice (pleated or frilled), cuffs, and collar. He would then assemble the parts himself and turn them in. The girls were charged for needles, electricity to run their machines, and lockers for their hats and coats. Their pay amounted to $3 to $10 a week. The contractor received about $28 to $30 weekly. Sometimes there would be a stretch of twenty-two weeks of work, and then a slowdown for five or six weeks occurred.

Out of this precarious income, Clara and girls like her— many of whom had emigrated to the United States by themselves—paid for their lodgings, about $4 a month, for a small portion of a two-room tenement flat, shared with a family of at least five. Food cost about $2.25 a week. There might be a steerage ticket yet to be paid off, and whenever possible, $2 were sent to her parents in Russia. Night school was free, but it often produced a need for eyeglasses, which cost at least $3. Illnesses—treacherous, feared—ate up any savings quickly. If a girl contracted tuberculosis—all too frequently the case— then she had either to throw herself on the mercy of Hebrew Charities and hope to be sent up to the Catskills to recover or to try somehow to reach Denver's Jewish Consumptive Relief Society, opened in 1904 by East European Jews (with six tents and a frame building) for the "poor sick," under the direction of Abe Cahan's friend, a former Am Olamite, Dr. Charle Spivak. Or if she was curable and had in some way arranged to be accepted by the Denver institution sponsored by American Jews, could afford the weekly charge of $6 to $9, and had no objection to nonkosher food, she could go to the National Jewish Hospital for Consumptives. Or she could give up and quietly die.

The girls at the Leiserson Shirtwaist Company on Tenth Street—among them Clara Lemlich—struck at the beginning of September; by the end of the month the girls at Triangle were out, too. The resources of the Waist-Makers' Local 25, of the International Ladies Garment Workers Union, hardly deserved the name. It had about 100 members and $4 in the treasury. The ILGWU, itself, only about nine years old, was by no means on a firm basis. Consequently, its secretary, John Dyche, opposed the demand for a general strike, urging, instead, an investigation of working conditions. Furthermore, Dyche had little faith in the sustaining powers of "irresponsible little girls" in a long strike. And to his disgust, others "butted in." The Women's Trade Union League, an organization of rich women with social consciences and activists in the women's suffrage movement—Mrs. O. H. P. Belmont, Ida Tarbell, and Anne Morgan (J. P.'s sister, no less) swept elegantly downtown to join the shirtwaist girls on the picket line. Soon bevies of Wellesley and Vassar students—undeniably Gibson Girls—marched up and down in front of Triangle and Leiserson's. Sympathy for the girls grew—except, of course, among the firms' management, the police, and municipal court judges. (Mrs. Belmont put up her $400,000 mansion at 477 Madison Avenue as security for bailing out four girls.)

On November 22 a mass meeting was held at Cooper Union. After two hours of solemn discussion by a podium full of notables Clara Lemlich rose from the audience and asked for the floor. She cried out passionately in Yiddish—"eloquently even to American ears"—"I am a working girl, one of those who are on strike against intolerable conditions. What we are here for is to decide whether we shall or shall not strike. I offer a resolution that a general strike be declared—*now.*"

For five minutes, the audience stood, shouting, waving hats and handkerchiefs. Finally, the chairman called for Clara's resolution to be seconded. This, too, inflamed the audience to a wild response. Carried away by the emotion, the chairman called out, "Do you mean it with all your hearts and souls? Will you take the old Jewish oath?"

Two thousand hands shot up, and two thousand voices chanted: "If I turn traitor to the cause I now pledge, may this hand wither from the arm I now raise."

The *Yahudim* position on the union activity of their East European brethren resisted easy classification; it had to be much more than simple adamant opposition. Throughout the whole forty-year immigration period, a multistrand of antipathies, inconsistencies, and reluctant pro tem unity constituted the fabric of their relationship.

In the eighties America had welcomed immigrants as the answer to an expanding labor market, but *Yahudim* urged immigration restriction. When Rabbi Joseph Krauskopf of Phil-

adelphia—an exemplar of *Yahudim* attitudes, he even lived
in Germantown—and Rabbi Joseph Silverman of New York's
Temple Emanu-El urged Jews to remain in Russia, the *Jewish
Gazette* reported their plea under the caption "The voice is
the voice of Jacob, but the hands are the hands of Esau."
However, from the beginning of the twentieth century onward, when American support for immigration evaporated
owing to a satiated labor market and then was reshaped by
prejudice into an ever more shrill cry for restriction, Mar-
shall-led *Yahudim* joined in battle against restrictive measures. It wasn't merely the insulting implication that Jews were
undesirable citizens, but that such measures might also set a
precedent for further government-sanctioned and enforced
discrimination against Jews, be they newly arrived immigrants
or already firmly rooted citizens.

At first, *Yahudim* sought to make the immigrants less visible—and thus less subject to attack. They financed the Industrial Removal Office to disseminate ghetto Jews over as
wide an area as possible, the Galveston Plan to route them
into the interior of the country by way of the Southwest, and
subsidized farming, which offered not only the concealment
of isolated communities, but the genesis of a field-laboring
Jew that would dilute—if not destroy—a prejudice-fomenting
stereotype.

The strategy failed to live up to expectations. Hundreds of
thousands of Jewish immigrants still packed the East Side:
visible—and grating, as well, on the other four senses of those
who considered themselves the Anglo-Saxon elite. And when
Clara Lemlich called her sister shirtwaist workers to arms at
the end of 1909 and set off a three-month strike, *Yahudim*
feared their Americanization efforts had been for nothing: the
lessons in English and citizenship, baseball, etiquette and
manners, elocution, cooking and love of flag—all designed to
make the immigrants disappear smoothly into the environment.

Moreover, at the end of the strike, the International Ladies
Garment Workers Union won such historic concessions—a
fifty-two-hour workweek, four paid holidays, and the right of
wage negotiation between employer and a shop committee—
that they inspired 60,000 workers in the cloakmakers' shops
to go out on an industry-wide strike in July, 1910. The employers united as the Manufacturers Association, and points
of view hardened on both sides. The daily, well-publicized
clashes between strong-arm strikebreakers (*shtarkes*) and

pickets—male and female—thrust Jacob Schiff and Louis Marshall into a dilemma. Both opposed union organization, which conjured up visions of civil disorder, class hostility, anarchy, and minimum wage laws. Furthermore to become involved in radical undertakings invited misconception. (During a Socialist meeting on the Lower East Side, a group of militant antiradicals milled about in the audience trying to break up the proceedings. One of their number reported to the police that the Socialists were rioting. The police bounded in, clubs swinging freely, whacking radical and nonradical alike. "But, Lieutenant," a nonradical complained indignantly, "I'm an anti-Socialist!" "I don't give a damn what kind of Socialist you are," the police officer bellowed. "Break it up!")

So when Schiff and Marshall stepped in to mediate the Cloakmakers' Strike, they knew that in the eyes of the average American, they—a millionaire investment banker and a deeply conservative lawyer—might very well be regarded as union sympathizers—*i.e.*, wild-eyed radicals. But that perennial Jewish catalyst, "It's a *shunda* [shame] for the goyim," made them attempt to bring about industrial peace. For both sides in the strike—the Manufacturers Association and an overwhelming majority of the leaders and members of the ILGWU—were Jews, and *Yahudim* feared that the spectacle of Jews fighting Jews would be embarrassing, a crass indication of Jewish disunity. (This concern was groundless. No matter how much evidence Christian America has of the Jew's propensity for argument and dissension, his penchant for clashing over minute issues, wrangling on matters of principle and boiling over with factionalism, American Jews hear one pronouncement repeatedly: "One thing about you Jews, you always stick together.")

Applying that old *shtadlonim* pressure, a blend of stern authority and honeyed words, Marshall, backed by the power of Schiff's wealth and prestige—maneuvered an extremely balky Manufacturers Association to agree to a fifty-hour workweek, ten paid holidays, time and a half for overtime, the abolition of inside contracting (in effect the end of sweatshops), *and* a minimum wage. For the signing of the agreement, two lawyers, Julius Henry Cohen for the Manufacturers Association and Meyer London for the ILGWU, met with Louis Marshall. The terms proved acceptable, but a dispute arose over what the agreement should be called. Cohen felt his clients would regard London's suggestion—"collective bargaining"—as entirely too heartening to the union, while London believed

Cohen's choice—"treaty of peace"—would strike his client as having the offensive air of surrender. Then Marshall, "shrewd as an old rabbi," broke the impasse. "Call it Protocol of Peace," he told them. "Neither side will know what it means and so will accept it."

The Protocol of Peace, a milestone in labor negotiations, ended the era of absolute power by the employer. Moreover, it entrenched the union in the shops and in the psyche of the workers. And for all this, *Yahudim*—conservative by disposition and conviction—could take a portion of credit, should they care to.

34

Azoy Geyt Es

Despite their good offices in settling the strike, the resentments between *Yahudim* and the immigrants weren't eased. But, paradoxically, anti-Semitism proved balm of sorts. The end of World War I brought the tide in favor of immigration restriction to its high mark, and restriction proponents buttressed their position with a burst of anti-Semitism. Jewish leaders, both native and immigrant, began to feel *tsitterdik* twinges, and a common enemy moved them to concerted action. The American Jewish Committee set up a Bureau of Jewish War Records to tabulate statistics concerning Jewish participation in the war. This enabled them to respond defensively with facts: Jews, only 3 percent of the population, had constituted 4.5 percent of the American armed forces and 5 percent of the casualty list. Jewish soldiers had to serve in a double capacity—on the battlefield and as examples of Jewish heroism. There were 150 Jewish Distinguished Service Cross holders. Of the 78 Congressional Medal of Honor recipients, 4 were Jewish; France had conferred 174 Croix de Guerre on American Jews, and 4 Medailles Militaires. One spectacular hero, Sam Dreben of El Paso, Texas, was given wide publicity. Formerly of Poltroe, Russia, an infantry sergeant during World War I, holder of the Distinguished Service Cross for attacking a German machine-gun enclave and killing twenty-three of its crew, he also received the Croix de Guerre and numerous other decorations. He had fought in the Spanish-American War, in the Boxer Rebellion, with Lee Christmas in Bonilla's Honduran revolution that had established Sam Zemurray firmly in the banana game, and in Mexico with General Pershing. Dreben had not been enthusiastic about the latter engagement. Mexico had no Jewish cemetery, he said, and he "did not care to start one." (Following World War I, a Jewish soldier could keep his religious identity even in a non-Jewish cemetery. The Monument Commission had originally marked the graves of all American soldiers buried in France with a cross, until the Jewish Welfare Board asked to have the Mogen David, the six-pointed Star of David, placed over the graves of Jewish soldiers.)

Then, in 1920, Henry Ford began a seven-year orgy of anti-Semitism, which made no distinction between *Yahudim* and East Europeans. During that period Ford's Dearborn *Independent* published ninety-one articles—including a regurgitation of the Protocols of the Elders of Zion—on the "International Jew," whom they pronounced "The World's Foremost Problem." Among the featured pieces were "The Jewish Associates of Benedict Arnold"; "Taft Once Tried to Resist the Jews—and Failed"; and "How the Jewish Song Trust Makes You Sing"—and not good clean toe tappers, either, like "Juanita" and "In the Baggage Car Ahead," but such unwholesome products of "Yiddish Tin-Pan Alley" as "Alexander's Ragtime Band" and "Everybody's Doin' It."

According to Ford and his newspaper staff, Jews or their "Gentile Fronts" controlled almost every aspect of American life. (Former President Taft loomed large, in their estimate, as a "Gentile Front.") Adding insult to injury was the charge —directed at *Yahudim*—that rich American Jews had *ordered* the huge influx of "caftan-clad East European Orthodox Jewish immigrants" to revive "the influence of Judaism"! Furthermore, readers were assured that "Jews were *not* the Chosen People."

What motivated this sustained outburst of malevolence? Ford, naïve, poorly educated, with little knowledge beyond the automobile industry (and in fact there were few Jews in that industry—the only Jewish car maker was André-Gustave Citroën, called the Henry Ford of France),* had branched

---

* Though not a car maker, John D. Hertz, a Czechoslavakian Jew, had founded the Yellow Cab Company in Chicago five years earlier and, at least in that area of transport, was number one.

out into world affairs in the recent past with his disastrous peace ship in 1915 and a futile run for a Senate seat in 1918. A former associate offered one explanation of Ford's venture into anti-Semitism. Ford, he said, planned to run for President and "hoped to win votes by attacking the Jews. He knew there were about three million Jews in the United States and he figured he would gain three or four or five votes of non-Jews for every Jewish vote he lost."

But when Jews stopped buying Ford cars and when a Jewish lawyer in Detroit sued him for $1,000,000, Ford agreed to make a complete recantation and apology. Louis Marshall wrote out a long penitent statement which Ford signed without reading. Marshall, whom the Dearborn *Independent* had characterized as "short, stocky and aggressive," and as "America's Jewish enigma," described a meeting with Ford to his son, with unenigmatic enjoyment: "On Thursday morning, at 9:30, *Mr. Henry Ford* by pre-arrangement called on me at the office and we spent a most interesting hour together. He said that he felt better now that he had relieved his mind of the burden of the 'great mistake and blunder that he had made' in his anti-Jewish publications. . . ." Ford also invited Marshall to see his new Model A "and asked me to select any of his products that I might desire." Marshall, however, declined, saying he preferred to walk.

Jacob Schiff died in 1921, and Louis Marshall in 1929.* With the exit of these two formidable figures, *Yahudim* were never quite the same. Little by little, East European Jews who had grown rich or influential began ascending the rungs of formerly *Yahudim*-ruled communal organizations. Henry Monsky, whose parents had been sent to Omaha, Nebraska, by the IRO, became a prominent lawyer, a close associate of Father Flanagan of Boys Town, a founder of the American Jewish Conference, and the first Jew of East European descent to be president of B'nai B'rith. Monsky had also figured in a romance broken by the antagonisms between *Yahudim* and East Europeans. In 1912 he met Daisy Hirsch, a niece of Adolf Kraus, who was one of the most prominent *Yahudim* and president of B'nai B'rith. They fell in love, but Daisy's

---

* Marshall had led the project to move Temple Emanu-El from Forty-third Street and Fifth Avenue to Sixty-fifth and Fifth. In the spring of 1928 he laid the cornerstone for the new building. By mid-September, 1929, he was dead, and his funeral was the first service to be held in the Moorish splendor of the $8,000,000 building.

mother, "a North German Jewess, shared a popular dislike
for East European Jews," and it was "understood" that suitors
of the Hirsch girls "should be the sons of German or Austrian
Jews." So when Henry called on Daisy at her Chicago home,
she entertained him on the front porch. But the prejudice
wasn't one-sided, for Henry admitted to Daisy that his Orthodox mother would be "as willing to have him marry a non-Jew-
ess . . . as she would be to receive a Reform Jewess. . . ." Because of their parents' opposition, they each married someone
else. But twenty-five years later, when Daisy was a widow and
Henry was divorced, they finally married.

As men like Monsky and Jacob Blaustein, who was approaching the giddy heights of the American Jewish Committee's hierarchy, and Sam Zemurray, the Banana Baron and
bestower of a half million dollars on Tulane University,
achieved prominence, a curious transformation took place.
These former *shtetl* dwellers and sons of *shtetl* dwellers took
on certain familiar characteristics. Men of achievement and
position, they exuded that quiet air of authority that had once
belonged exclusively to *Yahudim*. Who upon looking at a portrait of Samuel Goldwyn, for example, could deny, despite the
distinctively Russian cast of features, that there was a *Yahudi!*

As for the lesser East European immigrants, those who
hadn't as yet acquired the *balabatish* status of *Yahudim*, they
played a *Yahudim*-like role in the late thirties by organizing to
rescue German Jews from Nazi savagery. (One refugee recalled that as a child he had heard of the pogroms in which
"Russians were killing Jews," and his grandfather "explained
that in Germany, a civilized country, such a thing could never
happen to Jews.") Those who were able to escape were helped
by the Hebrew Immigrant Aid Society, the Joint Distribution
Committee (known simply as "the Joint"), and the Jewish
Agricultural Society, which undertook to direct some of the
refugees into farming—a project particularly successful in New
Jersey, where German exiles were helped by citizens of Alliance, the old Russian Jewish farm colony. (All this had a
definite *déjà vu*—or, at least, *nach amol* quality.) German
Jews approached this new occupation with Teutonic thorough-
ness, efficiency, and literalness. Before starting a chicken farm,
for example, they were likely to do extensive research, to really
find out everything about chickens—tabulate egg production
statistics, make comparative analyses of cost, explore the
various poultry diseases and the vaccines available to counter

them. As a result, the influx of German Jewish refugees revived the New Jersey poultry industry.

The same clash of personality often occurred between East Europeans as benefactors and German Jews, the recipients of philanthropy, as when the roles had been reversed. To German Jews, American Jews—in whom they clearly detected East European origins—were unrefined, materialistic. And former East European immigrants and their children—now established American citizens—applied equally harsh criticism: "ungrateful," "everything's coming to them." Though these German Jewish immigrants required financial help, no one suggested a campaign of "uplift" as had been the case with East European immigrants. Indeed, unlike Russian Jews of the eighties and nineties, the German exiles of the thirties were chiefly of the professional class—scholars, physicians, government officials, merchants, bankers—and it was resentfully observed by their American co-religionists that many of them were apt to dwell on their former status and to criticize by comparison American cultural and social standards. "It was better *bei uns*" (with us) was heard so frequently that American Jews took to calling Germans *Beiunsers*—among French Jews, they were *les Beiunsers*—and to circulate jokes about them. (A German dachshund snubbed a friendly Boston terrier, saying loftily, "Don't dink I alvays vas chust a dachshund, back home I vas a Saint Bernard.")

Fortunately, the hostility between Jews of East and West European origin has waned with the passage of time. Then, too, those alarming predictions made by *Yahudim* so many years ago—"In fifty years from now, or less, they will far outnumber us. Their children will far outnumber our children"—turned out to be accurate, for more than 85 percent of present-day American Jews are East Europeans or their descendants. But such evidence of God's will or the puzzling or the inevitable could be accounted for simply and quickly by one philosophical Yiddish expression, *Azoy geyt es*—that's the way it goes.

As another example of how it goes, no Jew—native or immigrant—could have foreseen some of the results of the future's homogeneity. In 1950, Robert Sarnoff, grandson of a desperately poor Russian tailor, married Felicia Schiff Warburg, great-granddaughter of the richest, most important *Yahudi* of his time. In 1970 the Sarnoffs were divorced, and the ex-Mrs. Sarnoff married Franklin D. Roosevelt, Jr. One wonders what their respective *zaydes*, Abraham Sarnoff and Jacob H. Schiff, and *bobbe*, Sara Delano Roosevelt, would have made of it all.

Selected Bibliography

Abbreviations
PAJHS Publication of the American Jewish Historical Society
AJA American Jewish Archives
JSS Jewish Social Studies
YIVO YIVO Annual of Jewish Social Science

ADLER, CYRUS, *I Have Considered the Days.* Philadelphia, 1941.
————, *Louis Marshall—In Memoriam.* New York, 1931.
ALEICHEM, SHOLEM, *Adventures of Mottel the Cantor's Son.* New York, 1953.
ANTIN, MARY, *The Promised Land.* Boston, 1912.
APPEL, J. J., "Trefa Banquet." *Commentary* (February, 1966).
ASBURY, HERBERT, *Gangs of New York.* New York, 1928.
BEN-HORIN, MEIR, Letters—Solomon Schechter to Judge Mayer Sulzberger. JSS, October, 1963; April, 1965.
BENTWICH, NORMAN, *For Zion's Sake.* Philadelphia, 1954.
————, *Solomon Schechter.* Philadelphia, 1938.
BERKSON, ISRAEL, *Theories of Americanization.* New York, 1920.
BERMAN, MYRON, "The Attitude of American Jewry Towards East European Jewish Immigration 1881–1914." Ph.D. Thesis, Columbia University, 1963.
————, "A New Spirit on the East Side." PAJHS, September, 1964.
BERNHEIMER, CHARLES, ed., *The Russian Jew in America.* Philadelphia, 1905.
BLOOM, BERNARD H., "Yiddish-Speaking Socialists on the East Side." AJA, April, 1960.

BLOOM, S. F., "The Saga of America's Russian Jews." *Commentary* (February, 1946).

BLUMENSON, S. L., "Utopia on Columbia St." *Commentary* (October, 1948).

BOGEN, BORIS D., *Born a Jew.* New York, 1930.

BORGENICHT, LOUIS, *The Happiest Man.* New York, 1942.

BRECK, ALLEN DUPONT, *The Centennial History of the Jews of Colorado.* Denver, 1960.

BREGSTONE, PHILIP, *Chicago and Its Jews.* Chicago, 1933.

BRESSLER, DAVID, *Distribution of Jewish Immigrants in Industrial and Agricultural Pursuits.* New York, 1907.

CAHAN, ABRAHAM, *Bletter fun Mein Leben* (Pages from My Life). New York, 1926–1931. 5 vols.

CARR, JOHN, ed., *Guide to the United States for the Jewish Immigrant.* Connecticut, DAR, 1912.

CHOTZINOFF, SAMUEL, *A Lost Paradise.* New York, 1955.

COHEN, J. H., *They Builded Better Than They Knew.* New York, 1946.

COHEN, M. R., *A Dreamer's Journey.* Boston, 1949.

COHEN, NAOMI, "The Abrogation of the Russo-American Treaty of 1832." PAJHS, January, 1963.

COHEN, SAMUEL S., "Recreational Enterprise on the Bowery." *Commentary* (November, 1952).

DAVIDSON, GABRIEL, *Our Jewish Farmers.* New York, 1943.

DAVIDOWITZ, LUCY, "Louis Marshall's Yiddish Newspaper." JSS, April, 1963.

DUBNOW, S., *History of the Jews in Russia and Poland.* Philadelphia, 1916–20. 3 vols.

EPSTEIN, MELECH, *Jewish Labor in the United States 1882–1914.* New York, 1950.

FINKELSTEIN, LOUIS, ed., *The Jews, Their History, Culture and Religion.* New York, 1950. 2 vols.

FISHBERG, MAURICE, *The Jews.* London, 1911.

FORD, JAMES, *Slums and Housing.* Cambridge, Massachusetts, 1936.

FREDERIC, HAROLD, *The New Exodus.* London, 1892.

GOLDHAFT, A., *The Golden Egg.* New York, 1957.

GOLDMAN, EMMA, *Living My Life.* New York, 1931. 2 vols.

GOREN, ARTHUR, "The New York Kehillah 1908–1922." Ph.D. Thesis, Columbia University, 1966.

GORDEN, B., *Between Two Worlds.* New York, 1952.

GRINSTEIN, HYMAN B., "The Effort of East European Jews to Organize Their Own Community in the United States." PAJHS, December, 1959.

HANDLIN, OSCAR, *Adventure in Freedom.* New York, 1954.

HAPGOOD, HUTCHINS, *The Spirit of the Ghetto*. New York, 1902.

HARTE, BRET, "The 'Ebrew Jew." AJA, June, 1954.

HELLER, JAMES, *Isaac Mayer Wise: His Life, Work and Thought*. New York, 1965.

HESCHEL, ABRAHAM J., "The Eastern European Era in Jewish History." YIVO, 1946.

HIGHAM, JOHN, *Strangers in the Land*. New Brunswick, 1955.

HILLQUIT, MORRIS, *Loose Leaves from a Busy Life*. New York, 1934.

HIRSCH, ABRAMOVITCH, "Rural Jewish Occupations in Lithuania." YIVO, 1947–48.

HOLLAND, SAMUEL H., "Arthur L. (Al) Welch." *The Record* (May, 1969).

HORWICH, BERNARD, *My First Eighty Years*. Chicago, 1939.

HOWE, M. A. DeWOLFE, *Letters of Barrett Wendell*. Boston, 1924.

HURVITZ, N., "Jews and Jewishness in the Street Rhymes of American Children." JSS, April, 1954.

JACOB, H., *The World of Emma Lazarus*. New York, 1949.

JACOBS, JOSEPH, ed., *The Persecutions of the Jews in Russia*. Philadelphia, 1891.

JOSEPH, SAMUEL, *The History of the Baron de Hirsch Fund*. Philadelphia, 1935.

———, *Jewish Immigration to the United States 1881–1910*. New York, 1914.

KARP, A. J., "New York Chooses a Chief Rabbi." PAJHS, March, 1958.

———, "Solomon Schechter Comes to America." PAJHS, September, 1963.

KASOVICH, ISRAEL, *The Days of Our Years*. New York, 1929.

KLIGSBERG, MOSES, "Jewish Immigrants in Business: A Sociological Study." PAJHS, March, 1967.

KOHUT, REBECCA, *My Portion*. New York, 1925.

KROPOTKIN, P., *Memoirs of a Revolutionist*. Boston, 1899.

LESSER, ALLEN, *Weave a Wreath of Laurel*. New York, 1938.

LEVIN, SCHMARYA, *Childhood in Exile*. New York, 1929.

LIFSCHUTZ, EZEKIEL, "Yiddish Autobiographies as a Source of American Jewish History." PAJHS, March, 1964.

LOWENTHAL, MARVIN, ed., *Diary of Theodor Herzl*. New York, 1956.

LYONS, EUGENE, *David Sarnoff*. New York, 1966.

MANDEL, IRVING, "The Attitudes of the American Jewish Community Toward East European Immigration in the United States." AJA, June, 1950.

MAY, MAX, *Isaac Mayer Wise: The Founder of American Judaism*. New York, 1916.

MCKENNA, M. J., *Our Brethren of the Tenements and Ghetto*. New York, 1899.

MEYER, AGNES N., *It's Been Fun*. New York, 1951.

MONSKY, MRS. HENRY, and BISGAYER, MAURICE, *Henry Monsky: The Man and His Work*. New York, 1947.

MORRIS, ROBERT, and FREUND, MICHAEL, eds., *Trends and Issues in Jewish Social Welfare 1899–1952*. Philadelphia, 1966.

MOSS, FRANK, *The American Metropolis*. New York, 1897. 3 vols.

NATHAN, MAUD, *Once Upon a Time and Today*. New York, 1933.

NATHAN, ANNE, and COHEN, HARRY, *The Man Who Stayed in Texas*. New York, 1941.

PANITZ, ESTHER, "In Defense of the Jewish Immigrant 1891–1924." PAJHS, September, 1965.

———, "The Polarity of American Jewish Attitudes Towards Immigration 1870–1891." PAJHS, December, 1963.

PHILIPSON, DAVID, *My Life as an American Jew*. New York, 1931.

———, "Strangers in a Strange Land." AJA, November, 1966.

POSTAL, B., and KOPPMAN, LIONEL, *A Jewish Tourist's Guide to the U.S.* Philadelphia, 1954.

PRINGLE, HENRY, "A Jonah Who Swallowed the Whale." *American* magazine, September, 1933.

RAGINS, SANFORD, "The Image of America in Two East European Hebrew Periodicals." AJA, November, 1965.

RAVAGE, M. E., *American in the Making*. New York, 1917.

REZNIKOFF, C., ed., *Louis Marshall: Selected Letters and Addresses*. Philadelphia, 1957. 2 vols.

RIORDAN, WILLIAM L., *Plunkitt of Tammany Hall*. New York, 1948.

RISCHIN, MOSES, *An Inventory of American Jewish History*. Cambridge, Massachusetts, 1954.

———, *The Promised City*. Boston, 1962.

ROBERTS, DOROTHY, "The Jewish Colony at Cotopaxi." *Colorado* magazine (July, 1941).

ROSENTHAL, R., "Fifty Years in the Canadian North." *Commentary* (May, 1949).

ROSTEN, LEO, *The Joys of Yiddish*. New York, 1968.

RUBINOW, I. M., "The Jewish Question in N.Y.C. 1902–1903." PAJHS, December, 1959.

RUDIN, A. JAMES, "Beersheba, Kansas: God's Pure Air in Government Land." *Kansas Historical Quarterly*.

SABSOVICH, K., *Adventures in Idealism*. New York, 1922.

SACHAR, HOWARD M., *The Course of Modern Jewish History*. New York, 1958.

SALTER, J. T., ed., *The American Politician*. Chapel Hill, North Carolina, 1938.

SAMUEL, MAURICE, *The World of Sholem Aleichem*. New York, 1942.

SANDERS, RONALD, *The Downtown Jews*. New York, 1970.

SCHOENER, ALLON, *Portal to America*. New York, 1967.

SCHPALL, LEO, trans., "The Diary of Dr. George M. Price." PAJHS, December, 1950.

————, "A Jewish Agricultural Colony in Louisiana." *Louisiana Historical Quarterly* (July, 1937).

————, "The Memoir of Dr. George M. Price." PAJHS, December, 1957.

SELDES, GEORGE, *Tell the Truth and Run*. New York, 1953.

SILVER, HAROLD, "Some Attitudes of the East European Jewish Immigrants Toward Organized Charity in the United States in the Years 1890—1910." M.A. Thesis, Graduate School of Jewish Social Work, 1934.

SOLOMON, BARBARA M., *Ancestors and Immigrants*. Cambridge, Massachusetts, 1956.

SOLTES, MORDECAI, *The Yiddish Press*. New York, 1925.

STEFFENS, LINCOLN, *Autobiography*. New York, 1931.

STEIN, LEON; CONAN, ABRAHAM, P.; and DAVISON, LYNN, trans., *The Education of Abraham Cahan*. Philadelphia, 1969.

STOLBERG, BENJAMIN, *Tailor's Progress*. New York, 1944.

SZAJKOWSKI, ZOSA, "The Attitude of American Jews to East European Jewish Immigration." PAJHS, March, 1951.

————, "How the Mass Migration to America Began." JSS, October, 1942.

TCHERIKOWER, ELIAS, ed., and ANTONEVSKY, A. trans. and revised, *The Early Jewish Labor Movement in the United States*. New York, 1961.

UCHILL, IDA LIBERT, *Pioneers, Peddlers and Tsadikim*. Denver, 1957.

WALDMAN, LOUIS, *Labor Lawyer*. New York, 1944.

WALDMAN, MORRIS D., "The Galveston Movement." *Jewish Social Service Quarterly* (March, 1928).

————, *Nor by Power*. New York, 1953.

WALLACE, WILLIAM S., "A Russian Incident 1894—1897." PAJHS, September, 1949.

WEIDER, ARNOLD A., *The Early Jewish Community of Boston's North End*. Waltham, Massachusetts, 1962.

WEITZMAN, CHAIM, *Trial and Error*. New York, 1949.

WELLS, H. G., *The Future in America*. New York, 1906.

WINTER, CARL, "The Influence of the Russo-American Treaty of

1832 on the Rights of American Jewish Citizens." PAJHS, December, 1951.

WIRTH, LOUIS, *The Ghetto.* Chicago, 1929.

WISCHNITZER, MARK, *To Dwell in Safety.* Philadelphia, 1948.

WISE, ISAAC MAYER, *Reminiscences.* Cincinnati, 1901.

WOLF, SIMON, *The Presidents I Have Known 1860—1918.* Washington, D.C., 1918.

WOLFF, FRANCES NATHAN, *Four Generations.* New York, 1939.

ZBOROWSKI, MARK, and HERZOG, ELIZABETH, "A Colony in Kansas —1882." AJA, November, 1965.

———, *Life Is with People.* New York, 1952.

———, "The United Fruit Co." *Fortune* (March, 1933).

Manuscript and Government Reports

Papers of the Baron De Hirsch Agricultural School; Emma Lazarus Papers; Records and Correspondence of the Industrial Removal Office; Meyer S. Isaacs Papers; Philip Cowen Papers; Lucien Moss Scrapbooks; Jewish Agricultural Society Records and Publications; Minutes of the Educational Alliance; William Jay Gaynor Papers; Interviews transcribed at the Oral History Center, Columbia University; Weber-Kempster Report on the Causes Which Incite Immigration to the United States, 1892; Reports of the Immigration Commission, 1901; Reports of the Industrial Commission, 1911.

Reference Works

The Jewish Encyclopedia, New York, 1901—1905, 12 vols.; *The Universal Jewish Encyclopedia,* New York, 1939—43, 10 vols.; *The Standard Jewish Encyclopedia,* New York, rev. ed., 1966; *Who's Who in American Jewry,* Vol. I, 1927, Vol. III, 1939; *The Jewish People Past and Present,* New York, 1946—55, 4 vols.; *American Jewish Yearbooks,* Philadelphia.

Newspapers and Periodicals

New York *Times;* New York *Herald;* New York *Daily Tribune;* Jewish *Messenger; American Hebrew; American Israelite; Jewish Gazette; Jewish Daily Forward; Arena; Century; Harper's Weekly; The Independent; Literary Digest; McClure's; North American Review; The Outlook; The Overland Monthly; Popular Science Monthly; Current Literature; Review of Reviews; Survey; World's Work.*

Index